Forerunners
of Revolution

By WALTER M. BRASCH

A Comprehensive Annotated Bibliography
of American Black English
(with Ila Wales Brasch)

Black English and the Mass Media

Before the First Snow

Cartoon Monickers;
An Insight Into the Animation Industry

Columbia County Place Names

The Press and the State:
Sociohistorical and Contemporary Interpretations
(with Dana R. Ulloth)

Sounds of Protest

Unionization and the American Journalist

A ZIM Self Portrait

Forerunners
of
Revolution:

Muckrakers and the American Social Conscience

by
Walter M. Brasch

UNIVERSITY PRESS OF AMERICA

Copyright © 1990 by Walter M. Brasch
University Press of America®, Inc.
4720 Boston Way
Lanham, Maryland 20706

3 Henrietta Street
London WC2E 8LU England

ISBN 0–8191–7967-1 (alk. paper)
ISBN 0–8191–7968-X (pbk. : alk. paper)

The paper used in this publication meets the minimum requirements of American National Standard for Information Sciences—Permanence of Paper for Printed Library Materials, ANSI Z39.48–1984.

Dedication

As always, to Milton Brasch and Helen Haskin Brasch
and to
*Those iconoclast reporters who refuse to be molded into
the image of corporate journalism.*

Acknowledgements

The publishing of anything involves the assistance of many people, and *Forerunners of Revolution* is no exception. A few need to be mentioned for their significant asssistance.

Rosemary R. Brasch reviewed the manuscript and provided many valuable suggestions that helped plug holes as well as make the copy flow a little better.

David M. Marra assisted in translating one computer format into another, then provided significant help in laying out the final book design.

Also assisting were librarians William J. Frost and Billie Aul.

At University Press of America, Helen Hudson, who has worked with me on several other projects, continually amazed me with her professional skills in getting the design through production.

Contents

"[The muckraker] sees a beautiful world about him, with stars and flowers and all sorts of things that interest him. He knows of many things he would like to do and to be, many ways in which he could amuse himself. And yet, instead of this, he begins to go about pointing out disagreeable truths to people. He says: "See, we are just like Rome. Our legislatures are corrupt; our politicians are unprincipled; our rich men are ambitious and unscrupulous. Our newspapers have been purchased and gagged; our colleges have been bribed; our churches have been cowed. Our masses are sinking into degradation; our ruling classes are becoming wanton and cynical.

This has been said in our country for a generation. Abraham Lincoln said it, for one. All earnest students knew it. But the public merely laughed incredulously.

And then comes the Muckrake Man. He says to himself, 'This is a serious matter. It cannot be neglected. The people will not believe it—but I will prove it to them!'

And so he proceeds to gather the evidence."

—Upton Sinclair, "The Muckrake Man,"
The Independent; September 3, 1906; p. 518.

Prologue

Samuel Hopkins Adams. Ray Stannard Baker. Christopher Connolly. Finley Peter Dunne. Benjamin O. Flower. Isaac Kahn Friedman. Benjamin Hampton. Will Irwin. S. S. McClure. Gustavus Meyers. Frank Norris. David Graham Phillips. Jacob Riis. Charles Edward Russell. George Kibbe Turner. Upton Sinclair. Lincoln Steffens. Ida Tarbell. Once, their names and stories about corruption and greed, monopolies, slumlords, and exploitation of the masses were known to almost every literate American. Today, they're largely forgotten, relegated to the catacombs of history, to be dug up every now and then by a journalism or history professor trying to instill in his or her students a foundation for social action in an era that is now more concerned with jobs and security than social and political justice.

For more than three decades, beginning in the 1880s, they were the finest journalists of the era, well-educated writers who cared about the society and the people they wrote about. Many had college degrees, at a time when the average American had a fifth grade education; many had studied philosophy and the creative arts in Europe. Many were socialists, seeing the problems of capitalist America not in its people, but in the social, political, and economic systems that had allowed for exploitation. They were concerned about the people, for what had happened to them in the last three decades of the nineteenth century, to what was becoming of the American dream; they were concerned if success in a corporate board room, the Congress, local politics, or on the streets, meant a loss of morality. To the country, they asked the question—must a person compromise principles to be successful? They cared about the people and believed through investigative reporting they could bring abuse to light, to help Americans reclaim their country.

They became a part of a social conscience of the people that would lead to sweeping state and federal reform and legislation that allowed urban lower- and middle-class America to regain their country from the exploitation by the robber barons and corrupt political machines, that, for awhile at least, would bring social, political, and economic reform. They were the muckrakers.

ix

Forerunners
of Revolution

CHAPTER 1
Killing the Revolution

Theodore Roosevelt was mad. In March 1906, *Cosmopolitan* magazine had begun a series of well-researched articles that reported that the U.S. Senate was composed of people who had placed personal greed above the needs of the people, and had sold out to the business interests; a month later, the magazine reported that one of the President's best friends was a "nothing [who] publicly came to nothing."

Roosevelt, who became president in 1901 upon the assassination of William McKinley, was an ambitious but honest and progressive politician, a reformer who cared about the people. For more than twenty years, in all levels of government, he was a vigorous opponent of corruption and graft. But now, in print, he was reading that his friends and political allies had betrayed the American people. The President had seen their flaws, but he had also seen their strengths. There might be some senators who were less virtuous than others, who could easily have been "bought," Roosevelt readily admitted, but to smear the Senate itself, accusing that body of treason, was itself wrong.

To Washington's Gridiron Club, an association of journalists, Roosevelt vented his rage, March 17. Referring to the "man with the muckrake" in John Bunyan's *Pilgrim's Progress*, Roosevelt said that there are journalists—he didn't name them—who were like Bunyan's pilgrim; they raked the muck from the earth, always looking down, always to some small spot, while rejecting a celestial crown. These journalists—these muckrakers—said Roosevelt, are necessary and important, but they see only a small part of life and never see the glory that could be America. Most important, said Roosevelt, "An epidemic of indiscriminate assault upon character does not good but very great harm. The soul of every scoundrel is gladdened whenever an honest man is assailed, or even when a scoundrel

3

is untruthfully assailed." When Roosevelt clarified his speech for the public April 14, 1906, at the dedication of the cornerstone for the office building for the House of Representatives, the nation added "muckraking journalist" to its vocabulary. It was not the first time that American journalists had attacked the nation's business and political communities.

The American Dark Ages

Several journalists had conducted investigations that predated the era of the muckraker. During the Colonial era leading to revolution, Thomas Paine, who would be called a muckraker had he lived more than a century later, dug out British excesses, and wrote impassioned pleas for the overthrow of the British government in the colonies; his *Crisis* papers and *Common Sense* pamphlet had prepared the Colonies for war. Other notable radical journalists included Isaiah Thomas of the *Massachusetts Spy*; Benjamin Edes and John Gill of the *Boston Gazette*; John Dickinson who used the essay form to solidify public opinion; and Samuel Adams, possibly the nation's greatest propagandist for social change, a journalist who combined his knowledge of the human mind and of class struggle to solidify radical opinion into unified action.

During America's "Dark Ages" following the Revolutionary War, a time when Federalist and Anti-Federalist (Republican) parties were fighting for control over a young country's ideology, many of the nation's printer-editors launched a series of attacks upon the nation's politicians.

From the Federalist press, led by John Fenno's *Gazette of the United States*, came wave after wave of attack upon Thomas Jefferson's Republican philosophy; from the Republican press, led by Phillip Freneau's *National Gazette*, came equally brutal invectives against Federalists Alexander Hamilton and John Adams. Not even George Washington was spared as the Anti-federalist *Philadelphia General Advertiser*, published by Benjamin Franklin Bache, declared in its December 23, 1796, issue, "If ever a nation was debauched by a man, the American nation has been debauched by Washington."

To control scurrilous charges of corruption, as well as to try to force the public and its press into printing truth, the Federalists under John Adams imposed the Alien and Sedition laws in 1797. Seizing the opportunity to champion the rights of unrestricted speech and of a free press, Thomas Jefferson, Adams' vice-president, launched his own counter-attacks that eventually led to Adams' defeat for a second four-year term and Jefferson's own election. Soon, it was Jefferson's Republicans who launched attacks upon free speech when the Federalist press attacked Jefferson.

Nevertheless, the nation's printer-editors continued their assaults, doing everything they could to dredge up fragments of evidence that would show that not only was the opposition corrupt, but it was also responsible for the destruction of the principles of the revolution. It made little difference if the British were the masters, or whether Federalism or Republicanism would prevail, there were greater social issues that would threaten the country. It was, alas, a revolution that would intensify the division between classes and races.

Revolution of a Different Color

While a few of the mass media were fighting for the continuation of a revolution, slave narratives and abolitionist literature—often written by Whites, but seldom published in the establishment media—pleaded for equality for *all* persons, no matter what their economic status or race. In 1827, a Black-owned newspaper arose to fight its own revolution, pointing out in its first issue, "We wish to plead our own cause. Too long have others spoken for us." *Freedom's Journal*, founded by Samuel Cornish and John B. Russwurm in New York City, lasted only thirty-one months, but during that time published innumerable stories about White oppression of the Black, as it tried to shame America into taking the chains off a race of people who were forced from their homeland and into subjugation. Several dozen other Black-owned antebellum newspapers—including David Walker's *Boston Appeal*, Phillip Bell's *The Colored American*, Martin Delaney's *The Mystery*, W. H. Day's *Alienated American*, and Frederick Douglass' *The North Star*—brought forth not only news of interest to the Black communities, but voices for social change.

In the antebellum North, William Lloyd Garrison, influenced by the Quakers' refusal to accept slavery, endured White invective to publish the *Liberator*, a weekly newspaper that would become the voice of unification for the abolitionist movement. A moderate when he first began speaking out against slavery, Garrison soon became a radical as others went to extraordinary lengths to silence him, throwing him into jail for seven months, destroying his press, and forcing him to run nearly naked through the streets of Boston. The more the anti-abolitionist North tried to chill

Garrison's First Amendment rights, the louder he spoke. Eventually, Garrison called for overthrow of slavery by violence if necessary.

But, it was in Alton, Ill., where anti-abolitionist mobs took a chunk from the First Amendment. In 1837, having defended and rebuilt his press after three separate attacks, the Rev. Elijah Lovejoy, a graduate of the Yale Divinity school, and owner of the *St. Louis Observer*, was murdered by a mob when he refused to silence his attacks upon slavery. It would be just one more thread that the public would unravel from a First Amendment it had fought to create.

Voices of Labor

For the most part, the establishment press, which had failed to support the abolitionist movement, or to report upon the newly-emerging industrial age and its eventual exploitation of the masses, concentrated upon news of business, targeting the merchant class and wealthy as their subscribers. However, a few newspapers emerged to plead the cause of the worker. In 1827, the *Journeyman Mechanic's Advocate* became the nation's first newspaper directed to the working class. Although it lasted only a year, it was a signal that the working class was about to become a viable force.

In 1828, with a nation suffering from an economic depression, and the populist election of Andrew Jackson to champion a "people's democracy," the *Mechanic's Free Press* was established, surviving until the depression of 1837 during the Martin Van Buren administration.

It was also during the Jacksonian age that John O'Sullivan's militant *Democratic Review* and William Cullen Bryant's *New York Evening Post* became voices for labor. Although no one could accuse Bryant of favoring oppressive industrial policies, it wasn't until 1834 when he took a temporary leave and left William Leggett in charge that the newspaper became an advocate of the poor and oppressed working class. In news column and editorial, Leggett led the newspaper even deeper into opposition to slavery and in being labor's advocate, declaring that *equality* would be the guiding philosophy of the newspaper. Upon his return from Europe, Bryant found that circulation and revenue had dropped, and he was forced to temper the newspaper's stand, but still maintained his support of labor.

A New Trend in Journalism

By the mid-1830s, a few journalists had begun to focus their energies into an organized and comprehensive look at American social issues. The "penny papers," named because they sold for one penny, as opposed to the six-cent dailies, emerged during the era of Jacksonian democracy, and had established a new trend in journalism. The "establishment papers" sold for six-cents, usually on long-term subscription; required as much as year-long contracts from advertisers; reported shipping and business news in dry monotones; and were identified as reading material for the elite of the East. The "penny papers" were targeted to the masses, and reported news that the "common person" would be interested in; the writing was brighter and easier to read than the "six cent dailies"; the newspapers were sold on the street corners where the people could buy it on a daily basis rather than by long-term subscription. Similarly, advertisers could now purchase single-issue or short-term contracts. Targeting the masses would lead to financial success—and a new direction for the mass media.

Benjamin Day (1810-1889) and George Wisner (1817-1849) of the *New York Sun*, often credited with being the founders of the "penny press era," had opposed slavery, launched campaigns to show the public that they were being lied to by the Board of Health on what could have been a cholera epidemic, dug into police and court records to prove that influence-peddling and bribes of police and judges were violations of the public interest, and established a standard that would eventually humiliate the other metropolitan newspapers into accepting the belief that a journalist's first responsibility is to all the readers, not special interests. Within six months of its founding, the *Sun* had reached eight thousand circulation daily, about twice that of its nearest competitor—and was subject to vilification by the other more "established" papers for catering to the masses.

In 1835, James Gordon Bennett (1765-1872) founded the *New York Herald* as a penny paper, and became known as "The Great Innovator" for developing the concept of what became the modern newspaper. Like Wisner and Day, Bennett targeted the masses for his circulation, creating sections that focused upon police and crime, sports, finances, and even religion, going so far as to have his reporters do reviews and analysis of sermons while also attacking the failures of established religion to meet the needs of all the people. Within a couple of years, the *Herald's* circulation topped forty thousand.

Horace Greeley (1811-1872) carried George Wisner's concern for social justice farther than any other editor of the nineteenth century. Whereas Bennett was the innovator, Greeley was the nation's social conscience. Greeley had begun his newspaper career as a penniless tramp printer at the age of fifteen. By the time he died in 1872, the nominee of the Democratic and Liberal Republican parties for the Presidency of the United States, he was the nation's most influential and respected editor, owner of the *New York Tribune* and the 200,000-circulation nationally-distributed *Weekly Tribune.*

Horace Greeley

In a journalistic career of more than four decades Greeley fought for the unionization of printers, eventually establishing a major typographical union in New York City at a time when unionism was considered to be not only a radical concept but possibly treasonous as well; vigorously opposed slavery; argued for the passage of the controversial Homestead Bill which allowed the federal government to give land in the Midwest to people who promised to develop it; opposed alcohol and smoking; advocated socialism as a way to help the masses achieve equality; and gave away to his employees, friends, and the poor, most of the stock of his newspaper.

Most didn't accept Greeley's philosophical views, but almost all respected him for having opinions, for challenging the established order—and most of all for assuring the public that his newspaper cared about the people, and was willing to look into all areas of society to expose greed and corruption.

Racism in a Separate But Equal Package

By the Civil War, the abolitionist attacks upon slavery, led by Horace Greeley, were so intense that Abraham Lincoln was eventually forced to issue the Emancipation Proclamation in 1863, after having said that he would have permitted slavery to exist if it meant keeping the union together. At the end of 1865, about four million Blacks were finally liberated by the passage of the Thirteenth Amendment to the Constitution. But, a law does nothing to change human relationships or human beliefs.

After the Civil War, America—both North and South—merely exchanged one kind of slavery for another. By segregating, America created a second class citizenry, claiming it was giving the Blacks everything the Whites had—"it's *separate* but *equal*"—while not having to work or live with what many thought to be "inferior beings." By refusing to employ Blacks in anything but menial labor, and by denying them an adequate education, America forced many into becoming sharecroppers and domestics. By requiring "literacy tests" that were arbitrarily enforced, white America could deny Blacks even the chance to try to help change the Jim Crow laws of subjugation. And by violence, by tar and feathers, by torture and lynching, America could show that it could handle the Black "problem."

Carl Schurz (1829-1906), one of the nation's most-respected editors and politicians, by Presidential directive had investigated conditions during reconstruction. Reflecting upon that time, Schurz pointed out:

Armed bands of white men patrolled the country roads to drive back the negroes wandering about. Dead bodies of murdered negroes were found on and near the highways and by-paths. Gruesome reports came from the hospitals—reports of colored men and women whose ears had been cut off, whose skulls had been broken by blows, whose bodies had been slashed with knives or lacerated with scourges . . . A veritable reign of terror prevailed in many parts of the South. The negro found scant justice in the local courts against the white man. He could look for protection only to the military forces of the United States still garrisoning the "States lately in rebellion" and to the Freedman's Bureau—that Freedman's Bureau, the original purpose of which was to act as an intermediary between the planters and the emancipated slaves, the white and the black, to aid them in making of equitable contract arrangements, and, generally, in organizing the new free labor system for the benefit of both. It would have been an institution of the greatest value under competent leadership, had not its organization been to some extent invaded by mentally and morally unfit persons. ["Can the South Solve the Negro problem?" *McClure's*, January 1904, p. 261.]

During the 1880s and 1890s, several hundred Black-owned newspapers were formed, their voices not only unifying the Black community but also attacking the racism that was not eliminated by a Civil War or constitutional amendments.[1]

What America had done to the Blacks was only a part of what it was doing to the Native American population. Racist, and exalting its "manifest destiny," the American government, supported by the people, pushed westward, destroying Indian villages, killing and maiming large populations, and then writing worthless treaties that were violated more by the American government than all the Indian nations combined. And when certain Indian nations responded to the betrayals and encroachment upon the land, which it was willing to share with the Americans but not be pushed off of, the American government sent in the military to "protect American lives." That "protection," inflamed by a civilian population that often had to be *controlled* by the military, led to genocide and eventual subjugation of an entire race. But, the press, for the most part, with notable exceptions by Greeley and a few others, didn't object—after all, the press was largely written and edited by white men for a White American population; in their own worldviews, the press, like their readers, believed that the Indians, by stopping wagon trains of settlers, were savages who kept America from experiencing its potential.

On the West Coast, the monopolistic and corrupt railroads imported thousands of Chinese to become slave labor in the linking of the nation's transportation. Like the Blacks and other minorities, the Chinese were treated poorly and subjected to innumerable acts of ridicule and embarrassment while the White majority felt psychologically secure that it was a lot better than those "immigrants."

Creating an American Underclass

Like Black and Native Americans, urban America was also oppressed, alienated from being a part of the country, as waves of immigrants—more than half of them Jews—poured into the country, and found that America wasn't yet truly a land of freedom from discrimination. At

---

[1] For a fuller treatment of the Reconstruction Cycle, and the proliferation of magazines for or about Blacks, see *Black English and the Mass Media* (1981, rev. 1984), by Walter M. Brasch: *The Afro-American Press and Its Editors* (1891), by I. Garland Penn: *A Register and History of Negro Newspapers in the United States* (1950), by Armistead S. Pride; and *The Black Press, USA* (1971), by Roland Wolesly.

Ellis Island, where most immigrants were processed, they found that officials often stole their money to process their applications, then arbitrarily "Americanized" or misspelled their names. In New York, Boston, Philadelphia—wherever there were mills and mines—entire families were put into one or two filthy roach-infested rooms in apartment buildings that had impure water, little heat, and walls that were thin and broken. Matthew Josephson in *The Robber Barons* (1962) described some of the immigrants' existence:

In hard times, the manufacturers were not responsible for the souls of their hired hands, like the manorial lords of the Middle Ages; few measures of safety were provided in the mines and mills, where hundreds and even thousands were killed and maimed annually. Little heed was paid to quarters in which workers and their families resided, the food they ate or the water they drank. With the passing of time, toward 1890, 10 percent of the population of our great cities were housed in slums as terrible as those of the wretchedest places in the Old World. And in the neighborhood of the big manufacturing works, stockyards, and mines, the unlovely shacks of laborers' communities clustered, like the cottages of servants and hired hands in feudal times.

A great steel manufacturer noted for his lavish philanthropies would acquire an additional mill in Pittsburgh, and in taking this over would also take possession of the row of company houses in which the workers resided. Thus Carnegie, buying Painter's Mill in Pittsburgh, renovated its producing plant thoroughly; but the notorious "Painter's Row" on the south side of the town was left untouched—with its five hundred people living in back-to-back houses, without ventilation, having cellar kitchens, dark, overcrowded sleeping quarters, no drinking water whatsoever, and no sanitary accommodations worth the name.

In [the steel mills of] Pittsburgh, in the coal fields of Pennsylvania, in the New England textile cities and in the neighborhood of the Chicago stockyards laborers lived huddled together in company "patches" [of varying quality]. . . . The very enterprising Pullman Company [created a model town outside Chicago,] expended some $5,000,000 per annum in wages, at an average rate of $600 per year [and] contrived through the model town [in Chicago] in which its subjects were housed to win back a great part of this sum, renting them houses, selling them food, gas, water and a variety of compulsory services or conveniences at what were afterward proved to be enormously profitable rates. Thus not only from the employees' labor were famous profits taken, but even from their hours of rest and refreshment. . . . Here as in the mining communities with their "company stores" he might receive almost nothing in his pay envelope, after "deductions," or might labor in debt until evicted. [pp. 363-364]

Not long after they were processed and settled, the immigrants learned they had traded one kind of tyranny for another when the "ward healers" promised to take care of them, giving them jobs, helping them become adjusted to their new country, in exchange for regular "contributions" and the right vote at election time. However, the jobs were little better than slave labor, usually for a few pennies a day in "sweat shops" that forced them to work ten- and twelve-hour days in buildings that reeked of filth. Pharmacists and doctors, teachers, lawyers, and writers. They all worked in the sweat shops, or in the low-paying clerical and janitorial jobs, or selling fruit or vegetables from carts on the streets of the Lower East Side. They, like the Blacks, were outcasts.

Jacob Riis (1849-1914), who had come to America as an immigrant from Denmark, found that he could use his skills as a photographer and journalist to help America understand what it was doing to itself. In article after article, first for the *New York Tribune* (1878-1890), then the *Evening Sun* (1890-1899), Riis told of the conditions of New York's tenements, of poverty and crime, of slumlords who didn't care and of tenants who had

given up the American "dream," hoping that it would be their children, through education and perseverance, who would become a part of the America that had excluded them.

In 1890, his book, *How the Other Half Lives*, shocked a complacent urban America that had lived in ignorance of the conditions in its own cities. Two years later, *The Children of the Poor* became a best-seller. In 1901, Riis completed *The Making of an American*; the following year, his fourth book, *The Battle with the Slum*, was published. Through public exposure of the problems, Riis was able to force the politicians—who had counted on those "right" votes—to tear down many of the

Jacob Riis

tenements, to build public parks and playgrounds, and to provide lights in the alleys and streets.

Nevertheless, Riis was not satisfied that a small part of America was being corrected, for he knew that there were other problems, and if those problems could not be solved, neither could poverty. He turned his attention to enforced child labor, and pointed to eight- and nine-year olds working ten and twelve-hour days in factories, earning pennies to help their families survive. He looked at the environment and reported that the industries were contaminating the water; his articles and public outrage eventually forced the city to spend millions of dollars to clean up its drinking supply. He continued to pound at the causes of the problem, discussing why slums occur, why child labor and pollution tear down what he believed was the finest country in the world. But, he also knew that when the people tired of hearing about the slums, of child labor problems, of pollution, the same problem would reemerge.

For the August 1903 issue of *McClure's*, Lincoln Steffens wrote:

[Riis] did not go about merely to see and help, he went back and reported it. When he had done that he struggled with corrupt city officials for relief. The chicaneries he saw; he caught them red-handed at their sordid tricks. Then, too, he was fighting other reporters [who either refused to believe his stories or] who had combined to "beat the Dutchman," and who were willing "to fake to do him." Severest test of all, he was wading up to his neck in police corruption, knowing well men who lived by blackmail and profits shared with thieves, gamblers, and prostitutes. None of this soiled this man outside or in, neither himself nor his ideals nor his belief in his fellow-man. ["Jacob A. Riis," *McClure's*; August 1903; p. 421.]

After a decade of suffering with heart disease, Riis died on the eve of World War I, praised by Theodore Roosevelt as "closer than a brother," honored by a nation for having written the stories that had led to reform.

Riis wasn't the only one to speak out against what America was doing to its immigrants and the poor. Economist Henry George, in *Poverty and Prosperity*, demanded an end of New York's slums, and campaigned for taxation reform that would probably have eliminated the worst of the city's tenement housing. Riding a wave of popularity, George was probably cheated out of being mayor of New York City in 1886 by a massive case of vote manipulation engineered by the power brokers opposing his plans for taxation reform.

George had been aided in the struggle by the crusading eloquence of the Rev. Edward McGlynn, a parish priest from the city's East Side. Defying orders from his archbishop, Father McGlynn continued to fight against tenement housing, and in support of George's economic policies, only to be excommunicated and defrocked for insubordination. A few years later, Father McGlynn was again ordained, but exiled to a rural parish well outside the city.

In Chicago Jane Addams (1860-1935), one of America's pioneer social workers whose work in tenement districts would earn her the Nobel Peace Prize in 1931, learned early in her career that change will not occur until the masses are informed of the problems, but that once informed, they will provide the base for change. To provide that knowledge, she wrote several magazine articles pointing to the causes of poverty, and what poverty was doing to an America that reluctantly accepted immigrants, then cast them into what was a permanent underclass. Then, for a decade, beginning in 1896, Addams issued *The Hull House Bulletin*, a periodical originated to provide continuous information about the problems that poverty caused, as well as to inform the people of the existence of a settlement house to aid those in poverty.

Ernest Crosby (1857-1907), born into wealth, graduated from New York University and the Columbia University Law School, then became a state legislator, poet, critical biographer of Shakespeare and Tolstoy, and justice on the International Court of Law. After long meetings with Tolstoy, from whom he became even more sensitive to the problems of the oppressed masses, Crosby organized the Social Reform Club, spending much of his life working at the local level to help the urban immigrants and at the international level toward the elimination of war. Strangely enough, it was his hatred of the military, fostered by eight years in the New York National Guard and his discussions with Tolstoy, that had led to national recognition; his cause was that of the anti-militarist.

After two mildly successful books—*Garrison the Non-Resister*, and *Precedent for Disarmament*, Crosby turned full-force to a biting denunciation of the military and America's imperialism. *Captain Jinks, Hero*, published in 1902, showed the regimentation of the army, the psychological demands and terror of following orders while trying to rise through the military bureaucracy; at the end, Crosby left his fictional hero in a psychiatric ward playing with toy solders.

'Consumed in a Butterfly Existence'

While the workers languished in squalor, working six-day weeks, twelve hours a day for not more than a few dollars, the robber barons, proclaiming their adoration for the free enterprise system, pumped out money to influence legislators and mayors, and made friends with newspaper editors, giving them "choice" beats and "inside" information to buy their complicity. While masses lived and died in their poverty, the nation's four thousand millionaires soon became the multi-millionaires. Benjamin O. Flower, editor of *The Arena*, looked at these four thousand as "idlers who eat, drink, dance, and are consumed in a butterfly existence [while surrounded by] the gaunt, hungry, hollow-eyed millions to whom life is an awful curse." [February 1891, p. 341.] Had these millionaires only been the "idle rich," had they only been the "social butterflies" of society, America probably would not have had the class warfare of the latter nineteenth century that led to the era of the muckrakers. However, these millionaires, for the most part, were the exploiters of the underclass, and by their example, a part of the reason why the near-millionaires and struggling-to-be millionaires often became as involved with the exploitation of human life as had the millionaires.

The industrial age had spawned the worst in human nature, and the Civil War had killed off the emerging middle-class youth while giving rise to the upper-class. While many youth, trapped by the spirit of patriotism died for their beliefs, there were also "more practical youth," wrote Richard O. Boyer and Herbert M. Morais "who lived for the mammoth plunder in ventures which ranged from profiteering war contracts to Congressional bribery necessary to gaining railroad rights-of-way. . . . While staying safe as others died these men laid the basis of the great American fortunes, some of which still dominate American life." [*Labor's Untold Story*, p. 20] By theft, deception, bribery, and fraud, these newly-minted millionaires, changing the nature of the country from an agricultural society to a mass production economy during the quarter-century after the Civil War, controlled America's industry, transportation, and natural resources, hired the underclass at poverty wages and forced them to live a substandard life in slums, shanties, and mining patches that would shame the country that was boasting it was the "world's "melting pot." In his annual message to congress at the end of 1988, Grover Cleveland boldly stated that the "trusts, combinations, and monopolies [were trampling the people] to death beneath an iron heel."

John D. Rockefeller (1839-1937), founder of Standard Oil, had a net worth of almost a billion dollars when he retired about 1912, after decades of breaking smaller companies, then absorbing the remains. George Jay Gould (1836-1892), who bribed his way into control of most of the rail transportation in the Southwest, also owned both the *New York World* (1879-1883) before Joseph Pulitzer gave it a moral conscience; and Western Union, the most efficient medium for the transmission of news between and to newspapers. Phillip D. Armour (1832-1901) and Gustavus F. Swift (1839-1903) had given America efficient meat packing companies—and they also gave it disease and death from spoiled meat. James B. Duke (1856-1925) and Benjamin N. Duke (1855-1929), founded the American Tobacco Co., made North Carolina the center of the tobacco trust and, like Rockefeller, developed efficient and brutal techniques to stop competition. Collis P. Huntington (1821-1900) controlled the Southern Pacific Railroad and through it, also controlled California and a large chunk of the West. Commodore Vanderbilt (1794-1877) established a transportation empire, leaving more than $100 million for his son, William Henry Vanderbilt (1821-1885) who, using business tactics then common, doubled his father's fortune, and left his sons a half-billion dollar series of conglomerates, along with multi-million dollar "Summer Cottages" in Newport, Rhode Island. J. P. Morgan (1837-1913), a financier and banker, through a system of interlocking directories, managed to influence almost all of America's major businesses.

A few multi-millionaires, while earning deserved reputations as robber barons, also turned to public service. Andrew Mellon (1855-1937) earned his millions as a financier in western Pennsylvania, not far from where Rockefeller began his conglomerate; in 1921, he began eleven distinguished years as secretary of the treasury under presidents Harding, Coolidge, and Hoover. Andrew Carnegie (1835-1919) earned his fortune in the steel industry in western Pennsylvania, and became head of one of the nation's largest trusts; however, by the time he died, he had donated more than $350 million to charity, much of the money used to build public libraries. Edward Albert Filene (1860-1937), department store owner, founder of the credit union concept and one of the founders of the Chamber of Commerce, unlike most the owners of America, believed that workers had certain rights—he tried to organize profit-sharing within his company—and that business and government should not only serve the public interest, but must also be the servant, not the master, of society. It was part of a libertarian philosophy that had led to the American revolution; a century later, it was a philosophy few business leaders and publishers believed.

Using tactics perfected by their corporate trusts, the millionaires and would-be millionaires pillaged the public treasury. Throughout the era, as America and Americans proclaimed the benefits of the free enterprise system, as the nation expanded after the Civil war, the "robber barons" stole from the people. Needing coal and lumber to fuel their railroads and industries, these robber barons stripped the land of its riches, denuded the forests, polluted the water, and tore the coal and metals from the earth, sending miners into the earth where they would die from cave-ins and gasses; if they survived, they would soon die of "Black Lung."

Whenever there was a natural resource—coal, zinc, aluminum, iron, lead, copper, boron, lumber—company towns instantly appeared. At the end of the month, when the company deducted the rent for the tar-paper shanties they forced the workers to live in, work supplies, food and household goods bought for exorbitant prices at the company store, and required monthly payments for the doctor and priest, the miner and his family were fortunate to have a couple of dollars left, not enough to move elsewhere to find other work. And when it was no longer profitable to rape the land, the "robber barons" moved on, to other places, to where there were forests, to where the land had not given up its resources; there, they once again built company towns and found workers, who for a few dollars and a place to live, would continue the process of tearing apart what had been an ecological balance.

To workers who tried to organize, the millionaire owners hired goons and thugs, men who first broke up meetings, then broke bodies. It was the fault of the workers, screamed many newspaper publishers, themselves businessmen concerned more in profit than human rights. If the workers wouldn't demand so much, wouldn't try to destroy a company by outrageous demands that could only force prices up, cried the tycoons, then the company wouldn't have had to hire detectives.

During the latter two decades of the nineteenth century, with the proliferation of newspapers and magazines, and the emergence of a militant America not willing to accept the excesses of the industrial giants, labor (and the newspapers necessary to unify the movement) emerged under the leadership of Terence Powderly and the Knights of Labor which claimed membership of about 750,000, and the subsequent American Federation of Labor, under the direction of Samuel L. Gompers. With their own newspapers, the labor movement was able to unify the workers and bring stories about exploitation to the public's attention. Their pleas were finally heard by a few major newspapers during the latter two decades of the nineteenth century.

$50,000 REWARD.—WHO DESTROYED THE MAINE?—$50,000 REWARD.

The Journal will give $50,000 for information, furnished to it exclusively, that will convict the person or persons who sank the Maine.

EDITION FOR GREATER NEW YORK
NEW YORK JOURNAL
AND ADVERTISER.

The Journal will give $50,000 for information, furnished to it exclusively, that will convict the person or persons who sank the Maine.

NO. 5,572.   Copyright, 1898, by W. R. Hearst—NEW YORK, THURSDAY, FEBRUARY 17, 1898.—16 PAGES.   PRICE ONE CENT In Greater New York and Jersey City.   TWO CENTS.

DESTRUCTION OF THE WAR SHIP MAINE WAS THE WORK OF AN ENEMY

$50,000!
$50,000 REWARD!
For the Detection of the Perpetrator of the Maine Outrage!

The New York Journal hereby offers a reward of $50,000 CASH for information FURNISHED TO IT EXCLUSIVELY, which shall lead to the detection and conviction of the person, persons or government criminally responsible for the explosion which resulted in the destruction of Havana of the United States war ship Maine and the loss of 258 lives of American sailors.

The $50,000 CASH offered for the above information is on deposit with Wells, Fargo & Co.

No one is barred; be he the humble but misguided seaman sting out a few miserable dollars by acting as a spy, or the attache of a government secret service, plotting by any devilish means, to revenge fancied insults or cripple menacing countries.

This offer has been cabled to Europe and will be made public in every capital of the Continent and in London this morning.

The Journal believes that any man who can be bought to commit murder can also be bought to betray his comrades. FOR THE PERPETRATOR OF THIS OUTRAGE HAD ACCOMPLICES.

W. R. HEARST.

Assistant Secretary Roosevelt Convinced the Explosion of the War Ship Was Not an Accident.

The Journal Offers $50,000 Reward for the Conviction of the Criminals Who Sent 258 American Sailors to Their Death. Naval Officers Unanimous That the Ship Was Destroyed on Purpose.

$50,000!
$50,000 REWARD!
For the Detection of the Perpetrator of the Maine Outrage!

The New York Journal hereby offers a reward of $50,000 CASH for information FURNISHED TO IT EXCLUSIVELY, which shall lead to the detection and conviction of the person, persons or government criminally responsible for the explosion which resulted in the destruction, at Havana, of the United States war ship Maine and the loss of 258 lives of American sailors.

The $50,000 CASH offered for the above information is on deposit with Wells, Fargo & Co.

No one is barred; be he the humble, but misguided seaman, sting out a few miserable dollars by acting as a spy, or the attache of a government secret service, plotting by any devilish means, to revenge fancied insults or cripple menacing countries.

This offer has been cabled to Europe and will be made public in every capital of the Continent and in London this morning.

The Journal believes that any man who can be bought to commit murder can also be bought to betray his comrades. FOR THE PERPETRATOR OF THIS OUTRAGE HAD ACCOMPLICES.

W. R. HEARST.

POWDER MAGAZINE

NAVAL OFFICERS THINK THE MAINE WAS DESTROYED BY A SPANISH MINE.

George Eugene Bryson, the Journal's special correspondent at Havana, cables that it is the secret opinion of many Spaniards in the Cuban capital that the Maine was destroyed and 258 of her men killed by means of a submarine mine or fixed torpedo. This is the opinion of several American naval authorities. The Spaniards, it is believed, arranged to have the Maine anchored over one of the harbor mines. Wires connected the mine with a powder magazine, and it is thought the explosion was caused by sending an electric current through the wire. It then can be proven, the brutal nature of the Spaniards is the fact that they wanted to spring the mine until after all the men had retired for the night. The Maltese cross in the picture shows where the mine may have been fired.

Hidden Mine or a Sunken Torpedo Believed to Have Been the Weapon Used Against the American Man-of-War---Officers and Men Tell Thrilling Stories of Being Blown Into the Air Amid a Mass of Shattered Steel and Exploding Shells---Survivors Brought to Key West Scout the Idea of Accident---Spanish Officials Protest Too Much---Our Cabinet Orders a Searching Inquiry---Journal Sends Divers to Havana to Report Upon the Condition of the Wreck.

Was the Vessel Anchored Over a Mine?

BY CAPTAIN E. L. ZALINSKI, U. S. A.

(Captain Zalinski is the inventor of the famous dynamite gun, which would be the principal factor in our coast defence in case of war.)

Assistant Secretary of the Navy Theodore Roosevelt says he is convinced that the destruction of the Maine in Havana Harbor was not an accident. The Journal offers a reward of $50,000 for exclusive evidence that will convict the person, persons or Government criminally responsible for the destruction of the American battle ship and the death of 258 of its crew.

The suspicion that the Maine was deliberately blown up grows stronger every hour. Not a single fact to the contrary has been produced.

Captain Sigsbee, of the Maine, and Consul-General Lee both urge that public opinion be suspended until they have completed their investigation. They are taking the course of tactful men who are convinced that there has been treachery.

Washington reports very late that Captain Sigsbee had feared some such event as a hidden mine. The English cipher code was used all day yesterday by the naval officers in cabling instead of the usual American code.

CHAPTER 2

The People's Champions

Like society itself, most newspaper publishers supported establishment policies, becoming sycophants of Big Business and the nation's socio-political economy. However, during the latter nineteenth century a few of the nation's most powerful media giants used their newspapers to attack the nation's social ills, launching myriad crusades to help the people, attacking corruption while vigorously pushing for better housing and working conditions.

Populism, Publishers, and Regional Responsibility

In the Midwest, the railroads and utilities, which had dominated and often destroyed the individual farmers, found that they couldn't control all of public opinion as many publishers tied their newspapers to the growth of agricultural reform following a national depression in the early 1870s. The Farmers Alliances, and the Union Labor, Socialist, and Populist political parties called for massive agrarian reform and launched vigorous crusades against the corruption of the trusts. By the end of the century, the Midwestern press tied its rising influence to the Populist Party which represented a "grass-roots" movement in democratic representation. The spread of the Populist philosophy was reflected within almost one thousand newspapers, many of which supported Populist beliefs while not supporting the political party itself.

During the 1880s and 1890s, three Midwestern publishers— William Rockhill Nelson (1841-1915), William Allen White (1868-1944), and Edward Willis Scripps (1854-1926)—emerged as champions of the people.

In Kansas City, Nelson gave the readers of the *Star* one of the nation's better newspapers, a crusading politically-independent newspaper un-afraid of challenging the large railroads, the utilities, and a well-en-trenched and highly effective political machine, leading Kansas City out of the "Wild West" image. Believing it wasn't enough just to expose corruption, Nelson became the leader for a number of non-political municipal improvements, including the building of viaducts, sidewalks, wide streets, parks, and low-income rental housing.

William Allen White had bought the struggling *Emporia* (Kansas) *Gazette* in 1895 for only $3,000. Within the next two decades, he had made the newspaper one of the most popular in the Midwest, and himself one of the nation's most respected commentators of American social issues. A staunch conservative Republican and businessman, White was a vigorous opponent of the Populist philosophy that would have increased govern-mental control over private industry, although in 1897, he called for gov-ernmental control of the privately-held utilities. He was also a strong en-vironmentalist and equally strong opponent of child labor and worker exploitation, and supported not only innumerable liberal and socialistic programs, including large chunks of Theodore Roosevelt's Square Deal proposals and Sen. Robert La Follette's Progressive philosophy, but in another era, Franklin D. Roosevelt's New Deal legislation—while oppos-ing Roosevelt for re-election.

E. W. Scripps developed the *Cleveland Press* and *Cincinnati Post* into mass circulation afternoon giants; together they became the base for what would emerge as one of the nation's largest media empires. Although among the nation's wealthiest, Scripps became identified with the work-ing class—although he paid average wages—and was a vigilant crusader against establishment policies and the capitalist economy that allowed the emergence of the robber barons. Like Greeley, he distributed his wealth and fought for the establishment of unions and collective bargaining principles for the working class, earning the respect and admiration of the workers while receiving enmity from fellow owners and publishers. According to Scripps, "The first of my principles is that I have constituted myself the advocate of that large majority of people who are not so rich in worldly goods and native intelligence as to make them equal . . . in the struggle with individuals of the wealthier and more intellectual class." To represent the workers, he had to attack governmental and business corrup-tion, monopolistic utilities and the trusts, and religious authoritarianism.

To build his empire, Scripps looked at industrialized cities with weak newspapers, hired strong editors and business managers to carry out his policies, and quickly replaced them if they slowed the pace or were unable

E. W. Scripps

to improve the quality of his property. Like Horace Greeley, Scripps believed that the workers should own a part of the company, and gave his editors and senior staff as much as forty-nine percent of each newspaper. By World War I, Scripps had control of almost thirty newspapers in nine states. By the 1920s, the Scripps empire was second only to that of William Randolph Hearst.

In New England, Samuel Bowles III (1826-1878) took the *Springfield* (Mass.) *Republican,* founded by his father in 1824, to greatness immediately before the Civil War with his backing of the abolition movement and opposition to business and governmental corruption. One of Lincoln's strongest supporters, Bowles was able to influence a large chunk of New England into accepting Lincoln and his policies. After the Civil War, the newspaper continued its leadership role against corruption at all levels.

On the West Coast, Fremont Older (1856-1935) earned the reputation as one of the nation's better reporters and most influential editors, becoming known as "The Great Reformer" for his campaigns to improve California government. In a six-decade career in journalism—he had dropped out of school after the third grade, and began working in various jobs by the age of ten, and in journalism by the age of fifteen—Older had taken *The San Francisco Bulletin* and the *San Francisco Evening Call* from mediocrity into greatness. He gave the *Bulletin,* where he was managing editor from 1895 to 1918, a reputation as a well-written, expertly-edited crusading newspaper which exposed bribery, blackmail, and graft between city officials, the public utilities, and the municipal streetcar company. At the *Evening Call,* where he was editor from 1918 to 1929, he increased that newspaper's crusading spirit, while raising its circulation 13,000 within a year, to 111,000, bringing it past the *Bulletin,* which began a long decline after he left. Among Older's long-term campaigns were to establish gun control laws, bring about prison reform, and abolish capital punishment. In 1929, the *Evening Call* and the *Bulletin* merged, and Older became editor-in-chief of the combined newspapers.

About sixty miles northeast of San Francisco, Samuel Seabough's *Sacramento Union* launched an all-out war in 1867 against the corruption of the Central Pacific Railroad which had bought politicians and effectively dominated California transportation and politics. In retaliation, the railroad squeezed the newspaper into isolation by banning it from the vast transportation and communication system that could have delivered it throughout the northern part of the state, while at the same time giving favorable treatment to the San Francisco dailies to expand into the Sacramento Valley. In 1874, a year after the *Union* was able to get an independent elected to the U.S. Senate, it was bankrupt, victim of a political economy that had punished it for its crusading independence.

Southern newspapers, many of which had long histories of activism, were also swept up in the developing muckraking era, often taking strong editorial positions opposing majority interest. In North Carolina, Josephus Daniels (1862-1948), first with the *Raleigh State Chronicle*, then as owner of the influential *News & Observer*, crusaded not only against the tobacco trust of the Duke family, owners of the American Tobacco Company, but against what he believed could have been health problems associated with smoking. To counteract Daniels, the tobacco trust and the Southern railway, which had a long history of economic and political corruption, created another newspaper which gained some success before failing, as the middle-class stayed loyal to the pro-labor *News & Observer* which campaigned for tax equality, shorter working hours, the abolition of child labor, and mandatory education of all people. Although a believer of racial segregation, Daniels also vigorously argued for the improvement of education for all Blacks, claiming that although there should be separation, there must be *equality*, not just words but in reality.

Other Southern editors, including and Francis W. Dawson (1840-1899) of the *Charleston News and Courier* and brothers Ambrose (1857-1926), N. G. (1859-1903), and William Gonzales (1866-1937) of *The State* of Columbia, S.C., went even further than Daniels, crusading for an equality that would more than a half-century later would lead to the abolition of the "separate but equal doctrine." But in their own era, Dawson and the Gonzales brothers found that the more they crusaded against intolerance, bigotry and inequality, the more they fought the sweeping tides of corruption and greed, the more they challenged the established order, the more they were vilified. In 1903, N. G. Gonzales was murdered by Lt. Gov. James H. Tilman whom *The State* had previously refused to support for nomination for the governorship. A hand-picked jury later acquitted Tilman on a plea of self-defense. Gonzales was forty-four years old when he was killed.

On the East Coast, articles in the *New York Sun* had led to an end of widespread corruption in the administration of U. S. Grant, although Grant himself probably had no knowledge of the corruption. Also during the 1870s, several articles in the *New York Times* and Thomas Nast's searing political cartoons of the "Tammany Tiger," published in *Harper's Weekly*, brought to light the corruption of New York, as practiced by Tammany Hall and William "Boss" Tweed. In 1884, reporter Frank Keenan uncovered the reason why New York awarded a 999 year franchise to a street car company—twenty-two of twenty-four city aldermen had each been bribed $20,000. Two years later, with the aldermen feeling rather secure, the city's district attorney was finally able to put together Keenan's evidence, along with an undercover confession from the vice-president of the Board of Alderman; several aldermen fled to Canada, nine were sent to prison.

In April 1890, the *New York Evening Post*, edited by E. L. Godkin, published its first of a major series of articles exposing the members of Tammany's executive committee. From Lincoln Steffens, a young police beat reporter who would soon become one of the nation's leading muckrakers, the public learned about a police department which allowed crime to flourish for a price; Steffens "break" occurred when a police captain confessed not only to his own acceptance of bribes, but to the system that had pervaded the entire New York City police department, reaching to the superintendent of police. From other reporters, the public learned about huge bribes paid to the city's politicians to allow favored position for some businesses and the destruction of others. The series led to an investigation by the New York legislature and the eventual defeat of many of the Tammany politicians; eventually, Theodore Roosevelt would become the city's police commissioner, a reform politician whose mission was to rid the city of widespread graft, while restoring public acceptance of a department that had become identified more with protecting criminals than protecting the public.

However, the media are a part of society and can only be as courageous as the people—and only as independent as their publishers allow. John Swinton, managing editor of the *New York Sun*, former chief editorial writer of the *New York Times*, often risked his job and public wrath for publishing the truth about governmental and corporate incursion upon the rights of the people.

He had been a militant abolitionist before the Civil War and an advocate for worker rights his entire journalistic career. His writings, although not always popular or acceptable to a majority, nevertheless forced them to recognize the principles of democracy and equality that the Revolution, less than a century earlier, had struggled to incorporate within a written constitution. Describing a police massacre upon thousands of the unemployed who had gathered at Tompkins Square in 1874, demanding jobs not charity, Swinton risked public censure as a defender of "Communist foreigners" to label events as they were:

> But now, about ten o'clock, when they were standing around peaceably, waiting for the mayor, platoons of police suddenly appeared [and] rushed without warning whatever on the helpless and unarmed multitudes, violently assailed them with their clubs, struck at heads right and left, wounded many, dragged off some thirty or forty who were flung into station houses, not unlike the Black Hole of Calcutta.

> The editorial funks [other newspapermen] and intellectual policemen have aroused prejudices against these [union workingmen] by saying they were Communists, in league with the impending earthquake! Be not alarmed by mysterious words, and let not the epithet 'Communist' stir up the same kind of hydrophobia that the epithet 'Abolitionist' once did. Suppose the ideas of these hapless people were the sort which editors and policemen call 'communistic,' does anybody suppose that the thing can be scribbled out of their hearts or clubbed out of their heads?

For more than two decades, Swinton, one of the most energetic and capable of all journalists, covered every kind of story from amusing incidents to governmental corruption, always concerned about the truth, always concerned about the people. And, as important, concerned about his profession, about the colleagues and friends who chose to make journalism their way of life. But now in 1880, as guest of honor at a banquet attended by leaders of New York journalism to honor him, he turned his attack not to the injustices of American society, but to the abuse of authority. His target was not the Industrial Age nor its practitioners, but the publishers of American thought. "There is no such thing in America as an independent press, unless it is in the small towns," Swinton declared. "You know it and I know it," he continued, as many in his audience nodded in silent or amused agreement, waiting to find out just what he was going to say, now that he had gotten their attention. "There is not one of you who dares to write his honest opinions, and if you did you know before hand that they would never appear in print," he said, raising a few more mumblings in the audience. It was a reality that many refused to accept. Of all the jobs available, the American journalist believed that his was one the one that fostered independence and individualism more than any other. They listened, quickly becoming annoyed at what might have been a political speech said during a time for frivolity. Years of outrage at the system was about to explode before the leaders of American journalism, as Swinton fearlessly declared:

... The business of the New York journalist is to destroy the truth, to lie outright, to pervert, to vilify, to fawn at the feet of Mammon, and to sell his race and his country for his daily bread. You know this and I know it, and what folly is this to be toasting an 'Independent Press.' We are the tools and vassals of rich men behind the scenes. We are the jumping-jacks; they pull the strings and we dance. Our talents, our possibilities and our lives are all the property of other men. We are intellectual prostitutes." [Quoted in *Labor's Untold Story*, by Richard O. Boyer and Herbert M. Morais, p.81]

His audience was outraged, indignant. They had heard similar comments from others, from "Communists" and other "rabble," but not from one of their own, not from one who had commanded so much respect that they had voluntarily united to honor him. In one impromptu speech, he had not only betrayed his colleagues, he had given public voice to a those who would attack what they believed was a sanctified institution for the people! They hadn't wanted to believe it, they had fought against it, yet within the recesses of their hearts, the better journalists had to know that they had been prostitutes of the rich, that they were a part of society that was as establishment as their owners.

Not long after having delivered his attack, Swinton founded his own newspaper to be a voice against the excesses of the trusts and for bringing injustices to the people's attention. The front page of *John Swinton's Paper* carried the proclamation of principles:

1. Boldly upholding the Rights of Man in the American Way, 2. Battling Against the Accumulated Wrongs of Society and Industry, 3. Striving for the organization and interests of workingmen, and giving news of the Trades and Union, 4. Warning the American people against the treasonable and crushing schemes of Millionaires, Monopolists, and Plutocracy.

John Swinton had the energy, enthusiasm, and concern for the people to bring about change. But, he lacked the one ingredient to make his newspaper a force for social change—he didn't have the financial support. It would now take two millionaires and their newspapers to extend Swinton's beliefs that the people deserve better than their society is willing to offer, who would sensationalize the nation and change not only the course of American journalism, but American history as well.

'Devoted to the Public Welfare'

Joseph Pulitzer (1847-1911), like Horace Greeley and James Swinton, threw his editorial support behind the nation's working class, first in St. Louis where he made the *Post-Dispatch* one of the nation's greatest newspapers, one which boldly exposed municipal corruption, then in New York City where the *New York World* eclipsed the *Tribune* as the nation's most influential newspaper.

Pulitzer was born in Hungary, and came to America at the age of  seventeen, a volunteer in the Union cavalry during the last year of the Civil War. It was an experience that would lead him into a lifelong opposition to militarism. After the war, with minimal English language skills, facing discrimination not only because of being an immigrant but because he was a Jew, Pulitzer went to work on the docks, and was eventually hired as a reporter for the *Westliche Post*, a German-language daily in St. Louis. Sixteen hours a day, seven days a week, he was one of the reporters who wrote stories opposing the powerful while supporting the poor and impoverished. Eventually, he was able to buy a struggling newspaper, combine it with another, and became owner of the English language *Post-Dispatch*. Soon, Pulitzer and editor John A. Cockerill (1845-1896) led campaigns against police corruption, crooked politicians, and the abuse of public trust, and eventually succeeded in mobilizing small business and the middle class to rise in protest.

Joseph Pulitzer

In New York, he took over the struggling *World*, and declared in his first editorial:

[The *World* is] dedicated to the cause of the people rather than that of the purse-potentates [and will] expose all fraud and sham, fight all public evils and abuses [and] will serve and battle for the people with earnest sincerity. [May 11, 1883]

Outlining a ten-point program of reform, Pulitzer, on the verge of becoming one of the most affluent people in the country, declared that he and his newspaper supported massive economic reform that would tax income, inheritances, luxuries, and monopolies, forcing the rich to take the burden of supporting the nation's social and economic necessities.

Within months, the *World* was crusading against the excesses of the wealthy and helping the oppressed classes, including immigrants and labor, publishing myriad articles about the New York City sweatshops that exploited immigrants, of corporations that owned tenement housing, of public officials whose first loyalty was to Big Business and their own bank accounts.

Expanding the concepts of the penny press, and resorting to sensationalism, Pulitzer pushed the *World's* circulation to 250,000 within four years, up from about 15,000 when he took over. Under the editorial leadership of Cockerill, chief editorial writer William H. Merrill, Sunday editor Arthur Brisbane, managing editor Ballard Smith, and city editor Solomon S. Carvalho, the *World* became the largest circulation newspaper in the country. By the end of the century, the *World* would have more than one million circulation, much of it from its reputation as a supporter of the poor and oppressed. Every Christmas, the *World* provided dinners for the poor; every winter, it provided coal to the needy; every summer, it brought free ice to the city's tenements; and always it tried to provide for free medical care for those unable to afford even the lowest fees of the "horse and buggy" practitioner. In 1895, the *World* campaigned against industrialist-financier J. P. Morgan, forcing the federal government to sell bonds to the public rather than special-interest corporations; shortly after the birth of the twentieth century, the *World* attacked William K. Vanderbilt and the New York Central Railroad, one of the largest and most corrupt monopolies in the nation.

As expected, Pulitzer continued to campaign for the rights of labor, declaring his opposition to the nation's aristocracy by proclaiming:

Our aristocracy is the aristocracy of labor. The man who by honest ernest toil supports his family in respectability, who works with a strong heart and a strong hand, who fights his way through life courageously, maintains his good name through privacy and temptations, and winning from his children in respect as well as love, is the proudest aristocrat in the American public. The new *World* is his organ.

The *World* campaigned for eight-hour work days, only a half-day of work on Saturdays, and weekly salaries, rather than the monthly salaries corporations were paying.[1] In 1892, the *World* gave front-page play to the murder of striking steelworkers by Carnegie-hired Pinkerton guards in Pittsburgh; on its editorial pages, William H. Merrill, one of journalism's crusading editors, attacked the steel trusts and the abuses of management, at a time when most newspapers were linking labor strikes with treason.

In 1902, the *World* was one of the few publications in the country to support Theodore Roosevelt's decision to assist the coal miners in their determination to force the mine owners, most of whom were owned by the trusts, to forced arbitration. Ironically, when it came to his own newspapers, Pulitzer had difficulty accepting the necessity for journalists to join labor unions, believing that unions were important—but for the skilled and semi-skilled trades.

Pulitzer's newspapers also helped develop the era of the undercover reporter, a method of acquiring information about widespread governmental abuse. In the 1880s, while a reporter for the *Pittsburgh Dispatch*, Elizabeth Cochran had uncovered corruption in Mexico, leading to her expulsion from that country. Now at the *World*, Cochran, writing under the name of Nellie Bly, went undercover to learn the truth behind some major societal problems; for these stories, she got herself committed to a mental asylum in order to write about the squalor and inhumane conditions in the city's mental health system, had herself arrested to investigate abuse of women prisoners, posed as the wife of a pharmaceutical manufacturer in order to expose bribes given by lobbyists, and worked in several jobs to learn then report about sweatshop conditions. In 1889 as a promotion stunt for the *World*, Bly, who helped usher in the era of the participant-journalist, proved that a person could go around the world in less than the eighty days imagined by Jules Verne. Pulitzer's crusades on behalf of the people continued into the twentieth century. In 1904, Frank I. Cobb, soon to

---

[1]Workers who were paid monthly often found that the last few days of the month they had to borrow from their employers, usually at inflated rates, and were forever in debt to the company. Further, corporations that paid monthly were able to use the workers' money in the interim, earning additional interest or for buying and selling stocks and commodities, increasing corporate profits.

become one of the nation's most influential editorial writers, began replacing John Merrill who was nearing retirement. Under Pulitzer's and Cobb's direction, the *World* continued to attack corporate excesses and corruption.

In 1907, Pulitzer, less than four years from his death, formalized the creed that had dominated his newspapers' editorial policies:

I know that my retirement will make no difference in its cardinal principles; that it will always fight for progress and reform, never tolerate injustice or corruption, always fight demagogues of all parties, never belong to any party, always oppose privileged classes and public plunderers, never lack sympathy with the poor, always remain devoted to the public welfare, never be satisfied with merely printing news, always be drastically independent, never be afraid to attack wrong, whether by predatory plutocracy or predatory poverty.

Pulitzer's statement appears every day on the editorial page of the *St. Louis Post-Dispatch.*

'Upsetting the Settled Order'

William Randolph Hearst (1863-1951) who inherited his first millions from a miner father who later was accused of buying himself a U.S. senate seat from California, first fought for the people, showed concern for his employees, supported media unions and the goals of the American Federation of Labor, in direct opposition to the markedly anti-union philosophy of the American Newspaper Publishers Association,[2] and organized crusades against corruption and for the poor. Like Pulitzer, Hearst also recognized that helping the poor and oppressed also resulted in newspaper credibility—and increased circulation among the masses.

In 1887, having been expelled from Harvard for having sent gift-wrapped chamber pots to his professors—with each chamber pot having a picture of the professor pasted on the bottom—and after a year on the staff of Pulitzer's *World*, Hearst persuaded his father to let him take over the struggling *San Francisco Examiner*, a poorly-written and edited newspa-

---

[2]The *Los Angeles Examiner*, which Hearst created in 1903, was given the full support of the labor movement which had been involved in wars with the anti-labor *Los Angeles Times*. Ironically, it was a strike against the *Examiner*, when the Hearst chain had turned away from labor, that eventually led it to fall well behind the *Times* and its eventual death in 1989. The *Times* remains a non-union newspaper.

per which had become part of the family fortune several years earlier as partial compensation for a gambling debt.

Within weeks, the younger Hearst began modeling the *Examiner* after Pulitzer's editorial philosophy, and soon not only bought himself excellent reporters—among them Mark Twain and Ambrose Bierce—but initiated innumerable crusades, speaking out on behalf of the middle-class and the poor. If there was any kind of a tragedy in San Francisco, Hearst spared no expense to rush food or clothes or whatever was necessary to assist, making sure, of course, that everyone knew that the assistance came from the *Examiner*.

Using a Pulitzer-inspired technique, Frank Peltret created a situation that caused him to be committed to Napa State Hospital for a month; the result was a sensational, and highly accurate, look at criminal abuse of mental patients. Winifred Black (later known as Annie Laurie, a "sob sister" feature writer), feigned illness to investigate management and health care practices of a San Francisco hospital; the stunt, as in New York, helped bring an end to a social problem. Other undercover stunts included living with the Mormons in order to report on the problems of polygamy and working in a fruit cannery to report about oppression of women in industry.

However, one of the most powerful and enduring newspaper crusades was the *Examiner's* incessant condemnation of the Republican-owned Southern Pacific Railroad of Collis Huntington, which had established a stranglehold upon California. In articles and editorials, Hearst tore into the railroad and Huntington's business practices. The crusade had proven to be politically embarrassing to Hearst's father, a friend of Sen. Leland Stanford, partner in the Southern Pacific.

Unable to get Hearst's father to influence the son, or Hearst to reduce his attacks, the railroad attempted to destroy the publisher's credibility by admitting that, yes, it was true that the Southern Pacific did "occasionally" resort to bribes, but that Hearst's attacks were provoked not by concern for the people, but by the Southern Pacific's refusal to pay the last $8,000 on a $30,000 bribe it had given Hearst. However, the young millionaire was able to show that not only was the money paid for advertising but that there was absolutely no less of an editorial attack against the monopoly after it published the advertisements; Hearst proudly pointed to the fact that his own business manager had even deleted a clause in the advertising contract, one agreed to by almost all other newspapers, that would have required the *Examiner* to restrict its criticisms if it wished to get the advertising. Nevertheless, the railroad's vicious attacks had cut into

Hearst's credibility for quite some time.

In 1895, Hearst—having made the *Examiner* one of the better newspapers on the West Coast, while seeing its circulation top 750,000, up from about 24,000—bought the struggling *New York Journal*, and boldly moved into New York City to challenge the leadership of Pulitzer's *World*. Never forgetting that a powerful newspaper needed excellent reporters and writers, Hearst raided the *World*, buying the reporters' and editors' loyalties with salaries that not even Pulitzer could match.[3] In the *Journal's* November 8, 1896 issue, Hearst let his readers know about that newspaper's direction, stating, "It is the Journal's policy to engage brains as well as to get the news, for the public is even more fond of entertainment than it is of information." Within months, Hearst's *Journal* and Pulitzer's *World*, each trying to outsensationalize the other, launched circulation wars that led to an era of "yel-

William Randolph Hearst

low journalism" that mixed muckraking with sensationalism, and gave muckraking its connotation of vile and intruding journalism. On the streets, rival circulation staffs were known for violence, overturning delivery carts, destroying newspapers as efficiently as they bloodied opposing carriers' bodies.

---

[3] Hearst essentially bought the best of Pulitzer's *Sunday World* staff, including Arthur Brisbane who would become the *Journal's* editor-in-chief and chief architect of the Yellow Journalism era. With salary and bonuses for circulation increase, Brisbane would earn more than $250,000 a year shortly after the turn of the century. However, salaries outside Hearst's publications were often low. Most New York reporters, by the turn of the century, were paid $40-60 per week, but thousands of journalists throughout the country were averaging only about $20 per week, with no job benefits or security, and were definitely second-class citizens to the printers and compositors who were members of unions.

It was his encouragement of the nation's imperialism that had led the
Journal to promote first what would become the Spanish-American War
in 1898, then the invasion of the Philippines which led to more than
200,000 Filipino casualties, in the nation's imperialistic quest for annexa-
tion. The power and influence of Hearst was such that the nation began
referring to the popular Spanish-American War as "Mr. Hearst's War."

Whether or not Hearst created the situation that made war inevitable,
Americans were willing to go to war. In American history, every generation has had a war to fight, opportunities for young men to earn their
ribbons of valor floating on seas of blood. The country was caught up in
a spirit of expanding nationalism and the glory of the military, something
the yellow journals were able to exploit. During the previous century, few
attempts were made to show problems within the military or of a military
life; most magazine articles and novels had shown the glamor of military
balls, the glory of the battle. The Civil War was three decades old; the glory
of battle was enhanced by the old soldiers' recollections, the destruction
of life now softened by time. During the Westward Expansion, "Dime
Novels" brought to even the remotest part of the country the adventures of
the cavalry fighting what were believed to be savage Indians. Almost all
media support the government's action in matters of war, and so it was that
within the nineteenth century, almost no establishment voices spoke out
against the senseless War of 1812 or Mexican-American War of 1847; no
one spoke against the annihilation of the American Indian nations.

Beginning in March 1895, with news about a revolt of Cubans against
Spanish rule, and continuing for more than three years, the nation's
media—often fed their information by Cubans who had escaped to
America and had established a massive information network—published
innumerable stories about the Cubans' "struggle for freedom," exaggerat-
ing even the Cubans' exaggerations. When the Spanish began a systematic
series of reprisals against the Cuban guerrillas, American media were there
to report on atrocities, many of which existed only in reporters' imaginations. In 1897, artist Frederick Remington, who had been sent to Cuba by
Hearst, cabled "the Chief" that there were no atrocities, that war didn't
seem likely, and that he was coming home. Hearst is believed to have
cabled, "Please remain. You furnish the pictures, and I'll furnish the war."[4]
During 1897, the New York media increased their muckraking news about
the Cuban insurrection.

----

[4]Reported by Hearst correspondent James Creelman in *On the Great Highway*
(1901).

By now, the American public, fueled by the media, demanded governmental intervention in Cuba. But still the government of William McKinley refused to act. The possibility of war was even further reduced when Spain sent a new prime minister to Cuba and promised greater autonomy for the island, eventually giving to Cuba almost everything the American government had demanded.

Still stirring war clouds, the *Journal* published a secret message from the Spanish ambassador to the United States, stating that McKinley was "weak and catering to the rabble," the same thing Theodore Roosevelt, assistant secretary of the Navy, and many others were saying. With the *Journal's* publication of the diplomatic message intended only for dissemination among the Spanish rulers, and extensive revelations of what the *Journal* claimed were Spanish atrocities, Americans were hyped for war. On February 15, 1898, the American battleship Maine was sunk in Havana harbor, with the loss of 266 lives. There were two probable causes for the explosions—a Cuban revolutionary agent could have placed explosives at the ship's waterline, retaliation against the possibility that America would support Spain in its plans to give Cuba autonomy rather than independence; more likely, the sinking of the Maine was the result of an internal explosion.

On February 17, 1898, the *World* speculated across eight columns, "MAINE EXPLOSION CAUSED BY BOMB OR TORPEDO?" It *thought* Spain was involved, but wasn't sure. The *Journal* was. In that day's issue, the *Journal* reported in a full-page banner, "DESTRUCTION OF THE WAR SHIP MAINE WAS THE WORK OF AN ENEMY." A caption under an eight-column drawing informed the Americans, "Naval Officers Think the Maine was Destroyed by a Spanish Mine." The next day, the *Journal* reported, "THE WHOLE COUNTRY THRILLS WITH WAR FEVER."

Both the United States and Spain launched immediate investigations; the *World* and *Journal* sent investigators to Cuba, then incorrectly reported the two countries' official statements that stated Spain was not involved in the sinking. During the next two months, Americans prepared for war, forming volunteer militia, and pressuring Congress into appropriating a $50 million defense fund. In March, Sen. John M. Thurston of Nebraska candidly added another reason for the war:

> War with Spain would increase the business and earnings of every American railroad. It would increase the output of every American factory. It would stimulate every branch of industry and commerce.

On April 18, the Congress called for American intervention in Cuba, action supported by the *Journal, World*, and *Sun*, and most major American newspapers, although opposed by the *Herald, Tribune*, and a few other metropolitan newspapers. Six days later, the U.S. declared war.

The Spanish-American War—with Col. Teddy Roosevelt leading his Rough Riders regiment up San Juan Hill, Adm. Dewey seizing Manilla, William Randolph Hearst leading a small flotilla of private boats in the Battle of Santiago Bay, and several hundred American reporters, photographers, and artists on Cuban battlefields—was over in four months, with the loss of about 2,500 American lives, most from malaria or yellow fever. However, the victory placated the expansionist Americans who triumphantly noted that from the war the country acquired the Philippines, Guam, and Puerto Rico. Within a year, America in its imperialistic destiny also annexed Hawaii, Samoa, and Wake Island.

It was the alleged Spanish atrocities against Cubans that had been a major factor leading to war with Spain; ironically, proven atrocities by Americans against the Filipinos were not heard, as only a few muckraking journalists were able to get to the truth behind the Americans' subjugation of the Philippines. It was during the Filipino uprising in 1899 that 70,000 Americans committed atrocities, leading to more than 200,000 Filipino casualties, at a cost of less than 10,000 American casualties. However, a few journalists used their influence to dig out stories about American concentration camps and torture, atrocities that far exceeded anything the Spanish did to the Cubans. Soon, the voices of journalists Samuel Clemens and Carl Schurz, social worker Jane Addams, business executive Andrew Carnegie, and labor organizer Samuel Gompers were heard along side that of U.S. Sen. George Hoar of Massachusetts, founder of the 500,000-member Anti-Imperialist League. Eugene Debs, socialist leader of the American Railway Union, was denounced for anti-war views. Responding to the nation's people and its press, Debs said, "In 1894, the press denounced [the railroad strikers] for the alleged reason that we were murderous and bloodthirsty, and now the same press opposes us because we are not." Even the *Journal* had doubts about the Americans' actions. However, as during the Mexican-American and Vietnam wars, the dissenters were smothered by the establishment press which had advocated what it had believed to be America's imperial destiny. One hundred and thirteen days after it began, the "splendid little war," as Secretary of State John Hay had declared it, was over, America had expanded its imperialistic destinies, and the Spanish empire was finally dissolved.

The war had done nothing to diminish Hearst's crusading spirit, and may actually have given him the psychological stimulus to realize that a great newspaper could effect both political and social change. In 1899, the *Journal* increased its attacks upon the trusts. The Sherman Anti-trust Act of 1890, although a powerful piece of legislation, had done little to break the trusts which skirted the laws by creating holding companies or single corporations with innumerable subsidiaries. And, by payoffs to governmental officials and the various legislatures, Big Business was able to pull the teeth of the law. Under Brisbane's editorial direction, and with Hearst's full encouragement, the *Journal* broadened its sweep, launching a vicious series of attacks against political corruption and the Tammany Hall machine. It was this attack which would eventually lead Tammany into launching an all-out war against Hearst's ambition to become President of the United States. In 1902, with the assistance of the Tammany machine, he was elected to the U.S. House of Representatives where he sponsored several bills that reflected his personal philosophy of reform; the following year, he showed political strength by his second-place showing in the national Democratic convention for the presidency. Still in Congress, Hearst ran for mayor of New York City in 1905, only to lose by about 3,500 votes. A subsequent investigation indicated that had there not been massive fraud in registration of illegal voters, combined with thousands of persons voting up to a dozen times each, Hearst would probably have won election as New York's mayor. The following year, he received the Democratic party's nomination for governor, only to lose to Republican Charles Evans Hughes whose Republican party was able to invoke not only traditionally-Democratic Tammany loyalty but a wave of Hearst-hatred.

Hearst had the political ambition, but it was his media empire that had helped bring about change. Almost a lone voice among the media, as he had been in the Congress, Hearst not only called for destruction of the trusts, but for the nationalization of the mining and transportation industries, public ownership of franchises, aid to the indigent, an annual tax based upon people's incomes, and the direct election of U.S. senators, as opposed to the selection within party caucuses. They were policies that led many to call Hearst a "socialist" or "Communist," not long after calling him a hero for exposing what they thought were Cuban atrocities. Eventually, the nation would respond by destroying the trusts, regulating the franchises, establishing a welfare system designed to benefit the poor and oppressed, initiating a graduated income tax, reforming municipal elections, and electing their senators by popular vote.

Although William Randolph Hearst used the power of a mass circulation daily newspaper to help the people, he was attacked for using the crusades to selfishly increase his profit, and the power of a mass circulation empire to force compliance to his wishes. According to muckraker Lincoln Steffens, writing in his 1939 autobiography, Hearst was "like a reformer in politics; he was an innovator who was crashing into the business, upsetting the settled order of things, and he was not doing it as we would have done it. He was doing it his way." Steffens condemned Hearst for discovering "that there was room at the bottom, and with sensational news sensationally written and pictured, he did reach for and get the people. He was a demagogue; he was pro-labor." [pp. 539-540]. However, in 1906, Steffens would write an excellent profile of Hearst, one so balanced that his own staff had accused him of having been "taken in" by the charismatic Hearst.

Louis Filler, in *Crusaders in American Liberalism* (1939), in an era of Hearst-hatred, furthered the attack:

He dived to the bottom of the reader's mind and stirred up the filth and despair that had lain so quiet before. . . . Indeed, Hearst lied, distorted, sensationalized. But throughout the later years of the Nineties, and particularly during the muckraking period, there was hardly a reformer or revolutionist of note whose thoughts were not at one time or another woven into the skein of newspapers and magazines which carried the stamp of Hearst's personality. . . .

Hearstism, then, meant stirring the prevailing muck. [pp. 133-134.]

Nevertheless, the Hearst of the 1890s believed in the people, cared about their problems, and wanted to make things right in a world controlled by the rich and politically adept. That he would become the greatest media power in the country, that he had become cynical and eventually turned from labor and some of the socialist causes he supported, that he would abuse the power he had inherited, should not detract from the crusading spirit he brought into American journalism.

CHAPTER 3

The Receiver of Ideas

By the turn of the century, with the rise of progressivism—an activist libertarianism that emphasized that not only was government was an extension of the people, but that the people must change the government in order to improve society[1]—muckraking spilled out of the newspaper columns and into other media. From newspapers, magazines, and books, the public was learning about crime, corruption, and the major social problems that America had yet to recognize, let alone correct. It would now be a national magazine that would take muckraking farther than ever, pounding story after story of poverty, worker exploitation, corporate excesses, political corruption, and consumer abuse until the public demanded regulation and the federal government finally had to yield.

In 1893, Samuel S. McClure (1857-1949), John S. Phillips (1861-1949), and Albert Brady, friends since their days as students at Knox College, established *McClure's Magazine*, nine years after McClure and Phillips had founded the nation's first newspaper syndicate; Brady was recruited from a job as publisher of the *Davenport* (Iowa) *Daily Times*. Although *McClure's* developed a circulation of about forty thousand the first year, it was in precarious financial condition, even after a $6,000 initial capitalization by Col. J. Pope, one of McClure's former employers, and subsequent loans of almost $10,000, including $5,000 from Arthur

---

[1] The Progressive movement, with Theodore Roosevelt, and Sens. Robert La Follette and Albert Beveridge as its best-known spokesmen, were able to bring about significant social legislation during the first decade of the twentieth century, and were primarily responsible for the establishment of the initiative, referendum, and recall in the political process to force government to be more responsive to the needs of the people.

Conan Doyle whose Sherlock Holmes mysteries were enchanting American audiences.

McClure, Phillips, and Brady believed that a well-written, well-edited magazine always had a place in the American market, and *McClure's* quickly earned that reputation, as McClure and Phillips hired the best writers, paid them well, and gave them wide latitude to develop, with few time constraints, significant articles that were both accurate and thorough.[2]

In fiction, *McClure's* would publish the stories of both not-yet-discovered as well as many of the most popular American writer-journalists, including Willa Cather, Stephen Crane, Theodore Dreiser, Bret Harte, Jack London, O. Henry, Robert Louis Stevenson, and Booth Tarkington; among the British authors were Arthur Conan Doyle and Rudyard Kipling. Others on the staff would include Frank N. Doubleday, soon to become founder of one of the nation's most respected book publishing companies; and John H. Finley, who would become editor-in-chief of *The New York Times*; artists Dan Beard, A.B. Frost, and Charles Dana Gibson—as well as Samuel Hopkins Adams, Ray Stannard Baker, Albert A. Boyden, Burton J. Hendrick, Lincoln Steffens, Ida Tarbell, and George Kibbe Turner, among the best investigative reporters the nation had ever produced.

As he had done with the best short story and serial writers, McClure went after the best in science writing. The first science story—written by Ida Tarbell (1857-1944), whom McClure had met in Paris (after he had read a manuscript of hers in the States) while she was developing her writing skills—was an exclusive interview with Louis Pasteur. During the next four years, *McClure's* published in-depth stories about X-rays and wireless telegraphy, and exclusive interviews with Thomas Edison and Alexander Graham Bell.

A year after its founding, with the publication of Ida Tarbell's nationally-acclaimed biographical series about Napoleon, circulation doubled to about 90,000. In November 1895, Tarbell's second series of sketches, "The Early Life of Lincoln," combined with a literate mix of general stories, sent circulation past 250,000, and monthly advertising pages to about 150. In 1898, *McClure's* published Tarbell's series about Lincoln's later life, and circulation shot up another hundred thousand.

---

[2]At the time, freelance writers were paid by the word or by the page; McClure paid them by the story—"on such a salary as would relieve him of all financial worry . . ." [*My Autobiography*, p. 245.]

With its strong editorial content, and a cover price of only ten cents, at a time when most magazines sold for at least twenty-five cents, *McClure's* was able to draw a strong circulation base. By 1900, it had more than 350,000 paid subscriptions; in 1906, at the height of the muckraking era, circulation topped 500,000.

With that foundation of editorial quality and high circulation, *McClure's* added a strong advertising base, leading all American magazines in pages of advertising, and insulating it somewhat from advertiser abuse as it led the pack of muckrakers.

For the first few years, *McClure's* had preached the American dream, publishing profiles of outstanding corporate executives whose names were known to the middle class. Four years after its founding, McClure wrote in the October 1897 issue:

S.S. McClure

The purpose of the founders of this magazine has been and is to bring within reach of a greater mass of readers than before enjoyed the opportunity, the fresh product of the best writers of fiction, the clear presentation of the latest and most far-reaching developments of science, the most vivid and human pictures of the great men and events of our history—in short, to give our readers from month to month a moving living transcript of the intelligent, interesting, human endeavor of the time. We . . . wish to gain material success, but we want to gain it by those means which appeal to our intellectual as well as to our moral self-respect. ["McClure's Magazine: Reminisces and Insights," p. 1101]

To Rob the Bees

It was S.S. McClure's spirit that drove his staff, that brought forth the muckraking era, that gave boldness and dimension to the first decade of the twentieth century. "On his way up," said Ida Tarbell in her autobiography, McClure "had gathered about him a horde of dependents with whom he was always ready to share his last dollar. He was reckless with money as with ideas." [p. 255] Editorially, said Tarbell, McClure "cared above all for the soundness, the truthfulness of the magazine."

Willa Cather, *McClure's* managing editor from 1906 to 1912, remembered that McClure "could take an average reporter from the daily press, give him a 'line' to follow, a trust to fight, a vice to expose—this was all in that good time when people were eager to read about their own wickedness—and in two years the reporter would be recognized as an authority . . . The strangest thing was that [these reporters], staring at their own faces on newspapers and billboards, fell to venerating themselves." ["Ardessa," *Century*, May 1918.]

Lincoln Steffens, writing in 1931, recalled:

McClure was a good journalist, one of the best I ever knew . . . Smiling, enthusiastic, [he] was the receiver of the ideas of his day.

He was a flower that did not sit and wait for the bees to come and take his honey and leave their seeds. He flew forth to find and rob the bees. He was rarely in the office. "I can't sit still," he shouted. "That's your job. I don't see how you can do it." One reason that he could not stay in the office was that we checked him. That, too, was my job, the job of us all, to hold down S. S. But, his nerves drove him, too; his curiosity, his love of being in it, his need to wonder, and to be wondered about. He followed the news, especially big, personal news. If a new author rose on the horizon, or an explorer started for it, or a statesman blew in over it, S. S. went forth to meet him and "get him into *McClure's*." To Africa he traveled, to Europe often, to the west, south, east, and the north of the United States to see things and men, to listen and to talk. Field work was his work. Ideas were his meat, and he never knew where he got them. He told an explorer once what the explorer had seen in the Antarctic; he picked out a few suggestive remarks of the dull man's short account and, taking the story away from him, described the man's own trip to him . . . [*Autobiography*, p. 362.]

Ray Stannard Baker, agreeing with Steffens, remembered that the nation's greatest muckraking publisher "had a highly creative mind . . . and was all intuition and impulse, bursting with nervous energy, one of the most unorganizible, impatient, and disorderly men I ever knew."

However, the success of *McClure's*, as his staff knew and Baker recalled, was the presence of McClure's genius "as edited and condensed by J. S. Phillips, and guided and bounded on the business side by the clear-running intelligence of Albert Brady." [*American Chronicle*, p. 94]

Phillips, who had studied at Knox and Harvard colleges and the University of Leipzig, ran the day-to-day operations of the magazine, functioning as both editor and general manager. Ida Tarbell, in her autobiography, remembered Phillips as "an invaluable aid. . . . He was no easy editor. He never wheedled, never flattered, but rigidly tried to get out of you what he conceived to be your best. . . . I never had an editor who so quickly and unerringly spotted weakness, particularly in construction." [*All in the Day's Work*, p. 158]

Ray Stannard Baker agreed, recalling that Phillips was . . .

. . . was the most creative editor I ever knew [who] could tell wherein an article failed and why; he could usually make fertile suggestions for improving it. . . . He was thoughtful, sensitive, critical, with a deep love for the genuine, the thorough, the sincere in literature and art. There was nothing flamboyant about him. He had a strong sense, in which S.S. McClure was deficient, of cooperation with his associates. . . . [*American Chronicle*, p. 95.]

Insight Into a Criminal Mind

By the turn of the century, *McClure's* had begun its investigations that showed the public that the government and corporate America had conspired to violate the public trust.

In 1900, McClure published "Stories from the Underworld," a series written by Josiah Flynt Willard (1869-1907) and Alfred Hodden, writing under the names Josiah Flynt and Francis Walton. The series was the first major study of the nature of the criminal. According to McClure, the series was a "philosophical [study] about a [social] class . . . which the great mass of people know nothing, except that they are law-breakers." Willard had spent several years within the "underworld" and wrote from that knowledge, revealing great insight into the human condition. Known as "Cigarette," Willard had been born into wealth, but chose the life of a tramp, running away from home several times before he was out of school. According to historian Louis Filler:

The roads were not safe, as the growing and well-favored Josiah soon learned. But they held a fascination for him and he returned to them again and again. Each time he was wiser than he had been before, and bolder in his dealings with the criminals and tramps who were his companions. Fortunately for him he was a born actor and mimic and was able to conform to the ways of hobo society. As it was, being small and slight, he was always in danger among people for whom brute force was a ready resort. Several times, Josiah narrowly escaped injury at the hands of vicious tramps who suspected him of not "belonging" or simply did not like him. . . .

[In Europe, he] became intimately acquainted with the dregs of German . . . and French society, of Russian and Italian and Swiss. His ability to adapt himself to strange situations was amazing. Friends later told how he could take them with him to the slums of a city, then change completely before their eyes merely by shifting his gait, altering the movements of his hands and eyes, and talking rapidly in a strange, unfamiliar language. It was, in fact, at such times that he became creatively alive; he was otherwise a quiet young man, unassuming and attentive to others, who never thought any thoughts but his own. [*Crusaders for American Liberalism*, pp. 69-70.]

In 1894, at the age of twenty-five, Willard had begun writing about the people who moved from place to place, existing in poverty, often only steps ahead of the police. The success of his articles, published in some of the nation's leading publications, led to *Tramping With Tramps* (1899). Now, in 1900, with *McClure's* sponsorship, Willard, assisted by Alfred Hodder, a brilliant young writer who would become a part of the reform movement of New York City, was telling the people about a social class they had known about only through dime novels and rumor. The series, which had begun in the August issue, was eventually collected into book form as *The Powers That Prey*.

In 1901, McClure published Willard's series about crime in several American cities; it was a series that finally brought many of the problems of urban crime to the attention of the public. According to Willard, the underworld felt secure that the public accepted crime since it accepted corruption among its own police. Later that year, McClure published Willard's second book, *The World of Graft*, a thoroughly-documented study of municipal corruption at all levels, detailing the relationships between police and the criminal class. Most readers were shocked at Willard's revelations, many refused to believe them, a few—notably the New York police—believed them, and were out to "get" him, although Willard knew how to blend into the underworld to avoid retribution. *The World of Graft* became one of the most popular books of the new century, and eventually led to municipal reform in several cities.

With Willard's articles and books proving that parts of America were searching for a change, and willing to accept journalistic thrusts at its own society, McClure increased his magazine's emphasis on pointing out social problems previously unknown to most people.

To Live in the Coal Shadow

Shortly after the turn of the century, Isaac Kahn Friedman had looked at the steel industry, of worker exploitation and immigrants forced into their own ghettos, and wrote *By Bread Alone* (1901), a powerful revolutionary novel set on a bed of truth, and published by McClure. For the base, Friedman used the violent Homestead strike in Western Pennsylvania which had shown the nation the uncontested power of Big Business, with the security of the National Guard to enforce capitalism's wishes, to crush the workers.[3]

With governmental protection, the mine and mill owners were able to increase their wealth at the expense of the lives of their workers. Journalist-historians Richard O. Boyer and Herbert M. Morais, in *Labor's Untold Story*, reported:

When a man left in the morning dark for the mine neither he nor his wife nor his children knew if they would ever see him again. Working up to his knees in water, the slow drip of falling drops soaking him as he labored, he never knew when he would hear the dreadful rip of cracking timbers as rotten scaffolds buckled under the weight of sliding tons of falling coal. Nor did he know at what instant he might see that flash of searing fire that began with an explosion of poisoned gas, the blaze leaping through the lethal air and flashing down the black tunnel until it enveloped and killed the working miners. He knew only that the mine owners without one exception had refused over the years to install emergency exits, ventilating and pumping systems, or to make provision for sound scaffolding. [p. 46]

The problems were no better for the children of the miners, for like their fathers, they, too, had to work the mines, and after them, it would be their children trapped in the darkness of exploitation. In February 1902, in one of its first articles about labor, *McClure's* highlighted the problems associated with enforced child labor. In "Children of the Coal Shadow," a powerful indictment of child-labor in the mines of Pennsylvania's anthracite coal industry, Francis H. Nichols reported:

Almost the first words which [a miner's] baby can grasp are his mother's complaints of the exorbitant prices charged for the necessities of life at the "company's store," or his father's curses at the injustice of some "docking boss," or his sister's sobs when a ten-per-

---

[3]During the previous three decades, National Guard bases were often built near major industrial cities, not because of military or personnel necessity, but because some state and federal politicians, in the pay of the trusts, had made sure that the Guard units were available to protect the trusts when necessary.

cent wage reduction has been declared at the knitting mill. . . .

Painfully ludicrous and pitiful as it all is, it is perfectly understandable. The children of the Coal Shadow have no child life. The little tots are sullen, the older children fight; they rarely play, and almost their only amusement is . . . the union and the strike that is the logical result of the conditions of their existence. They have no friends. Their parents, driven by what they think is necessity, forswear them into bondage. Their employers, compelled by what they regard as economic forces, grind them to hatred. The State, ruled by influences, either refrains from amalgamating laws or corrective enforcement. The rest of the world doesn't care. So the shadow of the coal heap lies dark upon these "unionized" little ones [who have worked in the mines from the time they were eight or nine years old] . . . Within a few years the breaker boy will be a miner. It is the only trade with which he is familiar, and his lack of education will make a commercial or professional career for him almost impossible. He will have to live in Anthracite, because it is the only country where a hard-coal miner can follow his trade. The mill girl [who has also worked from the age of nine or ten] will marry early in her life; her husband will be a miner. They will both be American citizens. They will remain in the Coal Shadow.

In December 1902, *McClure's* published John Mitchell's summary of the strike by anthracite coal miners. President of the United Mine Workers of America, Mitchell could have discussed the brutal conditions in the mines and the contempt by the owners for the workers, as evidenced by meager pay, lack of adequate safety measures, and the subjugation of the workers to some of the most abusive work rules in the country in the country. Mitchell, however, focused upon the organization of the UMW:

The fundamental error of capital in the coal strike was the unwillingness of the companies to concede the right of labor to organize and to act through its organization as they act themselves. We are living in the age of combination, of consolidations, of federation; labor is following in the footsteps of its partner, capital. The labor organizations do not oppose, or even look with disfavor, upon combination of capital; they recognize it as a natural sequence of the evil effects of disastrous competition. Labor is simply keeping up with the industrial development of our times, and he is rash indeed who seeks to plant himself as an obstacle in the current of progress. Capital finds strength in unity, the average stockholder merging all his influence in the giant corporation. Following the same instinct, labor organizes, minimizing the individual for the good of the whole, and asserts its right to speak and act collectively. [p. 221]

... The great lesson which the coal strike has taught is that the individual is nothing, the good of society at large is everything, and that no man, no combination of men, no matter how many or how powerful, whether they belong to capital or to labor, can set their own interests or their own will against the common good. ...

The strike has taught both capital and labor that they owe certain obligations to society, and that these obligations must be discharged in good faith. ... [p. 220]

The union can no more be crushed than the "trust" can be crushed. The two must work side by side, and hand in hand go peaceably along together. Society's efforts should be directed not to crushing combinations of capital or combinations of labor, but to preservation of the good ones which wholesomely do their share of the world's work, and to regulation and reformation of those which show bad tendencies. ["The Coal Strike," p. 223]

Ulcers Upon the American Dream

Although *McClure's* was publishing stories that exposed greed and public corruption, it wasn't until the January 1903 issue that *McClure's* acknowledged that it had taken a new direction in magazine journalism, a direction that brought social issues into a realm that the people could understand and be affected. In that January issue—marked by an editorial written by McClure about this new direction—were articles by Lincoln Steffens, Ida Tarbell, and Ray Stannard Baker, soon to be identified as the era's leading muckrakers.

For several years, the urban newspapers and magazines had been probing municipal problems, often tying them to corruption. Albert Shaw, in the April 1892 issue of *Review of Reviews*, declared, " . . . the government of the City of New York is a stench and a stink of pollution, a hissing and a byword, a world-wide synonym for all that is iniquitous and abominable." [p. 286] Even a reform administration, with Theodore Roosevelt as police commissioner, had only short-term effects, as corruption and the political machines only "laid low" awhile. New York wasn't the only place where corruption bred.

Mark Sullivan, in "The Ills of Pennsylvania," published in the

October 1901 issue of *The Atlantic Monthly*, asked "What's the matter with Pennsylvania?" then answered, "Indeed, she hath more than one disease. But the principal one is, she is politically the most corrupt state in the Union." [p. 559] Citing several instances of blackmail and bribery by state and local officials, Sullivan pointed out that, "Every hospital, every institution, that depends upon state appropriations is compelled to yield tribute [bribes and concessions to state legislators.]" [p. 560]

However, a few refused to yield to official blackmail. To illustrate, Sullivan looked at John Wanamaker, who would eventually see his department store become one of the nation's largest. Wanamaker began with "an inadequate old two-story building, a transformed freight shed," rejected innumerable requests for bribes by Philadelphia city officials to allow improvements, and was subjected to powerhouse tactics to force him into bankruptcy. True to his beliefs of a moral code of integrity being far greater than political spoils, Wanamaker, who had been postmaster general under William Henry Harrison, was defeated for election to the U.S. Senate when, assured by the machine leaders that for a $200,000 payment they would get him the necessary votes in the legislative caucus, he refused; Boise Penrose, who apparently did buy the votes, was elected.[4]

Writing in the November 1901 issue of *Everybody's*, Percy Stickney Grant, a New York city minister, tore into the problems associated with the urbanization of America:

Cities have been called ulcers. They swell and fester on the surface of human population, which is healthy only by its sparser distribution. They are full of filth, poverty, and vice. They breed criminals. They graduate thieves, murderers, and panderers as naturally as universities graduate scholars.

This is not the worst. Cities not only produce vice and crime, they also consume virtue. More horrible than a disease, they appear like diabolical personalities which subsist upon the strength, health, virtue, and noble aspiration produced in the country. [p. 555]

When S. S. McClure hired Lincoln Steffens (1866-1936), city editor of the well-written and edited *New York Commercial Advertiser*, to be his managing editor, neither had any idea that "The Shame of the Cities," a three-year project that shook America apart, would be the result. Steffens had been one of the nation's better newspaper reporters; his work on the

---

[4] Wanamaker and Robert Ogden had founded *Everybody's* in 1899, owning it four years before selling it to a corporation headed by Erman J. Ridgway.

New York Evening Post more than a decade earlier had led to public awareness of police corruption—as well as his personal friendship with police commissioner Theodore Roosevelt. Now at *McClure's*, Steffens would develop as the nation's best-remembered muckraker. However, first he had to get into the trenches.

In his autobiography, Steffens recalled that "one day S.S. sat down by my side, and he told me very impressively that his brother [Robert, who had earlier objected to Steffens being an editor] was right":

"You may have been an editor," [S.S.] said very sincerely, very kindly. "You may be an editor. But you don't know how to edit a magazine. You just learn to."

"How can I learn?" I asked him, angrily.

He laid his hand on my knee. "Not here," he said. "You can't learn to edit a magazine here in the office."

"Where then can I learn? Where shall I go to learn to be an editor?"

He sprang up and waved his hand around a wide circle.

"Anywhere," he said. "Anywhere else. Get out of here, travel— go—somewhere. Go out in the advertising department. Ask them where they have transportation credit. Buy a railroad ticket, get on a train, and there, where it lands you, there you will learn to edit a magazine." [*Autobiography*, p. 364.]

The trail led to St. Louis where he met Claude Wetmore, *Post-Dispatch* city editor, whose reporting over the previous decade had exposed the city's corrupt government; and Joseph Folk, a prosecuting attorney who was trying to weed crime from a well-entrenched city machine. Folk had made several revelations, many published in Pulitzer's *Post-Dispatch*, but still the problems existed. Now, shortly after the turn of the century, Wetmore and Folk would be the guide for Steffens to learn more about the nature of city government.[5] In the October 1902 issue of *McClure's*, Wetmore's and Steffens' article, "Tweed Days in St. Louis," was published, the opening paragraph shocking some, amusing many:

St. Louis, the fourth city in size in the United States, is making two announcements to the world: one that it is the worst-governed city in the land; the other that it wishes all men to come there and see it.

---

[5]The article was originally to have been written by Wetmore, with Steffens as editor. However, Wetmore insisted on being a co-author after Steffens added significant information about corruption which Wetmore may have deliberately left out. Wetmore would eventually write *The Battle Against Bribery*, a round-up of corruption in St. Louis.

TWEED DAYS IN ST. LOUIS

Joseph W. Folk's Single-handed Exposure of Corruption,
High and Low

BY CLAUDE H. WETMORE AND LINCOLN STEFFENS

ST. LOUIS, the fourth city in size in the United States, is making two announcements to the world : one that it is the worst governed city in the land ; the other that it wishes all men to come and see it. It isn't our worst governed city ; Philadelphia is that. But St. Louis is worth examining while we have it inside out.

There is a man at work there, one man, working all alone, but he is the Circuit (district or state) Attorney, and he is "doing his duty." That is what thousands of district attorneys and other public officials have promised to do and boasted of doing. This man has a literal sort of mind. He is a thin-lipped, firm-mouthed, dark little man, who never raises his voice, but goes ahead doing, with a smiling eye and a set jaw, the simple thing he said he would do. The politicians and reputable citizens who asked him to run, urged him when he declined. When he said that if elected he would have to do his duty, they said, "Of course." So he ran, they supported him, and he was elected. Now some of these politicians are sentenced to the penitentiary, some are in Mexico. The Circuit Attorney, finding that his "duty" was to catch and convict criminals, and that the biggest criminals were some of these same politicians and leading citizens, went after them. It is magnificent, but the politicians declare it isn't politics.

The corruption of St. Louis came from the top. The best citizens—the merchants and big financiers—used to rule the town, and they ruled it well. They set out to outstrip Chicago. The commercial and industrial war between these two cities was at one time a picturesque and dramatic spectacle such as is witnessed only in our country. Business men were not mere merchants and the politicians were not mere grafters ; the two kinds of citizens got together and wielded the power of banks, railroads, factories, the prestige of the city, and the spirit of its citizens to gain business and population. And it was a close race. Chicago, having the start, always led, but St. Louis had pluck, intelligence, and tremendous energy. It pressed Chicago hard. It excelled in a sense of civic beauty and good government ; and there are those who think yet it

might have won. But a change occurred. Public spirit became private spirit, public enterprise became private greed.

Along about 1890, public franchises and privileges were sought not only for legitimate profit and common convenience, but for loot. Taking but slight and always selfish interest in the public councils, the big men misused politics. The riff-raff, catching the smell of corruption, rushed into the Municipal Assembly, drove out the remaining respectable men, and sold the city—its streets, its wharves, its markets, and all that it had—to the now greedy business men and bribers. In other words, when the leading men began to devour their own city, the herd rushed into the trough and fed also.

So gradually has this occurred, that these same citizens hardly realize it. Go to St. Louis and you will find the habit of civic pride in them ; they still boast. The visitor is told of the wealth of the residents, of the financial strength of the banks, and of the growing importance of the industries, yet he sees poorly paved, refuse-burdened streets, and dusty or mud-covered alleys ; he passes a ramshackle fire-trap crowded with the sick, and learns that it is the City Hospital ; he enters the "Four Courts," and his nostrils are greeted with the odor of formaldehyde used as a disinfectant, and insect powder spread to destroy vermin ; he calls at the new City Hall, and finds half the entrance boarded with pine planks to cover up the unfinished interior. Finally, he turns a tap in the hotel, to see liquid mud flow into wash-basin or bath-tub.

The St. Louis charter vests legislative power of great scope in a Municipal Assembly, which is composed of a Council and a House of Delegates. Here is a description of the latter by the February Grand Jury :

"We have had before us many of those who have been, and most of those who are now, members of the House of Delegates. We found a number of these utterly illiterate and lacking in ordinary intelligence, unable to give a better reason for favoring or opposing a measure than a desire to act with the majority. In some, no trace of mentality or morality could be found ; in others, a low order of

It isn't the worst-governed city; Philadelphia is that. But St. Louis is worth examining . . .

The article shook the St. Louis machine and let the people of other cities know that governmental corruption was not confined just to their own cities.

In his autobiography, published in 1931, Steffens recalled the effect his first major article had upon urban America:

The article on St. Louis brought forth letters, editorials, and all sorts of comment, explaining the extraordinary contributions described. Republicans blamed the Democrats; they overlooked the fact that the worst period in St. Louis had been under a Republican mayor. Eastern interpreters said St. Louis was a western city. New England remarked upon the large foreign population in St. Louis, a German town.

European newspapers . . . talked about youth; America was a young

Lincoln Steffens

country, and the political scandals were growing pains. The English spoke of democracy, with a complacent side glance at the aristocracy of governing class. Business men indicated the politicians and politics as the cause and offered business men and business as the cure. They did not note that it was businessmen who bribed the politicians in St. Louis and that prominent business men who had been elected to the city council to clean up the city were among the confessing boodlers. I myself had held some of these beliefs; I thought vaguely that there was something in them. And I had never for a moment questioned the great moral assumption which underlay all this thinking: that political evils were due to bad men of some sort and curable by the substitution of good men. I was on level with my time, my contemporaries, and our readers.

Joseph Folk eventually won fourteen of the fifteen cases he brought to court; however, the Missouri Supreme Court, strongly suspected of having been bought off by the state's machines, overturned the cases. The people didn't rise up against the Court, for they had long ago believed that there were "others" who were the corrupt ones, that the sweeping indict-ments Folk brought interfered with their right to do business. Ironically, a statewide reform movement swept Folk into the governorship of Missouri—and out of St. Louis. But even here, he found that the reformers began to become uneasy when he turned the spotlight against them. The people of the state, as had the people of St. Louis before them, couldn't believe they were guilty of what Folk was accusing them of. According to Steffens:

They thought they were innocent; they thought that bad men were deceiving and misleading them; they did not know that they them-selves were involved and interested in the corruption. St. Louis found out. Missouri would find out some day, too. When that day came, as it did, then the people of the State would unite with the citizens of St. Louis to stop Folk and his interference with their business. . . . [Folk] was a possibility for president at one time after he was elected governor of Missouri, when he could not have been reelected gover-nor. . . ." [*Autobiography*, p. 397.]

Steffens, who had graduated from the University of California, and had studied philosophy at the universities of Berlin, Heidelberg, Leipzig, and Paris, now determined that he could develop a scientific study of the American city by looking into social causes rather than personality:

The German universities had corrected my American culture to some extent: the laboratory work in psychology there had hammered into me that explanations of natural phenomenon—quick, superficial, common-sense convictions—were apt to be nothing but protective guards set up by the poor, weak human mind to save itself from the temptation and effort to think; that, if you know too surely, you cannot learn; and that, for the purposes of research, you may have theories, but never, never knowledge. I wanted to study cities scientifically, and I argued with Mr. McClure that it would heighten the interest in the articles [if] we were to start out with blank minds an search like detectives for the keys to the mystery, the clues to the truth. He would not have it so. Science did not interest the readers, except as a source of wonders; and besides he was sure of that which he had learned by experience on *McClure's Magazine* and by observation in all other business—that the dictatorship of one strong wise man . . . would abolish our political evils and give us a strong, wise administrator of cities . . . We had a pretty hot fight, and McClure won. What I went to Minneapolis to write about was that democracy was a failure and that a good dictator was what is needed. [*Autobiography*, p. 375.]

With a title for his story, "The Shame of Minneapolis" provided by McClure, Steffens began piecing together news stories that the local press had already published about the city, then tied them together by some brilliant interviewing of local officials. What Steffens found was that Minneapolis had been run by a tyrant who controlled all areas of government, and whose brother was chief of police. A Grand Jury was looking into the corruption, and the foreman had finally taken the role of benevolent dictator, with the grand jury appointing a reform mayor in order to rid Minneapolis of its "shame," just as McClure had said should occur.

In his first paragraph of "The Shame of Minneapolis," published in the January 1903 issue, Steffens outlined his basic belief about the nature of government, as well as the focus of the series:

Whenever anything extraordinary is done in American municipal politics, whether for good or for evil, you can trace it almost inevitably to one man. The people do not do it. Neither do the "gangs," "combines," or political parties. These are but instruments by which bosses (not leaders; we Americans are not led, but driven) rule the people, and commonly sell them out. But there are at least two forms of the autocracy which has supplanted the democracy here as it has everywhere it has been tried. One is that of the organized majority by which, as in Tammany Hall in New York and the Republican machine in Philadelphia, the boss has normal control of more than half the voters. The other [part] is that of the adroitly managed minority. The "good" people are herded into parties and stupefied with convictions and a name, Republican or Democrat; while the "bad people" are so organized or interested by the boss that he can wield their votes to enforce terms with party managers and decide elections.

The second article had hit the American public hard, and gave Steffens a national reputation. In his autobiography, he recalled:

My article on Minneapolis had succeeded beyond all expectations. The newsstand sales had exhausted the printed supply; subscriptions were coming in; and the mail was bringing letters of praise, appreciation, and suggestion. "Come here to this place," they wrote from many cities, towns, and even villages; "you will find scandals that make Minneapolis and St. Louis look like models of good government." [*Autobiography*, p. 392.]

During the next three years, with Albert Boyden (1875-1925) as the magazine's managing editor, Steffens concentrated upon exploring corruption and urban decay throughout American government, focusing upon

Pittsburgh, Philadelphia, Chicago, New York, Cleveland, and Cincinnati, as well as New Jersey, Rhode Island, Missouri, Illinois, Ohio, and Wisconsin. In 1904, his first book, *The Shame of the Cities*, a collection of the first few articles published in *McClure's*, became a best-seller, as well as a call for action.

For the May 1904 issue of *McClure's*, William Allen White reviewed Steffens' book, and the effect his articles had upon urban America:

> [Previously] the great mass of people ... have not known the real facts about real government. They have seen many unpleasant things in the papers, but as each side of the political contest was abusing the other side in telling these unpleasant things, the people have paid little attention to the clamor. But now, when a man comes as Mr. Steffens has come, with no party to advocate, with no reforms to promise or suggest, but with the plain facts—the people will eventually give heed, and sooner or later they will act upon the judgments which the facts force upon them ...

> The fact that after he had written the story of a town's disgrace, public sentiment rose in revolt—as it rose in Minneapolis—merely proves that if other cities knew what corruption is hidden beneath their unruffled fronts, other cities might also rise in virtuous indignation.

However, White also concluded:

> But certain cities did not rise; St. Louis did not; Philadelphia did not, and New York deliberately sat down in her former filth. Facts did not interest her. She was satisfied with the conditions as they were set forth. In the long run, probably most American cities will do as New York has done; turn away from the radical reform to gradual—almost imperceptible reform. [p. 221]

Reflecting upon his years as one of the nation's best investigative reporters, Steffens said he wasn't truly an investigator—a muckraker—but "had simply gone where someone else ... had been doing the work, and picking up the fruits of their labor and risk, described and interpreted their evidence [to a national audience.]" [*Autobiography*, p. 400] Nevertheless, without his skills as an interviewer and ability to hold a mirror to society, it is possible that it would have been many years before the people would have realized that their dirty linen was not only their own problem, but was also affecting their friends, neighbors, and community.

When Steffens left *McClure's* in 1906, George Kibbe Turner extended the series, writing about Galveston (September 1906), Chicago (April 1907), and Tammany Hall's continued control over New York City (June 1909).

With the investigations by Mark Sullivan and Lincoln Steffens as a base, Rudolph Blankenburg wrote a nine-part series for the January through September 1905 issues of *The Arena*. "Forty Years in the Wilderness; Or, Masters and Rulers of 'the Freemen' of Pennsylvania," was one of the nation's most thoroughly-documented and best-reported investigations into Pennsylvania corruption and its effects. U.S. Sen. Simon Cameron, charged Blankenburg, had "originated and laid the foundation for the unparalleled system of debauchery," and State Sen. Matthew Quay, who became the state's machine leader upon Cameron's death, was "a natural born schemer." His facts amply backed up the assertions, as he meticulously reviewed cases of fraud, deception, and graft in not only all levels of the political election process, but also in the awarding of franchises, licenses, and even building permits.

An editorial in the June 1906 issue explained what happened after the series was published:

The Arena containing this series of [articles] were regularly mailed to every important daily and weekly newspaper in Pennsylvania, while the morally alive men and women of the commonwealth were quick to read and circulate this story of political shame, in the hope—considered by many vain—that the people could be aroused from their lethargy. Their hopes were realized. The papers crystallized public sentiment. A tremendous moral awakening followed which shook the state machine to its foundations and overthrew Boss Durham and his corrupt hosts. And the revelations that came in the wake of this popular uprising and which have been disclosed since make the previous charges of Mr. Blankenburg appear tame in the extreme. ["The Muck-Rake Versus the Muck," p. 626]

While Blankenburg's series was exposing Pennsylvania corruption, the state's political structure arrogantly continued its plans to rape the public treasury, with the state capitol being the "golden egg." The *Philadelphia Press*, among other newspapers, brought the graft to the public's attention after several hard-hitting reformers set out to control the state's runaway budget. Owen Wister, leader of a reform movement in Philadelphia, reviewed the construction and subsequent state investigation, and reported in the October 1907 issue of *Everybody's* about significant cost overruns, blatant graft, and inferior workmanship that didn't meet specification:

The Capitol is not good work. Outside, it looks as much like all other Capitols as any banana looks like the rest of the bunch. Inside, it is a monstrous botch of bad arrangement, bad lighting, bad ventila-

tion, and the most bloated bad taste. . . . Pennsylvania learned that it
had paid for putty instead of mahogany. It had paid for plaster instead
of marble.

Pointing to specifics, Wister noted that the state paid over $200,000
for desks costing $49,000, $1.4 million for chandeliers costing $526,000,
and more than $2 million for office equipment costing only $412,000.

In the June 1906 issue of *The Arena*, speaking on behalf of the
reformers and muckrakers, Wister had concluded:

> So long as the public was in ignorance of the criminality and
> corruption that flourished by reason of the partnership between
> corporate and privileged interests and the politicians, the people were
> not morally culpable; but now that it has been made plain, the whole
> nation will be morally responsible and the ethical sentiments of the
> people will become blunted in an appalling degree of dishonesty,
> moral turpitude and corruption are not everywhere chased to their
> lairs and the unfaithful ones punished, be they rich or poor, to the
> fullest extent of the law. [p. 627]

With Blankenburg's revelations, combined with exposes in the Philadelphia newspapers, the state had been forced to launch an all-out investigation, leading to the indictment of seventeen persons. *The Arena's*
hopes were being met.

The Most Perfect of Monopolies

A month after "Tweed Days" appeared, *McClure's* published the first
article on the history of Standard Oil, founded in 1870 by John D.
Rockefeller, and under investigation by state and federal legislative bodies
since then, accused of innumerable violations of restraint of trade and
unfair business methods. However, most attempts to restrain Standard
Oil's avariciousness were blocked by prosecutors and legislators, many of
whom found it advantageous to their own financial and political security
to protect the Rockefeller millions.[6] "[The] sanctimonious . . . Rockefeller,
the slim little deacon from Cleveland, . . . knew what he wanted with an
intensity that was almost fierce," wrote Richard O. Boyer and Herbert M.
Morais in *Labor's Untold Story*, observing, "Secretive and soft-footed, he

---

[6]Among those who threw a cloak of protection around Standard Oil was U. S.
Sen. Mark Hanna, chairman of the Republican Party and widely accepted as the
"boss of the Senate."

liked to whisper if it were possible, and he was mildness itself unless money was involved and then he was as savage as a tiger. Her had an 'instinct of conspiracy'; the fact that it was against the law bothered him not a whit." [p. 73] Rockefeller had become a millionaire from oil, and was able not only to buy the loyalty of his friends and workers, but to silence his critics. Thomas W. Lawson, in "Frenzied Finance," published in the August 1904 issue of *Everybody's*, discussed a few of the reasons for Standard Oil's success, concluding it was . . .

. . . largely due to two things—the loyalty of its members to each other and to "Standard Oil," and the punishment of its enemies. Each member before initiation knows it's religion to be rewarded for friends and extermination for enemies. Once a man is within the magic circle [of corporate executives] he at once realizes he is getting all that anyone else on earth can afford to pay him for like services, and still more thrown in for full measure. The public has never heard of a "Standard Oil" man leaving the ranks. . . . While a "Standard Oil" man's reward is always ample and satisfactory, he is constantly reminded in a thousand and one ways that punishment for disloyalty is sure and terrible, and that in no corner of the earth can he escape it, nor can any power on earth protect him from it."

In 1881, the *Atlantic Monthly* had published "The Story of a Great Monopoly," Henry Demarest Lloyd's sweeping indictment of Rockefeller, calling the company "a public enemy." In 1894, Lloyd had broadened his attacks upon Standard Oil and the trusts with publication of *Wealth Against Commonwealth*, describing specific incidents of industrial corruption, graft, and sabotage. However, although the nation rose in indignation at Standard Oil, it was too busy to follow through, trapped by the great depression of 1894. Louis Filler says the failure to break Standard Oil in the late nineteenth century may have been because the nation had other things on its mind:

Worried middle-class Americans accorded Lloyd all honor, but they were too busy trying to elect Bryan to learn much from Lloyd's book. The times were desperate; there was another unnerving depression, and all the disturbances it produced held their attention. Messiahs were appearing; Coxey marched his army [of unemployed] to Washington; "Bloody Bridles" Waite of Colorado made loud and angry appearance at the Democrat convention; Populists, Free Silverites, and labor leaders filled the atmosphere with their slogans. But in the end there was little to show for all the protest and enthusiasm. The Populists disintegrated, Bryan lost the election, strikes were broken everywhere. With the middle-class thrust back, with labor pinned down, the great capitalists were now in the mood and able to push forward their enterprises with more aggressiveness than ever. [*Crusaders for American Liberalism*, p. 26.]

Less than a decade later, with America and its media now involved in a spirit of the great crusades, and with Lloyd's investigations as a base, McClure decided to conduct a thorough investigation of Standard Oil, far more systematic and far deeper than ever done before. In the late 1880s, while on the staff of *The Chautauquan*, Ida Tarbell had done some preliminary research on Pithole, the manufactured city of about 20,000 people that arose with the discovery of oil in Northwest Pennsylvania, and which became nothing more than stripped land thirty years later. Tarbell had a personal interest in getting to the truth—her father was one of the oilmen who was crushed by the developing Rockefeller trust. Now, in the 1890s, the premiere writer on *McClure's*, she was to research the story that would establish her reputation as not only one of the era's best feature writers but one of the best investigative reporters as well. Tarbell, said muckraker Ray Stannard Baker . . .

. . . was the best of us. . . . No one could have been more exacting than she was as a studious inquirer, or more devoted to the truth of the matter, letting the chips fall where they might. And no one was ever more determined as a fighter for the things she believed in, and lived for. She was steady and sound, never sensational in the manner of her writing or in the way she lived, and yet few series of articles in any American journal have ever been more fundamentally sensational that her history of the Standard Oil Company and the doings of John D. Rockefeller and his associates. . . .

She saw with clear eyes the evil in the world, and yet she believed in men; she believed in the "upward spiral of human progress." [*American Chronicle*, pp. 220-221]

For five years, with *McClure's* encouragement and financial support—later estimated at $50,000 including expenses—Ida Tarbell's primary assignment had been to investigate the Rockefeller empire, to dig into the history, workings and greed of Standard Oil, and report what it was doing both to and for the people. It would be the story that established her as one of the nation's best investigative reporters. McClure had believed that the series would be informative, not investigative. "The feeling of the common people [was that the Trusts] had a sort of menace in it," McClure wrote in *My Autobiography* (1913), noting that the public "took a threat-

ening attitude toward the Trusts, and without much knowledge." [p. 238]
According to Tarbell, "We were undertaking what we regarded as a
legitimate piece of historical work. We were neither apologists nor critics,
only journalists intent on discovering what had gone into the making of this
most perfect of monopolies."
[*All in the Day's Work*, p. 206.]

Ida M. Tarbell

For the first two years,
Tarbell had been given full cooperation of Standard Oil; for
the last three years, after asking innumerable pointed questions and having dug deeper
than Standard Oil found comfortable, she received no corporate assistance. But, now, in
the November 1902 issue of
McClure's, she opened what
would be a nineteen-part exposure of Standard Oil's un-
fair business practices. It would be a series that infuriated Rockefeller and
would shake apart his holdings—although Tarbell carefully outlined
Rockefeller's strengths and the benefits the country was getting from
many of the Rockefeller business practices which emphasized efficiency
while resorting to a web of deception and graft. With thorough documen-
tation, Tarbell showed what one monopolistic corporation could do to
destroy competition. It was a penetrating series into the nature of power
and greed, a series that laid open America's greatest monopoly, that
discussed crime and corruption, shady business dealings and little concern
for the people; there would be no libel suit—every fact Tarbell reported
was fully documented.

    At last it was open—there were trusts in the country that had
efficiently and often effortlessly managed not only to strangle the country,
but influenced enough legislators, governmental officials, and regulators
to overlook almost all the abuses the trusts directed against existing
legislation.

    Both Tarbell and *McClure's* were brutally attacked, not only by the
business community, but by other journalists as well. A vicious review
against Tarbell, which appeared in *The Nation*, was reprinted and distributed throughout the country. In *Gunton's Magazine*, a general circulation

magazine founded in 1891 and subsidized by the Rockefeller fortune, articles favorable to the trusts appeared frequently. With the brilliant advice of Ivy Ledbetter Lee, widely regarded as the nation's first professional public relations practitioner, Standard Oil and Rockefeller were able to present their sides of the story, while blunting some of Tarbell's facts. In 1904, after Tarbell's series was collected as a two-volume book, Gilbert Holland Montague wrote *The Rise and Progress of the Standard Oil Company*, a book which Tarbell later said "separated business and ethics in a way that must have been a comfort to [Standard Oil.]" [*All in the Day's Work*, p. 240] Complimentary copies of the book were widely distributed by the publisher, probably with funds provided by Standard Oil. More powerful was a pamphlet by Elbert Hubbard which glorified the advantages of the monopolistic control exerted by Standard Oil to bring efficiency to the industry, while targeting Tarbell and her research:

Ida Tarbell . . . is an honest, bitter, talented, prejudiced and disappointed woman who wrote from her own point of view. And that view is from the ditch, where her father's wheelbarrow was landed by a Standard Oil Wagon. . . . She shot from cover and she shot to kill. Such literary bushwhackers should be answered shot for shot. . . . Sniping the commercial caravan may be legitimate, but to my mind the Tarbell-Steffens-Russell-Roosevelt-Sinclair method of inky warfare is quite unethical . . .

The Standard Oil company should have nailed a few of the Ida Tarbell fairy tales ten years ago. [*The Standard Oil Company* (1910), pp. 13-14.]

Ida Tarbell said that she later learned "five million copies were . . . printed in pamphlet form by Standard Oil Company and were distributed . . . to school teachers and journalists, preachers and 'leaders' from the Atlantic to the Pacific." [*All in the Day's Work*, p. 241]

In 1908, William Randolph Hearst personally revealed several letters he had bought three years earlier—he never could adequately explain why he held them so long—from Standard Oil employees who had stolen then copied the letters from Standard Oil executives to several legislators and regulators; the content of the letters further nailed the company for having used its influence to bribe public officials. Eventually, Standard Oil of Indiana was found guilty of anti-trust violations, fined $29 million in U. S. District Court—a fine it never paid—and forcibly dissolved in May 1911 by a decision of the Supreme Court of the United States. At the same time, the tobacco trust was ordered dissolved. It was more than two decades after Sherman Anti-Trust Act was written into law.

Industrial Anarchy in the Mining Camps

While Steffens was investigating corruption in American cities, and Tarbell was continuing her probe into the nation's largest monopoly, Ray Stannard Baker (1870-1946) was writing articles for *McClure's* about American industry, focusing upon business and labor racketeering. Baker had come to *McClure's* in 1899 from the *Chicago Record*, with a reputation as one of the nation's better reporters, and the author of the recently-published *Our New Prosperity*, a highly-readable account of the nation's "boom" immediately after the Klondike Gold Rush and Spanish-American War of 1898. However, what wasn't in the book was what would expose Baker's blind side. Louis Filler justifiably asked:

Where was any mention of the labor unions, the excesses of the trusts, and the shame of the Southern Negro policy, subjects with which Baker was soon to deal? These were facts, too, but Baker was not anxious to have his faith in American institutions troubled. The labor question caught up with him, not he with it . . . [*Crusaders for American Liberalism*, pp. 87-88.]

For the October 1901 *McClure's*, Baker had profiled banker-financier J. P. Morgan. The following month, Baker documented the vastness of the U.S. Steel Corporation, composed of ten companies producing more than two-thirds of all steel in the United States, and which was which incorporated earlier that year for $1.1 billion:

[U.S. Steel] absolutely controls the destinies of a population nearly as large as that of Maryland or Nebraska, and indirectly influences twice that number. Its possessions are scattered over half a dozen states . . . with its chief interests centering at Pittsburg [sic], Chicago and Duluth, and the whole controlled from New York City. It owns or controls 115 fine steamships on the great lakes, and six important railroad lines and several smaller ones. In Pennsylvania, its coal possessions cover over 75,000 acres of land worth $1,200 an acre, besides 30,000 acres of other land and quarries, and 98,000 acres of leased natural-gas lands. It owns no fewer than 18,309 coke-ovens, being the largest coke producer in the world. Of blast furnaces, it owns eighty, producing 9,000,000 tons of pig iron yearly, and of steel plants it owns about 150. [p. 6]

However, Baker's relatively innocuous articles seemed to be more explanatory than investigative, and weren't the "bombshell" that Henry George had dropped with his earlier series in *The National Magazine*. After *McClure's* rejected "How Labor Is Organized" as being too general—Baker even admitted in his autobiography that "it was not in itself a very good article"—he submitted it to Walter Page's *World's Work* which did publish it in its August 1902 issue. In that article, Baker—who had grown up in an upper middle-class existence in Michigan, graduated from Michigan State and studied law at the University of Michigan—sounded his philosophy about organized labor:

To the historian of our time, two great events will stand out, each of which by some will be regarded as a grave danger to American institutions, and by others as the most perfect instrument of development and progress. . . . [One is] the

Ray Stannard Baker

organization of [U.S. Steel] the greatest corporation in the world, [the other is] the nearly complete unification of workingmen in coal-mining [the United Mine Workers]. . . .Both seek stronger and closer organization in order to crush out the non-unionist, whether company or "scab"; . . . they both seek to extend their own market—one by controlling sources of production, securing lower freight rates and so on, the other by the use of boycott and the union label.

It made no difference if he was reporting about coal miners of rural northeastern Pennsylvania, the miners of Colorado, or the Jewish tailors of urban New York, the same diligence, attention to detail, and ability to understand how great issues affected the people, went into his reporting. Although it seemed that he was anti-labor, he was in reality anti-*organized* labor. The subjugation of the people, Baker believed, was caused by both Big Business and organized labor. Yet, it was organized labor that was the force to bring the masses out of their exploitation, something Baker often alluded to, but was never comfortable with. "The Right to Work," an investigative feature of the coal strike of 1902, published in the January 1903 issue of *McClure's*, was a brilliantly-researched descriptive story of how the strike affected the 17,000 scab workers in northeastern Pennsylvania whom Baker had seen as pawns in the battle between the steel industry and the UMW. Nevertheless, no matter what his editorial opinions, Baker was one of the nation's best examples of the journalist as a brilliant interviewer and listener. In his autobiography, Baker talked about how he got the story of the non-striking miners:

> I used the same methods, as a reporter, that had proved so successful at the time of the Pullman strike in Chicago. I tramped out to the miners' homes, I went down into the mines where the men worked, I stayed at several of their long-winded meetings, and listened to their bitter discussions. I found the newly organized miners not only at war with the powerful owners of the mining properties, but even more angrily with the large numbers of their fellow workers who would not "come out" and support the strike. They hated these "scabs" to the point of murder. . . .
>
> It was easy enough to see the glaring injustices of the coal fields—low wages, company houses, company stores, poor schools, wretched living conditions: these had not only been widely publicized by the leaders of the strike, they were generally admitted. I did not need, at first anyway, to study these aspects of the situation. But why, if all these things were true, should 17,000 of the men in the anthracite fields, a sizable portion of the miners, doggedly refuse to support the strike? Why should they prefer to go on working in danger to their lives?
>
> What men I met during those fiery weeks! What stories they told me: what dramas of human suffering, human loyalty, and human fear I saw: all brilliantly lighted against the scorched and dusty background of the Pennsylvania hills. [*American Chronicle*, p. 167.]

Other articles by Baker, published during 1903 and 1904, focused upon labor racketeering, of the problems associated with the compulsory union-shop, and what he perceived as a conspiracy forged by Big Business and the Labor bosses working together. In 1903, he went to San Francisco to report that "the ancient master, the employer, had been hopelessly defeated and unionism reigned supreme." [*American Chronicle*, p. 180] In the Spring of 1904, he went to Colorado to look at "The Reign of Lawlessness: Anarchy and Despotism in Colorado," published in the May 1904 issue. True to his philosophy opposing Big Business and organized labor, Baker later noted that it was in . . .

... the mining camps and smelter towns of Colorado [where] I looked into the worst conditions of industrial anarchy than anywhere existing in America. Here neither capital nor labor obeyed the law and the local governments were unable to control the situation, or prevent riots, bloodshed, destruction of valuable property. . . .

In later articles I tried to present other aspects of these complicated and dangerous problems. Many of the conditions I reported were then absolutely new to the American people as a whole, and were therefore, at that time, highly sensational. I endeavored earnestly to see and set forth without prejudice, not only the point of view of the workers, but, with equal thoroughness and understanding, the side of the employers and the public. [*American Chronicle*, pp. 180-181]

In his autobiography, Baker reflected about "The Rise of the Tailor," published in the December 1904 issue of *McClure's*:

No one of the articles I wrote at that time more deeply aroused my interest and sympathy than the one [about the Jewish tailors or urban New York.] It concerned the effort of a number of far-sighted and idealistic labor leaders to organize the most poverty-stricken, unrecognized, and undefended laboring people in the country—masses of new immigrants who spoke little or no English, who were remorsely exploited and cheated at every turn. They were the Russian Jews of the slums of New York, the Southern Italians, and Poles and Portuguese and Greeks who were the workers in the garment industries. I recall the Yiddish sweatshop song I printed at the head of my article:

I work, work, work without end
Why and for whom I know not
I care not, I ask not
I am a machine

"These people," I wrote, "were cast into the turmoil of the let-alone civilization of America; no one paid any attention to them, or cared what happened to them—with the result that many of them were literally worked to death. [*American Chronicle*, p. 181]

But still Baker, while understanding the worker's problems, couldn't understand that organized labor wasn't as evil as he had believed, and that it was fighting hard to rid itself of internal corruption. Louis Filler suggests part of the reason for Baker's blind side:

[McClure] was highly pleased with Baker's work. The old formula sufficed for him: Baker had the facts—all of them, both sides of them, and he had a wholesome fear of a too powerful, too belligerent labor movement. McClure cherished Theodore Roosevelt's remark: "Yes! The White House door, while I am here, shall swing open as easily for the labor man as for the capitalist, *and no easier*." Why were Roosevelt and Baker so emphatic? Had labor hitherto had such easy access to the White House? What is certain is that they feared labor, encouraged, might clamor for more attention than they cared to give it. Here was the central reason for *McClure's* success: it was the unofficial organ of the Square Deal—the middle-of-the-road policy. If McClure himself was not like the President, intellectually Baker was; less heart, more earnest, but no less like him. *McClure's* printed John Mitchell's account of the coal strike, it printed Grover Cleveland's account of the Pullman strike, but it did not print [Eugene] Debs's account of the Pullman strike. Debs [thought McClure] was biased. [*Crusaders for American Liberalism*, p. 88]

If the necessity and value of organized labor was not within *McClure's* and Baker's philosophies, neither was it in the editorial philosophies of most media. Nevertheless, *McClure's*, unlike most the nation's press, at least was willing to give a part of its editorial space to the issues affecting the workers, and to assign one of the nation's best reporters to digging out the facts and trying to present them in as unbiased a form as could be done at that time.

Defection From a Proposed Conglomerate

During 1906, with both the muckraking movement and *McClure's* at their peaks, S. S. McClure announced a major expansion of his empire. To a startled staff, McClure announced that the magazine would continue to serve as a base for all operations, but there would also be a bank and life insurance company, an expanded publishing operation to include textbooks, a major new printing plant and, with excessive profits, housing projects for the impoverished. Although *McClure's* was the most popular of the American magazines, it was also in the middle of its decade of muckraking, an era that opposed the trusts and conglomerates of big business. *McClure's* staff—almost all of them frustrated with having to work with a man of genius whose mind was everywhere at once—tried to persuade him from going ahead with his plans. When he refused, Phillips reluctantly resigned in March 1906, selling all his shares to Sam McClure, his college buddy and twenty-year friend. Then, he arranged for control-

ling interest in the *American Magazine*[7], taking with him David McKinlay and John Trainor from the business staff, and Lincoln Steffens, Ida Tarbell, Ray Stannard Baker, John M. Siddall, and managing editor Albert Boyden from the editorial staff. Boyden
would become as important to *American Magazine* was Phillips was to *McClure's*. Ida Tarbell remembered Boyden as having a "genius for keeping things going and his gift for sympathetic friendship. . . . He was of the greatest value to the *American* in bringing together writers and artists. . . . Bert was so much younger than the rest of us, so full of energy and hope, so much more vital and all-shedding . . ." [*All in the Day's Work*, p. 261.] To the staff of *American Magazine*, they added William Allen White, who had written three significant investigations for *McClure's* and who was
becoming one of America's most respected

John S. Phillips

newspaper editors; and Finley Peter Dunne (1867-1936), the country's leading social satirist whose "Mr. Dooley" articles probed deep into the social problems in America.

Reflecting a different social outlook from *McClure's*, *American Magazine* announced that it would be a writers' magazine, one that would "reflect a happy, struggling, fighting world, in which, we believe, good people are coming out on top." Ray Stannard Baker recalled:

> It was a rare group we had there at the beginning . . . [They were people] genuinely absorbed in life, genuinely in earnest with their attitude toward it, and yet with humor, and yet with sympathy, and yet with tolerance, far more eager to understand and make sure than to dream of utopias. [*American Chronicle*, p. 226.]

The first significant article, a lengthy profile of William Randolph

----

[7]*American Magazine*, formerly known as *Frank Leslie's Illustrated Monthly*, was now under the editorship of Ellery Sedgwick who would become editor of *The Atlantic Monthly*; publisher was William Morrow who would soon become founder of a major book publishing company.

Hearst, written by Steffens for the November 1906 issue, was not the expose either the staff or the readers expected. Prior to the article's publication, Steffens was subjected to argument from most the staff, and accused by several of having been "taken in" by Arthur Brisbane, Hearst's editor-in-chief. Nevertheless, "Hearst, the Man of Mystery"—carefully researched by a master of the interview—was a thorough study of an intricate mind, a complex man torn by what he truly wanted to do, and what he was almost forced, perhaps destined, to do now that he controlled the largest media empire in America.

The addition of yet another competitor, even one with the pioneer muckrakers in America on its staff, combined with a national financial crisis in 1907, briefly cut into *McClure's* profits. But *McClure's* remained muckraking's leader with a half-million circulation, more than a million dollars in advertising—highest among the muckraking journals—and solid investigative articles by Christopher Connolly on the domination of Montana by the mining interests, Burton J. Hendrick on corruption and fraud in life insurance companies, Harry Orchard on union tactics among the miners, and several articles about America's multi-millionaires and of political corruption. In April 1907, *McClure's* published George Kibbe Turner's expose of prostitution and large-scale illegal gambling in Chicago; the story became the precursor to Reginald Kauffman's *The House of Bondage* (1910), one of America's most comprehensive studies of prostitution and its effects upon society. In December 1909, *McClure's* published Turner's powerful study, "Daughters of the Poor." The result was the passage of the federal Mann Act, prohibiting interstate transportation of women for immoral purposes. Other muckraking articles by Turner focused upon the problems of autos and drivers (September 1907), the Navy (February 1909), liquor control (September 1909), and the nature of American city government (May 1910).

RAILROAD REBATES

WHAT REBATES ARE, HOW THEY ARE PAID, WHO PAYS THEM, AND HOW THEY AFFECT INDUSTRY

BY

RAY STANNARD BAKER

"The people, sir, are not always right."
"The people, Mr. Grey, are not often wrong."
LORD BEACONSFIELD: "VIVIAN GREY."

IT is no exaggeration to say that the railroads of this country have infinitely more to do with the happiness and success of the people than the United States Government itself. They touch more people more intimately. "In America," says Acworth, the eminent British authority on transportation, "the railroad rate is a matter of life and death."

In its essence a freight-rate is a tax levied upon the people: a tax upon every mouthful of food we eat, every garment we wear, every timber in the house we live in, every shovelful of coal we burn. "A railroad," says President Mellen of the New York, New Haven & Hartford Railroad, "lives by a tax upon the community."

No other sort of taxation is so universal or so heavy as the freight-rate. In America each person pays about $7 annually for the expenses of the Federal Government, and this supports the army, the navy, pays the post-office deficiency, builds the Panama Canal, and provides for the entire machinery of government: president, congress, and supreme court; but the railroad tax in freights averages each year over $26 for every man, woman and child, nearly four times the government tax.

Now, taxation is an elemental function of government; it is, indeed, the foundation of government.

No money, no state.

One of the chief purposes of taxation is to build and maintain roads. The old Romans levied enormous taxes for roadbuilding — and conquered the world. All governments levy taxes in some form (road taxes, poll-taxes, toll-gate taxes, etc.) for maintaining highways. It is recognized as an essential function of government to keep open the public roads. President Roosevelt strikes this fundamental note in his message:

"Above all else, we must strive to keep the highways of commerce open to all on equal terms."

Railroads Are Highways

The railroad, by all the laws of the nations, is quite as much a highway as is a wagon road. But instead of levying direct taxes for keeping up the rail-highways (as do the people of Prussia, Austria, Switzerland and other countries) we Americans "farm out" the power of taxation to private individuals organized as a railroad corporation. The old kings farmed out the power of ordinary taxation to their favorite barons in the same way. The instrument that conveys this power upon a railroad company is a "charter." It gives the railroad company the right to operate the rail-highways and to charge a freight-rate (a tax) for doing it. Railroad presidents and directors are thus by appointment made the tax-collecting representatives of the people. For railroads are not now, and never were, private property, like a farm or a grocery store. They are *highways*.

The first essential of a tax is that it shall be just. To establish that point the Anglo-Saxon people have shed rivers of blood: our English ancestors revolted against the old barons who taxed both unequally and

CHAPTER 4

A Pandemic Invasion

Although middle-class urban America now realized it had been swept up in a pandemic invasion of business and governmental corruption, it had its own struggles of survival, and couldn't devote much of its time to squeezing the iniquities of society from its life. Besides, thought many, "we're only individuals—how does all this *really* affect me?" They would soon find out.

Railroads on Trial

The railroads were ripe for the muckrakers. Their owners had committed the grossest of offenses against the public, seizing choice private land by rules of eminent domain, restricting trade and barring competition, bribing state and federal officials and legislators, exploiting the workers and seeming not to care about safety, while using violence and threats against individuals, the unions, suppliers, and competitors to force compliance to the maintenance of the railroads' monopolistic purposes—all with governmental indifference. Although the emasculated Interstate Commerce Act of 1887 and the Sherman Anti-trust Act of 1890 were still on the books, the twenty-four general managers of the nation's largest railroads had formed an alliance of mutual interest that by the turn of the century would encapsule an association representing $818 billion in capital, more than 200,000 employees, and 40,000 miles of track, almost all of it protected by the federal government. Indeed, in one trust, muckrakers would find business and governmental corruption intertwined with a blatant disregard for the workers, as well as the public.

Part of that corruption was bound in the free passes issued by the railroads to persons who might have influence. Legislators and political bosses got annual cards for themselves and bushels of "trip tickets" for their constituents. In *Our Times*, Mark Sullivan pointed out:

Far from being seen as a bribe or impropriety, or a thing to conceal, the pass was regarded more nearly as an honor. Everywhere, to "flash a pass" on the railroad conductor was a gesture of distinction, of a sort—a sign of having arrived at some degree of power. To pay railroad fare was a mark of failure to emerge from the herd. . . .

The ability of a member of the legislature, or any other political leader, to get trip passes for his constituents or partisans, was perhaps the most potent form of patronage he had. Any important political boss, such as [Matthew] Quay of Pennsylvania, could command trip passes by the thousand for the accommodation of such delegates as would support him in a State convention, and such hundreds of henchmen as would cheer him from the galleries or chant his name in parades. [Vol. 3, pp. 206-207]

It was a neat arrangement—the legislators got unlimited free rides, the railroads got favored legislation, the public got the shaft. Even when free passes were outlawed, the railroads blatantly disregarded that law, as they disregarded most laws they didn't agree with. The 1874 Pennsylvania constitution specified, "No railroad, railway or other transportation company shall grant free passes, or passes at a discount, to any persons except officers or employees of the company." [Article XVII, Section 8]. However, for more than three decades, the Pennsylvania Railroad, among others, continued to issue yearly passes to whomever it wished, each card with the year in headline type. So arrogant were the railroads that many cards were even issued with expiration dates the day of the election.

However, the railroad passes were mild corruption compared to the railroads' blatant disregard for the people and their Constitution. In 1877, a few hundred railroadmen struck the pennsylvania railroad when they were told they would be suffering a ten percent pay cut—while the owners continued to live as highly as their opulent lifestyle would allow. Within a couple of months, the strike had spread to other railroads and hundreds of thousands of workers refused to cross the picket lines. By the time it was over, the militia of several states, combined with the railroad police, had seized control for the owners; in Pennsylvania, the state militia had fired into a crowd of thousands of moderately peaceful protestors, and killed almost two dozen workers, women, and children; the people retaliated, only to be crushed by the power of guns and bayonets. In 1894, against a relatively peaceful strike of the Pullman company, and against the wishes of the governor to Illinois, the federal government sent almost two thousand troops to Chicago force the workers back to their jobs, which now, for the third time, paid less than before. However, in an interesting twist of logic, the Supreme Court of the United States declared that the Sherman Anti-trust Act didn't apply to trusts—but did apply against the American Railway Union, and especially socialist Eugene Debs for having led the strike.

Reviewing the railroad trust, Louis Filler, in *Crusaders for American Liberalism* (1939), pointed out:

... No one needed to be told that there was a railroad problem. Most Americans had been reared among discussion of it. The immigrants and other settlers in the Midwest and Far West, especially, were very painfully aware of it. The railroads had absolute control over their lives: it told them how much they were to receive for their grain and cattle, dictated land values, settled the destiny of towns by passing through them or outside them, and otherwise showed its hand in nearly every phase, political, social, and economic, of national life. [p. 203]

Turn where he might, the citizen could not but see the evidence of their power and ruthlessness. ... They were strategically placed among the industries; they were the front-line representatives of the trusts; they were indomitable. Who or what could move them—short of an economic revolution? [p. 205]

Reviewing the history of the major railroads, David Graham Phillips noted:

... The New York Central had been one of the most industrious and extensive corruptors of the legislature. In the fourteen years up to 1867, it had spent upward of half a million dollars ... in buying laws at Albany to "protect its stockholders against injurious legislation"— which phrase always means to prevent just laws from being enacted, since an unjust law would be unconstitutional and would be upset by the courts. ...

On May 20, 1869, the Vanderbilts got, in one bill, the right to consolidate several railways, and a free grant of franchises worth hundreds of millions, and the right to water stocks and bonds practically as freely as they might choose. ["The Treason of the Senate," *Cosmopolitan*, March 1906, p. 497]

In *Labor's Untold Story*, Richard O. Boyer and Herbert M. Morais reported that Jay Gould, unscrupulous stock manipulator and owner of Western Union, the *New York World* before Joseph Pulitzer gave it a conscience, and a half-dozen railroads, including the Union Pacific, "was willing to spend huge sums with the Pinkertons [detective agency] to shoot down strikers but totally unwilling to increase pay and once said scornfully, when threatened with strike, 'I can hire one half of the working class to kill the other half.'" [p.72]

The New York, New Haven & Hartford Railroad, said Louis Filler:

... had corrupted politics so long that it could afford to leave the routine work of corruption to others. ... E. H. Harriman, the meteor of modern railroad history, in effecting merger after merger of railroad properties, left a wake of degraded businesses and political functionaries. Worth perhaps $10,000,000 in the late Nineties, when he died in 1909 he left an estate of some $150,000,000, which did not by any means represent the extent of the influence he had wielded or tell how he wielded it. [*Crusaders in American Liberalism*, p. 205.]

In *Labor's Untold Story*, Richard O. Boyer and Herbert M. Morais reported that Daniel Drew of the Erie Railroad and Cornelius Vanderbilt of the New York Central ...

... spent millions in bribing the New York City Council and the New York State Legislature, each seeking special privileges for his railroad at the expense of the other. The law was good for little beyond a laugh. When a judge remonstrated with Vanderbilt for prostrating the country for his own private profit, the old man said, "Can't I do what I want with my own?"

And when the railroads weren't exploiting their workers, bribing politicians, and stealing the public's lands, they were fighting with each other, each conglomerate, as Boyer and Morais noted, "hiring armies of thugs and fighting pitched battles for the possession of lines coveted by both," [p. 34]

During the latter nineteenth century, a number of newspaper and magazine writers had looked at the abuses of the railroad companies, pointing to instances of arrogant power in the settling of the country, but it was a muckraking novel, published in 1902, that brought national attention to the problem. *The Octopus*, Frank Norris's powerful indictment of what the railroads were doing to the people, became a national bestseller. Although a novel, it was so strongly wrapped in the truth that the California wheat farmers, upon whose land the Southern Pacific Railroad had cut its swath, found they were not alone in having been cheated and, in some instances, destroyed by the conglomerates. The following year, Norris wrote *The Pit*, a searing novel of romance and greed that, within a framework of a romantic novel, exposed the Chicago commodities market and the interrelationships with the railroads. Indeed, the railroads were truly the octopus, ensarling an entire nation in its tentacles.

In Wisconsin, a crusading Progressive squared off against the railroad trust. Robert M. La Follette had been a three-term Congressman when he ran for the governorship in 1894, four years after having been defeated for re-election to the House. Three losses later—with a well-oiled machine of Progressive and insurgent Republicans, combined with reactionary Democrats, and a reputation for his concern for the people and opposition to the trusts—La Follette was finally elected governor and able to carry through his promise to tax the railroads and eventually create a state commission to oversee transportation regulation. In 1906, La Follette was elected to the Senate where he carried on his campaign to break up the railroad trust. To further the cause of reform by bringing to the people the stories of business and governmental corruption and their greater social issues, La Follette founded *La Follette's Magazine* in 1909; the magazine, under the name *The Progressive*, is still being published, and still describing problems in the American social, economic, and political fabric.

"No man of my time in public life equalled La Follette as a fighter," recalled Ray Stannard Baker, " [He was] fierce, incorruptible, independent.... In his thorough-going way, he could know all the "folks" and count upon them for support." [*American Chronicle,* p. 269.]

For the July 1904 issue of *The Arena,* Benjamin O. Flower lashed out against the railroad trust, with the provocative title, "Twenty-Five Years of Bribery and Corrupt Practices, Or the Railroads, the Lawmakers, The People." The first few paragraphs set the tone for the thirty-seven page article, detailed with specifics:

For more than a quarter of a century the public service corporations have been steadily, insidiously, and subtly undermining the old Republican Order, corrupting the fountain-head of legislation, and elevating the interest of the corporate wealth over the rights and interests of the people. And during this time they have firmly established and entrenched a powerful plutocracy, which has not ineptly been called the new Commercial Feudalism, whose seat of power is in that paradise of modern gamblers and speculators, Wall Street, and whose strong hand is felt influencing, when not absolutely controlling, special legislation at Washington, in every State capital and in all the great municipal governments of the republic.

For more than twenty-five years the interests of the people have been systematically sacrificed, the producer and consumer have been shamefully oppressed and defrauded, and the moral sensibilities of statesmen and public servants from the highest elected and appointed offices, down to petty municipal positions, have been blunted and degraded from the Chief Executive, the State Superior Court judiciary, and the United States Senators down, the people's servants have reached a point where they unblushingly accept favors of great monetary value from public servant corporations, notwithstanding the fact that the companies are known to have in various ways sought to corrupt the people's representatives and defeat just and needed legislation, and, furthermore, to have systematically defied or evaded laws enacted to secure justice and bring relief to the public by curbing greed and avarice.

For more than a quarter of a century the public service corporations, chief among which have been the railroad organizations, through various corrupt practices, largely by bribery, direct and indirect, have steadily advanced to mastery of the government through an unholy alliance with political bosses and partisan machines. . . .

Two observations have been made about corporations that may be said to be axiomatic. *Corporations have no souls*—they are utterly devoid of the conscience element. Men who would shrink from any thought of personally resorting to bribery and other corrupt practices, men who consider themselves exemplary church members and pillars of society, in the capacity of directors and heads of great corporations, will wink at, countenance, and oftentimes even promote bribery and other corrupt acts on the part of their companies. Whatever corporations lack in conscience, however, they make up in greed and avarice. Cupidity promotes turpitude, but is never the parent of unselfish generosity, or of lofty patriotism. And this brings us to a second axiomatic statement. *Corporations bestow favors on outsiders only when benefits are expected in return, or when it is deemed important to obligate or silence some person who might become formidable either as a friend of rivals or as a champion of the producing and consuming public who are at their mercy, and whose relief must come through the sovereign power of government.* [pp. 13-14.]

In *Leslie's*, Ellery Sedgwick, elaborating upon earlier stories, pointed to innumerable instances of the failure of the railroads to provide for the safety of both its employees and passengers, citing statistics to show that many of the deaths from railroad accidents were avoidable if even the most basic safety precautions had been put into place. In several articles,

Sedgwick enumerated the facts that showed the cavalier attitude the railroads had about safety. The articles led to public outrage—after all, they were the ones who had to ride the trains—and eventual approval by the House of the Hepburn Act which established rudimentary oversight for railroads. However, the bill was stalled in the Senate. It would be a series in *McClure's* that would eventually break it loose.

In October 1905, *McClure's* fired a warning shot that the November issue would publish the first of a series of articles by Ray Stannard Baker exposing the railroad trust. In one of the most powerful editorials of the era, *McClure's* pointed out that the $13 billion railroad trust, which employed about 1.6 million people, controlled "about one-sixth of the entire wealth of the United States [and] have repeatedly broken and continue, to-day, to break the laws . . . not even secretly but with confessed openness." *McClure's* declared:

Charges of the utmost seriousness have been, for a long time, and are now being preferred against the men who control and operate the railroads of the country. They are at this moment upon trial, not merely because President Roosevelt has called a special session of Congress to decide whether these men have properly conducted the large interests intrusted to their care, but they are on trial before the higher court of public opinion. . . .

It is charged against the men who control the railroads that . . . they have secretly conspired with certain individual shippers . . . to do injustice to all other shippers in the same industries: that these conspirators, employing that sort of bribery called the railroad rebate . . . have now handed over the control of most of the great fundamental necessities of life—beef, coal, sugar, salt, oil, iron ore, coffee and the like—to a few men organized as "trusts,' and that these men, on their part, are dealing unjustly with the people. . . .

It is charged that ten men today control practically the entire transportation system of the nation . . . that they have conspired, secretly, unjustly and illegally, by virtue of their monopoly, to raise rates and impose onerous restrictions upon various industries of the country . . .

. . . By bribery of various sorts [these owners have] corrupted elections and prostituted legislators, and that through this corruption they have secured great influence in the Congress of the United States . . . [and] dominate not a few state and federal judges in this country. . . . The chief purpose of Mr. Baker, in the present work, is to make just such an investigation as every citizen himself would make if he could command the time. And he has brought to the investigation exactly the interest of any reader of *McClure's Magazine*—that of the American voter, who is deeply concerned with the welfare of his country. [October 1905, pp. 672-674]

By the time the "Railroads on Trial" series ended, Baker had carefully documented how the transportation industry manipulated legislators and public opinion, fixed freight rates that favored the large corporations, and put small business into bankruptcy. *McClure's* opening editorial had, indeed, been no dud.

Theodore Roosevelt, having read proofs of the first part of series, commented that he hadn't "a criticism to suggest," pleased that Baker had treated the railroad executives not as "exceptional villains but merely as ordinary Americans, who under given conditions are but the mere force of events forced into doing much of which we complain. I want so far as I can, to free the movement for their control from all rancor and hatred." [letter to Baker, Sept. 13, 1905.]

In a blunt message to Congress in December, Roosevelt demanded "government supervision and regulation of rates charged by the railroads." The bill, which had much earlier been passed by the House, was now stalled in a Senate composed of men already influenced by the trusts and private interests. However, the railroads themselves would do something that would force the bill out of committee. About the time McClure's editorial was published, the nation's major railroads had begun abolishing the free passes, not so much because they were concerned about exposure, but because, as Mark Sullivan reported in *Our Times*, they "came to doubt whether the friendship of those who received passes balanced the animosity of those who were denied them." Sullivan also reported that since the railroads had liberally sprinkled annual passes to politicians and daily passes to politicians to distribute to their favored constituents, "the practice had acquired such dimension that some trains did not carry enough paying passengers to defray their costs." [vol. 3, pp. 210-211].

Within a month, local, state, and federal governments had begun a renewed effort for greater regulation of the railroads. William Peter Hamilton, editor of the *Wall Street Journal*, later said that the railroads' voluntary abolition of passes, "was in its consequences perhaps the most devastating blow our railroads ever sustained ... Without a single exception, without distinction of creed, or color, the hands of every politician was turned against the railroads."

Aware that not only were the people indignant about railroad abuses and that they had been pushing their legislative bodies for reform, and even more aware of the dissatisfaction of many politicians with the railroads' recent action in arrogantly abolishing the free passes, Theodore Roosevelt again demanded the Congress to act against the tyranny of the railroads.[1] With some heavy back-room manipulation that would ally him with the Democratic minority, Roosevelt eventually convinced the Senate that it could either pass what would be a watered-down version of the House bill—or face a wave of American radicalism that could have led to militant and possibly violent confrontation as the public demanded full governmental regulation of the railroads, with significant criminal penalties against the railroad barons. The Senate, finally passed the Hepburn Bill in May which gave power to the Interstate Commerce Commission not only to regulate rates, but forced the railroads to diversify their holdings of steamship lines and coal companies; the bill also brought an end to the practice of giving free passes, except to employees and some non-profit agencies.

From Manipulator to Muckraker

Most of the muckrakers had looked at the problems in America from the outside—even the participant-journalists like Nellie Bly were outsiders. Thomas W. Lawson, however, used the knowledge he had gained as a millionaire businessman-financier, often operating close to or even barely exceeding the limits of the law, to write searing exposes of stock manipulation and fraud.

With the backing of Standard Oil, Lawson had initially established Amalgamated Copper in 1899 as a trust. Soon, Standard Oil and Lawson's other partners saw ways to increase profits by unprincipled business practices, and Lawson was forced into a secondary role by his partners who then swindled investors of more than $100 million, eventually leading about thirty persons to commit suicide.

Now, in early 1904, John O'Hara Cosgrave, *Everybody's* editor and an excellent journalist, began working with Lawson on a series of articles

---

[1]Ironically, the President's strong anti-trust message of April 18, 1906, which normally would have been published on the front pages of almost every American newspaper, was pushed to the inside. "Only an earthquake could move TR off the front pages" had been a jocular journalistic dictum. On April 18, an earthquake devastated San Francisco.

that would explain what had happened in the Amalgamated fraud, and would also, Lawson hoped, stun the nation into recognizing the extent of business corruption. The first article in the "Frenzied Finance" series, which would continue on an irregular basis for the next two years, and eventually be published as a book, appeared in the July 1904 issue. Lawson outlined the history and schemes of Amalgamated and the manipulation by Standard Oil. However, he didn't stop with a mere case history, as he meticulously set forth the facts proving that Amalgamated wasn't the only investment company that conducted shady business dealings. Soon, he was implicating most Big Business—including the nation's largest banks and life insurance companies—for stock manipulation, fraudulent accounting practices, and an arrogant disregard for a large chunk of criminal laws.

Muckraker Charles Edward Russell recalled that Lawson . . .

. . . told a story that for lurid details exceeded the imaginations of the wildest of shocker writers and in its disclosures of reckless viciousness seemed to show new capacities in the human spirit for the cruel and the avaricious. It was a nightmare of savagery, man returned to the jungle, still fashionably clad and boast of the ordinations and amulets of civilization—a staggering showing. Every paragraph contained material for a libel suit. What still puzzles me is that the men thus revealed in a delirium of lust and bestial conflict made no motion to protect themselves from the onslaught, made even no denial. [*Bare Hands and Stone Walls,* p. 132]

For his efforts, Lawson had wanted no fees, only that *Everybody's* commit itself to a massive promotion campaign that may have cost *Everybody's* as much as $50,000—and Lawson as much as $200,000-$250,000. On the strength of the articles, combined with the promotion campaign, *Everybody's* circulation went from about 300,000 to 500,000 in about three months, and averaged about 750,000 copies and 120-180 pages of advertising per issue during the next two years, as the magazine moved into the forefront of the muckraking movement.

Arthur and Lila Weinberg, in *The Muckrakers,* point out, "Lawson was to finance what Barnum was to show business. He was his own press agent. He knew every trick of publicity decades before press agentry became a profession in itself." [p. 261]

Mark Sullivan, in *Our Times,* pointed out:

What Lawson may have lacked in experience as a writer, or in conformity to conventional standards in his own decidedly bizarre business practices, he made up in a most extraordinary vividness of characterization, which caused crowds to clamor at news-stands for the monthly installments of *Everybody's*—the crowds including the financiers whom Lawson exposed, eager to end the suspense in which during thirty days of every month they wondered what ghastly secret of the underworld of high finance Lawson would tell next. [Vol. 3, p. 90]

The facts Lawson outlined were not only substantial but substantiated—none of the suits for libel were successful, and as Russell aptly noted, "the country gasped and wondered and gasped again. For a time it talked of nothing else . . . For a short time, Lawson was the most influential figure in the country . . ." [*Bare Hands and Stone Walls*, pp. 132-133].

In 1905, the *New York World* broke further ground in the expose of the life insurance industry when it reported how Equitable Life Insurance Co. executives were squandering the premiums on personal frivolities, including parties and liquor. *McClure's, The Arena, Collier's, The Era*, and *World's Work*, among other magazines and newspapers, weren't far behind in publishing damning information about the life insurance industry, often targeting excessive profits and the outrageous salaries and benefits paid its officers, as well as the large reservoir of funds that were used to bribe public officials. In March 1906, the New York state legislature finally passed a number of laws to regulate the life insurance industry.

"Frenzied Finance" had made Lawson a nationally-known muckraker; it also brought threats against him and his family. By the end of 1907, having spent much of his fortune on public reform during the previous three years, Lawson decided to stop his muckraking and return to a life on Wall Street, disillusioned that all his investigation and revelation hadn't truly changed the system, claiming that by quitting the series, he would now "allow the public to do their own reforming." Like many of the muckrakers, he had become bitter not only at having to defend his reputation and motives, and with having had to endure exaggerations and distortions of his personal life, but with the failure of the people to rise up in revolt of the existing order. He had put his time, money, and reputation on the line—and the people only became upset—for a short time—not enough to put their own necks on the line for reform. "The people, particularly the American people," wrote Lawson to Erman J. Ridgway, editor of *Everybody's*, "are a joke—a System joke."

During the next two decades, Lawson tried to remedy the problems of American Big Business from the inside, fighting for stock regulation. The proposals that Lawson outlined were eventually incorporated within the creation of the Securities and Exchange Act of 1934, three decades after his first articles exposed the problems. But, even the formation of the SEC did little to control the System that created the problem. Governmental investigations in 1939 revealed that the industry was even more entrenched, and better financed than at any other time. The corporate executives followed the law a little better, the people may have had better protection, but the industry was still in control of itself, and nothing was going to change that.

Alcohol-Laced 'Wonder Drugs'

For decades, Americans had been taking alcohol- and opium-laced drugs that were advertised as curing every medical problem ever discovered. Investigations of patent medicines and the packaging of meat would lead to what may have been the most sweeping reform of the first decade, for these exposes affected everyone. However, with initial opposition from Congress, and the medical and business lobbies, it would take the combined efforts of capitalists and socialists, the president of the United States, as well as the actions of several foreign countries and a massive protest by the American people to bring about legislation to protect America's health.

With the patent medicine quacks making more than $100 million year—and spending as much as $40 million just for various forms of advertising—it was too lucrative of a field to attack. Typical of the publishers was Harry K. Fox and the *Police Gazette*. After the Civil War, Fox had taken the easily-influenced *Police Gazette* at its deathbed, resurrected it, gave sports coverage a new dimension, and made the weekly magazine one of the most popular in America, making him one of the nation's richest publishers. An unscrupulous businessman, Fox spouted anti-Semitic and racist invective while accepting bribes not to run certain stories and pay-offs to run others. His classified advertising columns spouted come-ons for medicines to cure syphilis, cancer, and hair loss. His beliefs, like that of many nineteenth century publishers, was that as long as someone was willing to pay for an ad, he was willing to run it. However, Fox, the other publishers, and the major patent medicine companies would eventually experience the determination of the muckrakers.

Dr. Harvey Washington Wiley (1844-1930), a chemist not a journalist, in his own way was a muckraker and catalyst of some of the best muckraking in America. For twenty-five years, Wiley, chief chemist of the U. S. Department of Agriculture, had been fighting to get both his department and Congress to approve legislation that would regulate the manufacture of patent medicines. His careful analyses had shown that not only were the medicines useless, but could actually be harmful since many contained cocaine or alcohol. Unfazed by scientific analysis, and subject to intensive lobbying by the business and medical communities, Congress did nothing. It was now up to a very few journalists to bring the issues to the people.

Cyrus H. K. Curtis (1850-1933), who founded the *Ladies Home Journal* in 1883, and which soon became one of America's most respected magazines in an era that saw the proliferation of magazines, risked financial stability in 1893 when he declared that his magazine would no longer accept patent medicine advertising, at a time when most general circulation American magazines were growing fat with advertising from companies that claimed their elixirs could cure virtually every medical problem from "indiscretions of youth" to cancer.

Every now and then a newspaper or magazine would print something against the medicines, but nothing shook the heavily-financed patent medicine lobby that had Congress virtually locked up. In 1903, under intense pressure from some of the media, labor unions, and the Federated Women's Clubs, the House finally passed legislation requiring labeling of all medicines; the Senate killed it, probably convinced by the Proprietary Medicine Association and the National Wholesale Liquor Dealers Association not to pass restrictive legislation that could influence their own contributions to political campaigns. The fight continued, with Dr. Wiley increasing his efforts to get the patent medicines if not off the market at least properly labeled.

In 1904, the *Ladies Home Journal*, under the editorship of Edward Bok, one of the nation's most-respected editors, published three powerful article-editorials against patent medicines. In "The 'Patent-Medicine' Curse," published in the May 1904 issue, Bok told the magazine's one million subscribers:

> Every year, particularly in the springtime, tens of thousands of bottles of patent medicines are used throughout the country by persons who are in absolute ignorance of what they are swallowing. They feel "sluggish," after the all-winter indoor confinement; they feel that their systems need a "toning up," or a "blood purifier." Their

eye catches some advertisement in a newspaper, or on a fence, or on the side of a barn, and from cleverly-worded descriptions of symptoms they are convinced that this man's "bitters," or that man's "sarsaparilla," or that "doctor's" (!) "vegetable compound," or So-and-so's "pills" is exactly the thing they need as a "tonic."

"No use going to a doctor," argue these folks: "we can save that money," and instead of paying one or two dollars for honest, intelligent medical advice they invest from twenty-five to seventy-five cents for a box of this, or a box of that. And what do they buy, and what do they put into their systems? Few know. Fewer realize the absolute damage they are working upon themselves, and their households. For the sake of saving a physician's fee they pour into their mouths and into their systems a quantity of unknown drugs which have in them percentages of alcohol [usually 20-40 percent by volume], cocaine, and opium that are absolutely alarming. [p. 18.]

Bok's articles in the September and November issues added fuel to his demand for reform, calling for a national boycott of the medicines. The country was reacting to the disclosures, but still the lobbies held the Congress in a death grip.

With the *Ladies Home Journal* leading the opposition to the 'wonder drugs' other muckraking magazines and a few newspapers increased their attacks, risking advertising loss as the patent medicine lobby influenced other lobbies to pull ads from "offending" media. In its October 7, 1905, issue, *Collier's* published the first article of Samuel Hopkins Adams' powerful investigative series, "The Great American Fraud." Loaded with facts and analyses, and charging the patent medicine companies with criminal conspiracy, graft, influence-peddling, and anti-trust violations, the article shook apart the country. The second article of the series disclosed that most patent medicines included alcohol, the only "drug" of significance, and that numerous persons, including quite a number of "proper" ladies, were getting "better" by unknowingly getting drunk. "Maine, being a prohibition state," wrote Adams, "does a big business in patent medicines. So does Kansas. So do most of the no-license counties in the South." Other articles disclosed the presence of sulfuric acid and cocaine in the medicines, and re-introduced evidence of fraud. Ridiculing the claims of the patent medicine companies, Adams tore into Peruna, one of the nation's best-known:

What does Peruna cure? Catarrh. That's the modest claim for it; nothing but catarrh... What is catarrh? Whatever ails you. No matter what you've got, you will not only be enabled, but compelled... to diagnose your illness as catarrh, and to realize that Peruna alone will save you. Pneumonia is a catarrh of the lungs; so is consumption. Dyspepsia is catarrh of the stomach. Enteritis is catarrh of the intestines, Appendicitis—surgeons, please note before operating—is catarrh of the appendix. Bright's disease is catarrh of the kidneys. Heart disease is catarrh of the heart. Canker sores are catarrh of the mouth. Measles is, perhaps, catarrh of the skin, since "a teaspoonful of Peruna thrice daily or oftener is an effectual cure." . . . Similarly, malaria, one may guess, is catarrh of the mosquito that bit you. Other diseases not specifically placed in the catarrhal class, but yielding to Peruna . . . are colic, mumps, convulsions, neuralgia, women's complaints, and rheumatism. [October 28, 1905]

The following month, *Collier's Weekly* published Mark Sullivan's indictment of the media, "The Patent Medicine Conspiracy Against Freedom of the Press." In 1904, Edward Bok had commissioned Sullivan to conduct a sweeping investigation of the companies and their sales tactics. However, Sullivan's 7,000-word indictment of both the companies and the media was too long for the *Ladies Home Journal* format. Knowing a great story, and wanting to see it published, Bok then convinced Norman Hapgood, editor of the competing *Collier's Weekly*, at that time on the verge of greatness, to publish it. Sullivan's quest had taken him into several states, and into Massachusetts where he learned that Lydia Pinkham, from whom America's women bought millions of bottles of "tonic" each year, and to whom millions of women wrote for advice, had been dead for twenty-three years. The letters to Mrs. Pinkham, which the company had claimed were held in utmost confidence and read *only* by Mrs. Pinkham, were, in fact, answered by young clerks with no knowledge of medicine. Further, the names were often sold to other companies to be used for direct mail advertising. *Collier's Weekly* published a photo of Mrs. Pinkham's grave marker next to an advertisement that had urged Americans to write Mrs. Pinkham—"in her laboratory at Lynn, Massachusetts"—for professional advice.

Among Sullivan's other discoveries was that the companies had required the media to give substantial editorial support to the use of patent medicines if they wished to continue to receive advertising income from those companies.

"Fully forty millions [of the estimated $100 million gross sales] goes to the newspapers," Sullivan wrote, pointing out that there were "at least five patent medicine concerns in the United States who each pay out to the newspapers more than one million dollars a year." Because of the volume of advertising revenue, Sullivan charged that most newspapers didn't report on patent medicine abuses, noting that when the Massachusetts legislature debated the validity of patent medicines, March 15, 1905, only one newspaper, *The Springfield Republican*, already nationally known as one of the better newspapers in the country, even reported that such a debate had occurred—and most had fought against restrictive legislation that would have required patent medicine companies to label the contents of their bottles. The reason for vigorous opposition by the press, and by its silence of the debate itself, as Sullivan reported, was probably because of telegrams sent to all newspapers in Massachusetts by all the major patent medicine companies. Typical was a telegram sent by M. F. Cheney, owner of a Toledo-based patent medicine company and former president of the National Association of Patent Medicine Men:

> ... Should House bills Nos. 829, 30, 607, 724, or Senate Bill No. 185 become laws, it will force us to discontinue advertising in your State. Your prompt attention regarding this bill we believe would be of mutual benefit. ... We would respectfully refer you to the contract which we have with you. ...

That contract, which almost every daily and most weekly newspapers in the country had signed, included two unusual clauses that assured complicity with patent medicine goals:

> ... First—it is agreed in case any law or laws are enacted, either State or national, harmful to the interests of the ... company, that this contract may be canceled by them from date of such enactment, and the insertions made paid for pro-rata with the contract price. ...

> Second—it is agreed that the ... company may cancel this contract, pro-rata, in case advertisements are published in this paper in which their products are offered with a view to substitution or other harmful motive, also in case any matter otherwise detrimental to the ... company's interests in permitted to appear in the reading columns or elsewhere in the paper.

In New York, legislation regulating the patent medicine companies was also defeated; at its annual convention, the Association's Committee on Legislation was able to report:

> We are happy to say that though over a dozen bills were before different State Legislatures last winter and spring, yet we have succeeded in defeating all the bills which were prejudicial to proprietary interests without use of money, and through the vigorous cooperation and aid of the publishers. January 23 your committee sent out

letters to the principal publications in New York asking their aid against [these measures.] It is hardly necessary to state that the publishers of New York responded generously against these harmful measures. The only small exception was the *Evening Star* of Poughkeepsie, New York, the publisher which, in a very discourteous letter, refused to assist us in any way.

Presumably, the New York City metropolitan newspapers did assist. However, *Collier's Weekly*, the *Ladies Home Journal*, and a few other magazines were not intimidated by the patent medicine dollars or influence. *Collier's Weekly*, like the *Ladies Home Journal* the previous year, was attacked by politicians, government officials, and advertisers. In its November 10, 1906, issue *Collier's Weekly* reported that it had lost about $80,000 a year from not publishing patent medicine advertising, but still refused to yield to the pressure.

The hard-hitting editorials in the *Ladies Home Journal*, combined with Adams' and Sullivan's disclosures, finally shook apart America and forced the Senate into considering a bill that would regulate medicine. At first, the American Medical Association, always fearful of government regulation, and the American Newspaper Publishers Association, fearful of governmental intrusion into what was a lucrative advertising income for its members, vigorously lobbied against such a bill; the result of the intensive lobbying campaign led numerous senators to oppose any regulatory legislation. Finally, the AMA relented, now realizing that its support for regulation would benefit its own members by reducing the competition, and several senators changed their votes, following extensive public lobbying and a little arm-twisting by Theodore Roosevelt. The January 1906 issue of the *Ladies Home Journal* included articles by Bok and Sullivan, arguing against further delay. A weakened Senate bill now went to the House where it was stalled in committee, and tied up by the patent medicine lobby. It would take the shock of spoiled and infected meat being sold to the public as "government inspected" to finally move the Congress.

'The Most Brutal Novel Ever Published'

In 1899, A. M. Simons (1870-1968) wrote *Packingtown*, a study of the monopolistic practices of the meat packing industry which had exploited workers and sold diseased meats to the public. Within the next year, the Hearst empire began its battles against the beef trust, focusing upon issues of potentially diseased food, unfair labor competition, and the trust's terroristic threats against potential competitors. Hearst's fight against the meat packers had begun almost with the creation of the *Chicago American* in 1900. According to Charles Edward Russell, who was the first publisher of Hearst's *The American:*[2]

> When we started *The American* . . . there was a shortage of water supply in the city. Householders were begged and implored to conserve what we had and waste none of it, and for one summer the watering of laws was prohibited. This in a city bordering upon Lake Michigan seemed lunatic. We had on *The American* a bright and affable reporter named James O'Shaughnessy. He acquired a notion that the reason the water supply was short was because somebody was snitching it. Encouraged by the management, he obtained a permit to dig up the streets at certain intersections near the packing houses. Then with workmen he went at night, made the excavation and discovered that the city mains had been surreptitiously tapped and certain packing houses were drawing off millions of gallons for which they paid nothing. [*Bare Hands and Stone Walls,* p. 137]

But, the meat packers lobby was so well organized that it was able to bargain away its guilt—it would stop stealing water, but not pay anything for the water it had already stolen; all criminal charges were dropped. Within a couple of years, major American magazines were running stories highly favorable to the industry.

In 1905, the Interstate Commerce Commission finally investigated the "yellow cars" of the beef trust. The cars were railroad cars owned by the trust which then rented them to the railroads which, in turn, charged exorbitant rates for any packer, farmer, or cattleman not a part of the trust or willing to pay kickbacks. It was a mounting revolt by the independent packers, cattlemen, and farmers that led to the ICC investigation.

Spurred by the ICC probe, Erman J. Ridgway, editor of *Everybody's,* contacted Charles Edward Russell (1860-1941) and "the next thing I knew a muck-rake was put into my hand . . ." For most his career, Russell had been an iron-tough editor; first as a twenty-one year old managing editor of the *Davenport Gazette* (1881-1883), then as night editor of the *Minneapolis Tribune* (1883), managing editor of the *Minneapolis Journal* (1884), managing editor of the *Detroit Tribune* (1886), assistant city editor of the *New York Herald* (1889-1894), reporter (1887-1889) and city editor of

---

[2]The *American* was probably created as much to expand the Hearst empire as to give a voice for the Democratic party and William Jennings Bryan at the beginning of his second campaign for the Presidency.

Pulitzer's *World* (1894-1897), managing editor of Hearst's *New York Journal* (1897-1900), and publisher of Hearst's *Chicago American* (1900-1902). Now, as a muckraking journalist, Russell would earn his greatest fame and help bring about national reform.

"The Greatest Trust in the World," based upon Russell's own investigation as well as the revelations of J. W. Midgley to the ICC, ran in the February through September 1905 issues, and again shook the American public which now learned the extent of the industry's unfair business practices, violence against competitors, and its concern more with profits than health. Government inspected, wrote Russell for *Everybody's* and Samuel Merwin for *Success*, which was conducting its own investigation, meant only that Department of Agriculture inspectors, often inept or recipients of graft, looked at the livestock only *before* processing; they were unconcerned with what happened to it in the plant. The articles had forced the country to recognize the trust's brutal working conditions and lack of concern for the public health, but the beef packers had the ammunition to retaliate.

Knowing how easily money, the lure of "special considerations," and threats could intimidate, the packers increased their campaigns of buying editors and legislators in order to silence opposition and continue presenting their own fallacious version of the truth. However, mere bribery wasn't enough. As had Standard Oil done with Ida Tarbell's series, the trust sent forth a terroristic campaign against Russell. "[I was] astonished to find that I was . . . an unmitigated scoundrel," said Russell, "a hired assassin of character, a libeller of good men, an enemy of society and of the government, and probably an Anarchist in disguise." [*Bare Hands and Stone Walls*, p. 138]

The Independent would later editorialize:

> The short-sightedness of the "interests" always lies in their stupid belief that opposition to them is created by agitators. That they themselves create it by their own attempts to dictate, control or exploit is something which they can never get thru their fat heads. Were we of the betting fraternity, we would wager that not a dozen men controlling [the trusts] understand why their fellow citizens do not regard them as public benefactors. . . .
>
> The cause of our troubles has been *not the muck-rakers but the muck-makers*. If there is one thing absolutely certain about popular politics in America . . . it is that the people are no longer deceived. They are taking matters into their own hands, and whether attempts shall be made or not to put an end to free discussion in the press, on

the platform, in the pulpit, or from the teacher's chair, the exposures and the discussions will go right on. ["A Word to the Muck-makers," February 9, 1911, p. 320.]

The owners of the beef trust companies, including Swift and Armour, were eventually convicted of criminal terrorism, sentenced to one year each in prison—then released from sentence when the judge also ruled that officers of corporations were immune from conviction.

A subsequent government investigation against the packers became a "whitewash." Against intensive lobbying by the trust, the public outrage was not enough to shake loose the Pure Food and Drug Act, still bottled up in committee. Then Upton Sinclair (1878-1968), who would become the era's greatest muckraker, entered the picture.

Sinclair had graduated from college at the age of nineteen, having paid his expenses by writing pulp novels. By his mid-20s, however, his writing had gone well beyond the level of the dime novels, with *Manassas* (1904) regarded as one of the finest novels about the Civil War. A few probes into muckraking followed, then in 1905, with the storm developing over the meat packing industry's methods, *The Appeal to Reason*, a muckraking socialist magazine, commissioned Sinclair to become a worker in one of the plants, and to learn what no other journalist had been able to learn. In seven weeks, Sinclair had experienced the filth and exploitation, the willful disregard for both the government and the public. He wrote about the bribing of meat inspectors, and of the slaughter and selling of diseased animals; he told how the packing plants made sausage of meat that had fallen upon the sawdust floors, of how poisoned dead rats were dropped into the blades that blended the meat for the sausage. As Sinclair later pointed out, the practices he learned, the information he secured, weren't secret—they just hadn't been reported to the public:

"Why my dear fellow," said a Chicago packer to me, when I confronted him with certain matters, which convulsed two continents— "everybody knows these things. They are conventions of the trade. See, here, they are printed in catalogs"—and he proceeded to show me the prices of materials for adulterating and preserving spoiled meat. ["The Muckrake Man," *The Independent*; September 3, 1908; p. 518.]

The Appeal to Reason published Sinclair's book-length work serially, but the Macmillan company, which had previously accepted *The Jungle* for publication, now wanted changes. According to Sinclair:

Mr. Brett, president of the company, read the manuscript, and asked me to cut out some of the more shocking and bloody details, assuring me that he could sell ten times as many copies of the book if I would do this. So here again I had to choose between my financial interest and my duty. I took the proposition to Lincoln Steffens, who said: "The things you tell are unbelievable. I have a rule in my own work—I don't tell things that are unbelievable, even when they are true." [*The Brass Check,* p. 32]

Four other publishers rejected the book—a pack of lies, they cried— when novelist Jack London came to Sinclair's help "with his usual impetuous generosity," asked his fellow socialists for help, and secured $4,000 for publication. The series was already typeset when Walter H. Page of Doubleday, Page and Co. bought it, investigated the charges, found them accurate, and published the book, against heavy opposition.

As expected, the trust fought back, arm-twisting publishers into either silence or condemnation of Sinclair's charges. Elbert Hubbard, a Chicago advertising executive, wrote a scathing response which the Chicago meat packers bought, printed, and sent to the nation's physicians, clergy, and press. The *New York Evening Post* condemned the book as "lurid, overdrawn," then denied Sinclair a right of reply. In the *Saturday Evening Post*, owned by George Horace Lorimer who had worked for the Armour meat packing company for several years, staff writer Forrest Crissey ghosted a series of articles under J. Ogden Armour's signature refuting most of what Sinclair had said. Furious, Sinclair wrote "The Condemned Meat Industry" in a few hours then went into New York City, found Erman J. Ridgeway, publisher of *Everybody's,* and showed him the article which, said Sinclair:

... gave the affidavits of men whom the Armours had employed to take condemned meat ... and sell it in Chicago. It told the story of how the Armours had bribed these men to retract their confessions. It gave reports of the State health authorities, who showed how the Armours had pleaded guilty to adultering foods.

Ridgway stopped his presses, pulled a short story, and ordered Sinclair's article into that month's issue. This time, the media didn't even respond. "I had expected that every newspaper which boasted of public spirit would take up these charges, and at least report them," said Sinclair, "but instead of that, there was silence—silence almost complete!"

An investigation by the Department of Agriculture, itself implicated for conspiracy, complicity, and accepting of graft, became a whitewash. Articles scheduled to appear in *World's Work*, edited by Page, forced Theodore Roosevelt to order a new investigation by an independent committee which substantiated the charges of the muckrakers, after most newspapers still refused to acknowledge there was any problem with packaged meat. Sinclair, meanwhile, increased his campaign against the beef trust, writing several more articles for *World's Work*, *The Appeal to Reason*, and *Everybody's*, documenting the trust's disregard and contempt for the American people.

However, the revulsion of the people could no longer be contained. A weakened amendment to the Agriculture Act was an attempt to get "half a loaf" while protecting many of the nation's congressmen and senators, but the public would settle for nothing less than a massive reform. Americans had begun boycotting packed meat; soon, foreign countries began returning meat packed in America. It was then that the Pure Food and Drug Act, proposed by Dr. Wiley, and eventually pushed by President Roosevelt, was finally shaken loose of the committee. Faced by the boycott and the fury of the people who threatened to vote out of office anyone who didn't support the reform legislation, the House of Representatives finally rolled over, giving an overwhelming approval to the legislation that would require not only thorough inspections of all food, but the labeling of contents of all medicines.

The Jungle, regarded at the time as the "most brutal novel ever published," eventually became a best-seller, published in seventeen languages, and Sinclair would become the era's greatest muckraker. However, he mournfully noted that it wasn't for the revelations of the trust's business practices nor of its exploitation of the workers that the book became both popular and influential, nor was it successful because Sinclair proposed that socialism would be a way to curb the exploitation by business. "I failed in my purpose," Sinclair lamented in the October 1906 issue of *Cosmopolitan*, explaining, "I wished to frighten the country by a picture of what its industrial masters were doing to their victims; entirely by chance I had stumbled on another discovery—what they were doing to the meat supply of the civilized world.... I aimed at the public's heart, and by accident I hit it in the stomach."

As for Dr. Wiley—in 1912, after years of persecution by the Department of Agriculture, now under the Taft administration, he left governmental service to work for Hearst as the first director of the Good Housekeeping Bureau, a consumer protection division of the recently-purchased *Good Housekeeping*. The Bureau, with Hearst's mandate, was given the authority not only to test nationally-advertised products but to forbid Hearst's newspapers and magazines from running ads of products that were unsafe or unhealthy; products accepted for advertising in *Good Housekeeping* received the "Seal of Approval.

CHAPTER 5

A Conspiracy of Silence

by Upton Sinclair

A year had passed [since *The Jungle* was published] and I was living at Point Pleasant, New Jersey, when W. W. Harris, editor of the Sunday magazine-section of the "New York Herald," came to call on me, and explained a wonderful idea. He wanted me to go to Chicago secretly, as I had gone before, and make another investigation in the Stockyards, and write for the "New York Herald" an article entitled "Packingtown a Year Later."

He was a young editor, full of enthusiasm. He said: "Mr. Sinclair, I know enough about the business-game to feel quite sure that all the reforms we read about are fakes. What do you think?"

I answered, "I know they are fakes, because not a week passes that I don't get a letter from some of the men in Packingtown, telling me that things are as bad as ever." And I showed him a letter, one sentence of which I recall: "The new coat of whitewash has worn off the filthy old walls, and the only thing left is the row of girls who manicure the nails of those who pack the sliced dried beef in front of the eyes of the visitors!"

"Exactly!" said the editor. "It will make the biggest newspaper story the 'Herald' has ever published."

"Possibly," said I. "But are you sure the 'Herald' will publish it?"

"No worry about that," said he. "I am the man who has the say."

"But where is Bennett [James Gordon Bennett Jr., the newspaper's publisher]?"

"Bennett is in Bermuda."

Edited and reprinted from *The Brass Check*, published by the author in 1920.

"Well," said I, "do you imagine you could sign a contract with me, and put such a job through, and get such a story on the 'Herald' presses without Bennett's getting word of it?"

"Bennett will be crazy for the story," said the editor. "Bennett is a newspaper man."

"Well, you have to show me."

I explained that I was writing another novel, and was not willing to stop, but my friend Mrs. Ella Reeve Bloor, who had represented me with Roosevelt's investigating committee, would do the work. Let the "Herald" send Mrs. Bloor and one of its own reporters, to make sure that Mrs. Bloor played the game straight; and when the investigation was made, I would write an introductory statement, which would lend my name to the articles, and make them as effective as if I had gone to Packingtown myself. But first, before I would trouble Mrs. Bloor, or do anything at all about the matter, the editor must put it before Bennett and show me his written consent to the undertaking. "I am busy," I said. "I don't care to waste my time upon a wild goose chase." The editor agreed that that was reasonable, and took his departure.

James Gordon Bennett, the younger, was the son of the man who had founded the "New York Herald," establishing the sensational, so-called "popular journalism which Pulitzer and Hearst afterwards took up and carried to extremes. Bennett, the elder, had been a real newspaper man; his son had been a debauché and spendthrift in his youth, and was now in his old age an embittered and cynical invalid, travelling in his yacht from Bermuda to the Riviera, and occasionally resorting to the capitals of Europe for fresh dissipations. He had made his paper the organ of just such men as himself; that is to say, of cosmopolitan café loungers, with one eye on the stock-ticker and the other on their "scotch and soda." And this was the publisher who was to take up a new crusade against the Beef Trust!

But to my surprise, the editor came back with a cablegram from Bennett, bidding him go ahead with the story. So I put the matter before Mrs. Bloor, and she and the "Herald" reporter went out to the Stockyards and spent about two months. Mrs. Bloor disguised herself as a Polish woman, and both she and the reporter obtained jobs in half a dozen different places in the yards. They came back, reporting that conditions were worse than ever; they wrote their story, enough to fill an eight-page Sunday supplement, with numerous photographs of the scenes described. There was a conference of the editorial staff of the "Herald," which agreed that the story was the greatest the paper had ever had in its history. It must be read by Mr. Bennett, the staff decided. So it was mailed to Bermuda—which was the last ever seen or heard of it!

Week after week I waited for the story to appear. When I learned that it was not to appear I was, of course, somewhat irritated. I threatened to sue the "Herald" for payment for the time I had spent writing the introduction, but I found myself confronting this dilemma: the enthusiastic young editor was a Socialist, and if I made trouble, he was the one who would be hurt. So I decided to forego my money-claim on the "Herald." But I would not give up the story—that was a public matter. The public had been fooled into believing that there had been reforms in Packingtown; the public was continuing to eat tubercular beef-steaks, and I was bound that somehow or other the public should get the facts. I wrote up the story and submitted it to other newspapers in New York. Not one would touch it. I submitted it to President Roosevelt, and he replied that he was sorry, but was too busy to take the matter up. "Teddy" was a shrewd politician, and knew how hard it is to warm up to dead ashes, how little flavor there is in re-cooked food.

I knew, of course, that I could publish the story in the Socialist papers. That has always been my last recourse. But I wanted this story to reach the general public; I was blindly determined about it. There was a big Socialist meeting at the Hippodrome in New York, and I went up to the city and asked for fifteen minutes at this meeting. I told the story to an audience of five or six thousand people, and with reporters from every New York paper in front of me. Not a single New York paper, except the Socialist paper, mentioned the matter next morning.

But still I would not give up. I said: "This is a Chicago story. If I tell it in Chicago, public excitement may force it into the press." So I telegraphed some of my friends in Chicago. I planned the most dramatic thing I could think of—I asked them to get me a meeting in the Stockyards district, and they answered that they would.

Mind you, a little over a year before I had put Packingtown on the map of the world; I had made Packingtown and its methods the subject of discussion at the dinner-tables of many countries; and now I was coming back to Packingtown for the first time since that event. There was a big hall, jammed to the very doors with Stockyards workers. You will pardon me if I say that they made it clear that they were glad to have me come there. And to this uproarious audience I told the story of the "New York Herald" investigation, and what had been discovered. I stood, looking into the faces of these workingmen and women, and said: "You are the people who know about these matters. Are they true?" There was a roar of assent that rocked the building. I said: "I know they are true, and *you* know they are true. Now tell me this, ought they be made known to the American people? Would you like them to be made known to the American people?" And again there was a roar of assent.

Then I looked over the edge of the platform to a row of tables, where sat the reporters looking up, and I talked to them for a while. I said: "You are newspaper men; you know a story when you see it. Tell me now—tell me straight—is not this a story?" The newspaper men nodded and grinned. They knew it was a "story" all right. "The public would like to read this—the public of Chicago and the public of all the rest of America—would they not?" And again the newspaper men nodded and grinned. "Now," said I, "play fair with me; give me a square deal, so far as you are concerned. Write this story just as I have told it tonight. Write it and turn it in and see what happens. Will you do that?" And they pledged themselves, the audience saw them pledge themselves. And so the test was made, as perfect a test as anyone could conceive. And next morning there was just one newspaper in Chicago which mentioned my speech in the Stockyards district—the "Chicago Socialist." Not one line in any other newspaper, morning or evening, in Chicago!

A little later I happened to be on the Pacific coast, and made the test once more. I was putting on some plays, and it happened that a newspaper had played me a dirty trick that morning. So in my curtain-speech I said what I thought of American newspapers, and told this Chicago story. Just one newspaper in San Francisco published a line about the matter, and that was the "Bulletin," edited by Fremont Older, who happened to be a personal friend, and one of the few independent newspaper editors in America. Excepting for Socialist papers, the "Bulletin" has the distinction of being the only American newspaper which has ever printed that story.

CHAPTER 6

Treason Against the People

The investigations and quickly-enacted state and federal legislation against the railroads, meat packers, life insurance and patent medicine companies, had frightened many of the corrupt. However, as Upton Sinclair had so deftly pointed out, they also knew that laws that weren't enforced or were enforced selectively were no laws at all; further, they had the safety of a long history of political corruption to fall back upon. That soon would change, and the force behind it would be the power of the Hearst empire, now too large to bribe into silence.

William Randolph Hearst, who had led America into an age of "Yellow Journalism" during the 1890s, now looked at what *McClure's* was doing, and at his original goals that the media should lead America into greatness while helping the middle and lower classes, and gave *Cosmopolitan* a muckraking emphasis beginning in 1905 with a nine-part relatively-harmless series on "The Great Industries of the United States," and a two-page warning shot by Charles Ferguson in the October issue, "The Redoubts of Graft and How to Take Them." Attacking religious apologists of the robber barons, Ferguson sharply declared, "The monstrous treacheries of an age of graft will no longer bear to be explained on the theory of demoniac possession. Neither Mr. Rockefeller [nor the other robber barons] is a devil or a wizard. If they have betrayed the public it is because they had previously betrayed themselves." However, Ferguson also showed a humanistic side, perhaps a little naive, when he suggested, "There is no reason why they should be allowed to keep the spoils of treason, but neither is there any reason why we should bother to blacken their characters. Let them live and learn." But the robber barons and those who took the graft wouldn't just "live and learn." It would be a look at national corruption that led to a constitutional amendment.

Shortly after Hearst purchased *Cosmopolitan*, Charles Edward Russell suggested a series about the U. S. Senate:

> One day early in 1905, I was sitting in the press gallery of the United States Senate observing the proceedings . . . [Each senator] was there to represent some private (and predatory) Interest. Each was supposed to represent the people; each was in fact representing some division of the people's enemy. . . . I was struck with the patent fact that almost nobody in that chamber had any other reason to be there than his skill in valeting for some powerful Interest, and I thought a series of articles might well be written on the fact that strictly speaking we had no Senate; we had only a chamber of butlers for industrialists and financiers." [*Bare Hands and Stone Walls*, pp. 142-143.]

Russell had begun the research, but when another assignment took precedence, Hearst assigned David Graham Phillips (1867-1911) to the series.

For almost twenty years, Phillips had been a newspaper journalist, first for the *New York Sun*, then for Joseph Pulitzer's *World*. For the *World*, he was a cityside reporter, London correspondent, and an editorial writer, the position at that time considered to be one of the most prestigious in journalism. With a knowledge of the relationships between government and business—several of his incisive editorials probed the nation's trusts and power brokers—Phillips left newspaper journalism to write three muckraking novels detailing the control of private business upon the Senate. In 1905, with five of his novels published that year, he was comfortably secure in his role as a journalist-author.

Always able to spot bright enthusiastic journalists, Hearst lured Phillips out of freelance journalism and onto *Cosmopolitan* editorial staff. The story was to be an investigation of

David Graham Phillips

the U.S. Senate and its relationships with the trusts and power brokers. Gustavus Myers, formerly of *The New York Times*, was to be the principal investigator; Phillips, with a reservoir of knowledge about the art of political manipulation, would collect the data, analyze it, find the relationships, get additional evidence, then write a series of exposes. Both Myers and Phillips were given freedom to follow whatever leads turned up.

In an editorial preview, published in the February 1906 issue, *Cosmopolitan* explained why the series was important:

> We must never lose an opportunity to show that as private citizens we are opposed to public plunderers. We should interest ourselves in every scrap of information as to official treason that comes our way. We must be patient in the study of corruption as we are impatient of its creatures and their punishment. [pp. 477-478]

Phillips' first article detailing Senatorial greed and corruption was published in the March 1906 issue, available February 15. Titled "Treason in the Senate," the article told the American people that their senators "are not elected by the people; they are elected by the 'interests' . . . as hostile to the American people as any invading army." Phillips argued that when political caucuses, rather than the people, have the power to nominate senators, the chances are strong that there will be extensive control by the "monied" interests. According to Phillips:

> Politics does not determine prosperity. But in this day of concentrations, politics does determine *the distribution of prosperity*. Because the people have neglected politics, have not educated themselves out of credulity to flimsily plausible political lies and liars, because they will not realize that *it is not enough to work, it is also necessary to think*, they remain poor, or deprived of their fair share of the products, though they have produced an incredible prosperity. The people have been careless and unwise enough in electing every kind of public administrator. When it comes to the election of the Senate, how describe their stupidity, how measure its melancholy consequences? . . .
>
> The United States Senate is a larger factor than your labor or your intelligence, you average American, in determining your income. And the Senate is a traitor to you. [p. 488.]

Focusing upon Sens. Thomas C. Platt and Chauncey M. Depew, both of New York, Phillips attacked Platt as having a "long, unbroken record of treachery to the people in legislation of privilege and plunder promoted and in decent legislation prevented." [p. 490] However, most his attack was upon DePew. "His 'senatorial duties,'" wrote Phillips, "are like the duties of more than two-thirds of his colleagues—to serve his master, the plutocracy." In instance after instance, Phillips linked DePew to the Vanderbilt empire:

It would be a mistake to suppose that DePew had not a good brain. On the contrary, his brain was, and perhaps still is, far superior to the first Vanderbilt's, or to any of the first Vanderbilt's successors as chief custodian of the millions he got by robbing the people and 'milking' the New York Central [railroad] system. . .

[The Vanderbilts] have owned him, mentally and morally; they have used him, or rather, he, in his eagerness to please them, has made himself useful to them to an extent which he does not realize nor do they. [p. 496]

[While employed by the Vanderbilts prior to becoming a U.S. senator], DePew made himself a popular figure by generous, even wholesale distribution of [railroad] passes, by cultivating editors and reporters, by ingratiating himself with small politicians and the influential men of little towns and villages, by making popular addresses and after-dinner speeches, by the thousand and one devices which his ingenious mind and his expansive temperament and his passion for public applause suggested . . . [p. 499]

And for his reward [for loyalty to the Vanderbilt empire], the Vanderbilts have given him scant and contemptuous crumbs. After forty years of industrious, faithful and, to his masters, enormously profitable self-degradation he has not more than five millions, avaricious and saving though he has been. And they tossed him the senatorship as if it had been a charity. Of all the creatures of the Vanderbilts, none has been more versatile, more willing or more profitable to his users than DePew. Yet he has only five million dollars and a blasted name to console his old age, while his users are in honor and count their millions by the score. [p. 500]

In April, *Cosmopolitan*, with a circulation that had shot past a half million, published Phillips' second article in the series, an equally vicious polemic against Sen. Nelson W. Aldrich of Rhode Island, whom Phillips labelled as the "organizer of this treason [against the people]" [p. 628], pointing out that Aldrich was closely allied to the John D. Rockefeller empire, and claiming, "Before he reached the Senate, Aldrich had fifteen years of training in how to legislate the proceeds of the labor of many into the pockets of the few." [p. 632]. He concluded his attack by arguing:

Treachery has brought [Aldrich] wealth and rank, if not honor, of a certain sort. He must laugh at us, grown-up fools, permitting a handful to bind the might of our eighty millions and to set us all to work for them [the senators and trusts.] [p. 638]

In the same issue that the second of Phillips' articles appeared, *Cosmopolitan* published Alfred Henry Lewis's vitriolic attack upon Sen. Platt. Lewis (1857-1914) had been a lawyer and cattleman, and author of the highly-successful Wolfville tales about a rancher and the Old West, before turning to journalism. From 1891 to 1898, he was Washington correspondent for the *Chicago Times*, then became chief of Hearst's Washington bureau where he continued digging into government scandal, peppering his articles with personal bitterness and, on occasion, racial slurs. Now in one of the nation's most-respected magazines, he called Sen. Platt a weasel, and claimed that he was "a weak, vain, troubled, unhappy, unrespected man [for whom] the country owes him nothing, for he has given it nothing . . . One day he will die; and his epitaph might truthfully be, 'He publicly came to nothing, and privately came to grief.'" [p. 645] Echoing public rumor and accepted political intricacies of the time, Lewis charged that Platt manipulated Roosevelt into higher office—he was instrumental in Roosevelt's nomination for New York governor and, in 1900, vice-president—first to remove him as police commissioner of New York City then to remove him from the governorship where he had pushed for considerable social legislation.

Now President, Roosevelt was furious, charging that some of the nation's media had preferred only to look into the muck of society and failed to balance it by seeing the greatness that could become America. First to an audience of journalists, then to the public, Roosevelt tore into those he called "muckrakers." The nation now had a classification for all those investigative reporters who dug the muck from the earth. However, Roosevelt's classification swept broadly, and people assumed he meant not only Phillips and Lewis, but Baker, Steffens, and Tarbell as well. In a private letter sent to Ray Stannard Baker, April 9, 1906, about a week prior to the public announcement, Roosevelt had tried to explain the distinction; however, it wasn't made in the public speech:

I want to "let in light and air" [to the public's knowledge of government], but I don't want to let in sewer gas. . . . In other words, I feel that the man who in a yellow newspaper or in a yellow magazine (. . . Hearst's papers and magazines are those I have in mind at the moment, as well as, say the New York *Herald* and similar publications . . .) makes a ferocious attack on good men or even attacks bad men with exaggeration for things they have not done, is a potent enemy of those of us who are really striving in good faith to expose bad men and drive them from power. I disapprove of the whitewash brush quite as much as of mudslinging, and it seems to me that the disapproval of one in no shape or way implies approval of the other. This I shall try to make clear [in my public speech next week.] [Quoted in *An American Chronicle*, by Ray Stannard Baker, p. 203.]

Theodore Roosevelt

Later, Roosevelt wrote George Lorimer, editor-in-chief of the *Saturday Evening Post*, that the series included "so much more falsehood than truth that they give no accurate guide for those who are really anxious to war against corruption, and they do excite a hysterical and ignorant feeling against everything existing, good or bad." [Quoted in *The Letters of Theodore Roosevelt* (1954), edited by Elting E. Morrison, Vol. 5, p. 269]

Even muckraker Mark Sullivan thought little of Phillips' series of exposes. In *Our Times* (1926), Sullivan recalled:

[Phillips] was unfamiliar with his material and with the background of the picture he purported to paint. Instead of the austere setting down of fact, which had been the very essence of the literature of exposure, and which had carried conviction to the reader, Phillips substituted tawdry literary epithets . . . For the stark citation of documents that had given force to Miss Tarbell's exposures of railroad rebates, Phillips substituted—sure sign, in a writer, of haste and paucity of fact—lavish exclamation points. . . . The inaccuracy and hysteria of Phillips and others gave a justified opening to a Senator, Henry Cabot Lodge, to defend the body against "some of our irresponsible magazine writers whose only thought was to turn a penny by meeting what seemed a momentary demand for a sensational statement." [Vol. 3, pp. 92-93]

Ida Tarbell claimed that Roosevelt "was afraid that [the muckrakers] were adding to the not inconsiderable revolutionary fever abroad, driving the people into socialism." [*All in the Day's Work*, p. 241.] However, it seemed that Roosevelt, a Progressive as well as political opportunist, was merely trying to curb the excesses, and made sure that several of the nation's leading muckrakers knew that he was referring not to them, but primarily to what he considered inflammatory defamation of the Hearst reporting. More importantly, and often overlooked by the media, was that Roosevelt's speech also warned politicians that although some muckrakers had transcended the boundaries of decency, that corruption and graft would not be tolerated

Nevertheless, Phillips' ten-part series continued, each article citing innumerable cases of corruption, some petty, some substantial—some of it unsubstantiated—as he hammered at ties between senators and the nation's powerful lobbies. "Corporate lackeys!" Phillips called the senators he investigated. "Traitors!" he emphasized. While the Senate was trying to defend itself of charges of "cronyism," Phillips again lashed into the power brokers of America who had the wealth and were using it to influence politicians and legislation, both of which could not be expected to support the masses. As in his other articles, his vituperative writing, often stringing together a rage for reform, met with its critics. In its November 17, 1906 issue, *Collier's* reported:

> The articles made reform odious. They represented sensational and money-making preying on the vogue of the 'literature of exposure,' which had been built up by the truthful and conscientious work of writers like Miss Tarbell, Lincoln Steffens and Ray Stannard Baker . . . Mr. Phillips' articles were one shriek of accusations based on distortion of such facts as were printed, and on the suppression of facts which were essential.

Nevertheless, the facts Phillips cited were essentially accurate, and America rebelled in hatred. Throughout the country, the people began looking to their own elected officials to see evidence of corruption that Phillips had so carefully documented. However, most newspaper and magazine publishers, many tied to the politicians and Big Business, refused to run investigations; if they did, it was usually to praise their bought-for officials, and to condemn Phillips and the muckrakers for hyperbolic distortion, a not unfair charge. But still *Cosmopolitan*, as well as *McClure's, Arena, Everybody's, Collier's Weekly*, and some other national media persisted, pointing to innumerable instances of alliances between business and government.

Charles Edward Russell continued the *Cosmopolitan* investigation against political corruption, with "At the Throat of the Republic," a four-part series beginning in December 1907; it was a series that Hearst may have wanted published as much for its revelations about fraud as for vindication of his campaign in 1905 to be mayor of New York City. Unlike Phillips and Lewis, Russell, the careful and meticulous editor, carefully avoided vituperation while carefully positioning facts to let the people know that their votes were worthless:

> To the men that know how our elections are really conducted in the purlieus of great cities all these things are a tale twice told. They know that nine of every ten elections are decided solely by the methods of the vote-broker and the ballot-box stuffer; and the awful fact, familiar all their lives, has to them no appalling significance because they have never known anything else. But the respectable, intelligent, patriotic, right-minded citizen that has no knowledge of actual conditions, that dwells in a happy nimbus of things as they ought to be, that abides in peace and security by the shadow of the church and the university, whose world is bounded by an impeccable society—how shall I ever make clear to him that he has no real share in the government he lives under; that his vote is overwhelmed and his voice drowned by hordes of illegal voters; that the most often the issue at the ballot-box is not, as he fondly dreams, decided by the wills or preferences of his fellow-citizens, but by the purse that commands the largest army of professional criminals and by the word that goes farthest with the broker of votes?
>
> At every election in New York city every registration list in the poorer quarters is padded thickly with the names of men that have no right to vote—aliens, non-residents, dead men, myths, fictitious persons, dogs, cats, and ghosts. Almost every lodging house on the East Side is now and for years has been a busy and prolific factory of fraudulent and criminal votes. From some of these houses more men are registered as residents than the whole house ever held or ever could hold. [p. 150]

Based upon extensive interviews with those who bought and sold votes, Russell dealt specifics to the public, citing not only instances of fraud—he canvassed the polls and residences to learn of men who couldn't remember their assigned names—but how much they were being paid— the going rate was fifty-cents a vote, "but the opportunities were so good that . . . the average day's earnings for an active repeater were twenty-five dollars." [p. 266] "Precinct captains always know before the election how many normal opposition votes will be cast in their precincts," Russell wrote. "They know how many fraudulent votes have been bought. To ascertain how honestly the goods are delivered is a sum in simple arithmetic." [p. 260]

Although those who committed the fraud were important to Russell's series, more important was the organization and enforcement of the fraud by political leaders in collaboration with election judges, the police, and the courts. In the February 1908 issue, Russell discussed enforcement in New York City:

Much of the East Side was given over to violence. Prize-fighters, burglars, waterside thieves, highwaymen, and professional thugs were organized into bands to take possession of the polling-places and assault or disable the challengers or frighten them away. Voters approaching the polls were stopped, and if they would not promise to vote as desired [—the voting booth curtains often had holes in them—] they were set upon and beaten. Any man that proclaimed himself a worker for the other side did so at the imminent risk of his life. Riots, fighting, and bloody scenes followed one another all day. The hospitals were filled with injured men. Black-jacks and brass knuckles were the weapons most commonly used, but there was continual shooting. No resident of New York could recall another election accompanied by so much violence.

When the thugs had driven from the polls all the watchers and challengers of the opposition, almost unlimited frauds were perpetrated. At one precinct in the Third Assembly District, as soon as the watchers had been driven off, the ballot-boxes were opened and the opposition ballots taken out and thrown away. Ballots were picked up in the streets and found in ash-barrels. Misapplied ingenuity made many of these frauds safe as well as effective. . . . In New York city . . . they secured and deposited not fewer than sixty thousand fraudulent votes. [pp. 264-266]

At the end of 1908, Henry Raleigh, a New York City detective captain, shocked the nation with "Confessions of a New York Detective." Although most his articles in the series for *Cosmopolitan* was written in a "confessions magazine" style, with inside details of crimes and how the police solved them, some of it detailed graft and corruption within the police department—the same one Theodore Roosevelt as police commissioner in the late nineteenth century had tried to clean up.

But, the problems in New York City were no different than any other large city. In Louisville, "many precinct election clerks in the pay of the interests carried off the ballot-boxes to secret places, stuffed them full of fraudulent ballots, and returned enormous pluralities in favor of the interests." [p. 270] To assure compliance, said Russell, "the police worked on the side of the interests, intimidating, assaulting, and arresting members of the citizens' movement." In Buffalo, legitimate voters were disenfranchised when they were told "they were not on the [voting] lists or were registered in other precincts when such was not the fact." Russell investigated Maryland, and found one-third of the legitimate voters disenfranchised. In Cincinnati, Denver, Providence, Milwaukee, Newark, St. Louis, Detroit, Cleveland, the methods may have differed, but the results were the same, as Russell was able to accuse the utilities, railroads, and even vicelords of being the originators of the fraud. But, it was in Philadelphia where Russell documented 40,000 to 80,000 instances of fraud every year. Even backers of reformer Theodore Roosevelt were sucked into the buying and selling of votes. "The Second Ward of Philadelphia has 3421 qualified voters," Russell wrote, noting, "in 1904 it gave Roosevelt 4631 votes." The Eighth Ward, with 3199 qualified voters, gave Roosevelt 4472 votes; the tenth, with 4618 voters, cast 6705 votes for Roosevelt. According to Russell, "Mr. Roosevelt's majority in Philadelphia was about one hundred eighty thousand, of which more than eighty thousand votes were fraudulent." [p. 268]

With the complicity of the police, prosecuting attorneys, and courts, convictions were rare. In Philadelphia, there were only forty-one convictions for 81,000 instances; in New York, there were twenty-four convictions for 60,000 instances; it was little different in other cities.

With muckraking at its peak, reflecting a nationwide rebellion at the excesses of power and greed, election reform did come to the cities; by the 1908 election, fraudulent voting was significantly reduced.

For its May 30, 1908 issue, *Collier's* published William Hard's accusations against Joseph Cannon, speaker of the House, whom he claimed was "the most stationary political object ever exhibited within [the boundaries of the United States.] Not reactionary. That implies movement. Just stationary, fixed, embedded, like a rock in a glacier." One of the most knowledgeable people about the workings of the federal government and its budget, Cannon controlled appointments to all House committees, and was rightfully known as a benevolent dictator by those mildly opposed to him and an autocratical czar by his enemies. By the time the muckraking articles finished with him about 1910, the House had not only stripped the speaker of the power to appoint, but would strip Cannon of the Speakership as well.

Other articles in the muckraking magazines pointed to a plethora of violations of the public trust, but still there were abuses; by now, politicians had learned how to better disguise their graft. Then, in 1910, with managing editor James Keeley spearheading the crusade, the *Chicago Tribune*, Joseph Medill's conservative anti-labor newspaper, finally exposed the corruption that had led to the election of U. S. Sen. William Larimer. However, it took two more years before Larimer was eventually expelled from the Senate in 1912.

The following year, the people of the United States approved the sixteenth and seventeenth amendments to the Constitution. The Sixteenth amendment called for a graduated tax upon personal income, a tax that would take away some of the money of the rich, and give it to the government to be used to benefit all the people; those with little income would pay less than those with millions. The Supreme Court in 1895 had called such an action unconstitutional; others called it socialistic. But now, with the amendment, it was hoped that the income from the taxes would help all the people, while also diminishing the influence of the power brokers who, as David Graham Phillips claimed, had "bought" a senate.

The Seventeenth Amendment provided for the direct popular election of senators; no longer would state legislatures, their members often influenced by payoffs and favors, select the senator. In 1920, the people passed the Nineteenth Amendment, forbidding discrimination by sex in voting for office; numerous articles by Phillips and the other muckrakers had helped prepare America for the necessity of having all its citizens eligible to vote. However, Phillips never saw the reform his series had created. In 1911, in New York City, he was killed at the age of forty-two. By then, the muckraking movement had all but been buried.

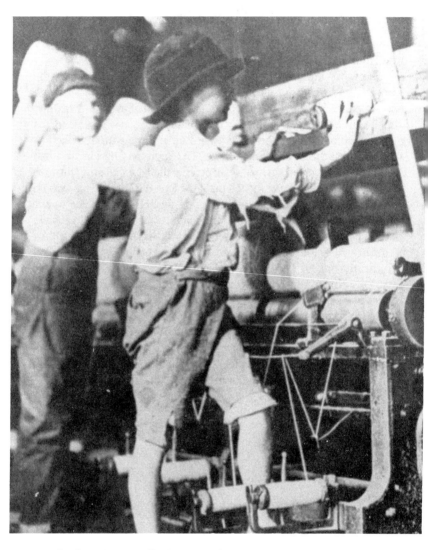

In the mines, mills, heavy industry, and the farms, children as young as four years old received an education in survival.

CHAPTER 7
A New Social Awareness

The year that Theodore Roosevelt had given the muckrakers their name had been the "highwater mark" of the movement as series after series pointed to the problems in America's social structure, exposing intertwining corporate trusts and corruption, shocking America into action. An editorial in the March 22, 1906, issue of *The Independent*, a month before Roosevelt made "muckraking" a national phrase, praised the movement:

All right thinking men must rejoice that the literature of exposure came into existence when it did, and all sane men will be glad if it gives place to something less fervid, in due time. It has accomplished a great purpose, and the American people will be sounder—more sincere, less fearful in right doing . . . because of it. the public conscience has been awakened and wrong-doers have been stricken with wholesome fear. ["The Literature of Exposure," p. 691]

Although unwilling or unable to become soldiers in the fight for better government and a more socially responsible corporate world, an oppressed and exploited urban America was willing to allow the reformers and the media to expose themselves to the battle to eliminate corruption and social injustice, and to cheer from the sidelines. Encouraged by the middle-class, and with it the lure of additional circulation, which in itself would lead to greater advertising revenue, a few more newspaper and magazine publishers were willing to give respectable salaries, spend the money necessary for comprehensive investigation, give their reporters freedom and time to dig into the issues critical to the preservation of democracy, then stand up courageously to advertisers and the public. With the encouragement of their publishers, journalists and would-be journalists also saw the lure of power and fame, reflected by the higher circulation. Soon, hundreds of would-be muckrakers began investigating just about

105

anything they could, leading the profession deeper into the sensationalistic days of yellow journalism and to abuses and excesses never imagined by the earlier journalists.

A year before the virulent "Treason of the Senate" series appeared in *Cosmopolitan*, *Collier's Weekly* was concerned that perhaps the proliferation of muckraking articles was having a negative impact upon the country. "Why listen to the facts [such as presented by Steffens and Tarbell]," said *Collier's*, "when diatribes are at hand?" [May 25, 1905] Even Upton Sinclair, the era's most prolific muckraker, lamented that "The Treason of the Senate," while a powerful indictment that led to sweeping political change, went too far, and charged Phillips with having crossed the line of solid investigative reporting and into a world of sensationalism.

In *The Critic*, a gossipy literary journal, F. Hopkinson Smith (1838-1915), near the end of a distinguished career as an artist and novelist, criticized the movement:

Publicity through the medium of the daily press and the magazines of the United States has assumed such a vicious form in some instances that it has done the American people much harm. Under the guise of exposing graft, corruption, and whatever title we may be pleased to give it, some of the mediums of publicity have magnified petty faults and grossly exaggerated conditions merely for the sake of commercialism—to increase their circulation. Agitation for reform has served as a pretext for attacks upon men and women which were entirely unwarranted, but one of the most baneful tendencies of this stuff, which is unfit to be called literature, is its wholesale slander of our country and our people. . . .

[The muckrakers] are on the scent for scandal and blackmail because that sort of stuff is salable, and in most cases for that reason alone. They are merely pandering to a public taste which craves these things . . .

We cannot afford to let this literary and mud-slinging continue— nor will we for long. Our people are very busy, and they have much to do. Much escapes us in our working hours because we are all absorbed in our labor. But when a thing is brought before our notice in all its force, we take hold of it with all our might and then the reaction comes. The cheap magazines and yellow press are not reformers—and that the masses will learn very soon. When they do learn this, there will be a revolution of popular beliefs which will counteract in measure the harm that is being done by these alarmists. But let us hope that the revulsion of feeling comes soon. ["The Muck-

Rake as a Circulation Boomer," June 1906, pp. 511-512]

Nevertheless, there were still magazines and reporters who cared about the truth and who meticulously researched public documents to form a basis for their stories exposing problems in America. Although solid well-researched articles began appearing in many of the leading general circulation magazines, including *The Atlantic Monthly, Century, Harper's, Popular Science Monthly*, and the *Saturday Evening Post*, it was the magazines now identified as muckrakers that pushed the country into a new social awareness. In addition to *McClure's*, the leading muckraking magazines now included *The American Magazine, The Appeal to Reason, The Arena, Cosmopolitan, Everybody's, Hampton's*, and *World's Week*.

Even the theatre became involved when several playwrights began using muckraking stories from the nation's newspapers and magazines for their subjects. Probably the best-known of the muckraking playwrights was Charles Klein (1857-1915) whose two dozen plays included *The District Attorney* (1895), a dramatized form of the newspapers' stories about New York City corruption; *The Hon. John Grigsby* (1902); and *The Lion and the Mouse* (1905), a thinly-disguised Rockefeller-Tarbell conflict that ran 686 performances on Broadway.

Other Broadway plays, most focusing upon governmental corruption, included *The Man of the Hour* (1906), by George Broadhurst; *The Power of Money* (1906), by Owen Davis; *The Stolen Story* 1906), by Jesse Lynch Williams; *The Undertow* (1907), by Eugene Walters; *Friends of Labor* (1907), by Julius Hopp; *The Offenders* (1908), by Bayard Veiler; *A Gentleman From Mississippi* (1908), by Harrison Rhodes and Thomas Wise; *The Writing on the Wall* (1909), by William J. Hurlbut; *The Nigger* (1909), by Edward Shelton; *A Man of Honor* (1911), by James S. Barcus; *Within the Law* (1912), by Bayard Veiller; and *The Lure* (1913), by George Scarborough.

The Inhumanity of Mankind

During 1908 and 1909, *Cosmopolitan* published Alfred Henry Lewis's probes into "The Owners of America," a fact-based, but still emotional series, detailing the lives of America's corporate goliaths. The nation's muckraking media were still concerned about the robber barons, but now they were after the fabric of the nation; it would be their attacks upon the social structure that would lead to its greatest glory—and eventual demise.

Behind a veil of religion, some of the nation's churches had been responsible for some of the worst poverty in America. The worst offender, however, was New York's Trinity Episcopal Church, founded in 1697. By the end of the nineteenth century, it was perhaps the nation's wealthiest church, with estimates placing its ownership of land and properties between $39 million and $100 million, with about one-third of it in tenement housing. For twenty-five years, social workers, reform politicians, and the New York newspapers, especially the *World*, had reported the abuses and excesses of the Trinity corporation; for a five-year period, the national muckraking magazines added their voices. All were largely ignored by the Trinity Corp.

In 1905, *McClure's* had published Samuel Hopkins Adams' investigation into tuberculosis as a social disease; in the article, he had attacked Trinity for owning tenements that bred tuberculosis. A flurry of correspondence between Trinity and *McClure's* produced few results. Then, in Spring 1908, following extensive investigations, Charles Edward Russell wrote two sharp articles that revealed that not only were church finances controlled by Wall Street brokers, but that much of the church's income came from renting slum tenements. For *Everybody's*, Russell carefully described the tenements, pointing out that houses a century earlier designed to house one family now housed five or six families, bred disease, had no fire escape, and very likely would burn quickly. Tearing into Trinity, Russell wrote:

Profit, much profit, very great profit, lies in property of this sort ... These are houses that old-time tenants built on land let from Trinity on short leases. When the leases expired, Trinity, following a consistent and profitable policy, refused to grant renewals ... It also refused to purchase the house that the tenant had built. The tenant, therefore, was confronted with this situation: he could tear his house down brick by brick and cart it away to the dump or the river or he could abandon it (as it stood) to Trinity, sometimes for nothing, sometimes for a nominal sum. These are houses, therefore, in which the investment of Trinity was almost nothing, possibly an average of $200 each, and now from these same houses she gathers $40 or $50 a month for rent, paying out nothing for repairs. ... Very few of [the houses] are fit under any circumstance for human habitation. ...

Why don't [the tenants] move elsewhere? ... Dear soul, so long as Trinity offers a tenement at $5.50 a month [per family] somebody (in the conditions of life that we create and maintain) is certain to live in it. ...

The management [of Trinity] is a self-perpetuating body, without responsibility, and without supervision. All these are strange conditions. But stranger than all is this: that a Christian church should be willing to take money from such tenements as Trinity owns . . .

For the May 1909 issue of *The American Magazine*, Ray Stannard Baker ripped into Trinity again:

There is no more barren, forbidding, unprogressive part of the city than the Trinity blocks south of Christopher Street. Trinity has sat still and waited for the increase of the value of its land. . . .

A distinctly higher standard of social morality has been built up in New York in the last twenty-five years. And in the work of improving conditions in the crowded districts of Manhattan Island the city authorities have repeatedly collided with Trinity. The first clash came in 1887. A law had been passed requiring that running water should be furnished on each floor of tenement houses. In most of the Trinity houses, the tenants had to go down stairs and out of doors to get their water supply. When a demand was made on Trinity to obey the law, the vestry objected and began a bitter fight in the courts, which finally reached the Court of Appeals. Of course this costly litigation was not paid for by the vestry-man or even the communicants of Trinity. This legal battle was financed out of the rentals of the very people who were to be benefitted by the new law. . . . Trinity has always been against improvement; it has always had to be lashed to its moral duty by public opinion or by the courts, or by fear of legislative action. . . .

It is difficult, indeed, to see how a group of men so intelligent and honorable should collectively exhibit so little vision, so little social justice. Whether judged as good morals or as good business, the results have been lamentable and disheartening. . . . [p. 10-11]

The attacks came against Hampton, Russell, and Baker, charging them not only with heinous crimes but with atheism—for having attacked a church's disregard for the poor. "The whole front of righteousness and Things as They Are was livid with rage," Russell reported in *Bare Hands and Stone Walls*. Benjamin Hampton, responding to his critics, asked them a point-blank question:

"You say that these tenement houses are not really bad. Would you like to live in one of them? Take the best of them all. Would you like to live in it?"

And the answer was always the same.

"No, but it is good enough for the people that dwell in it."

"How do you know it is good enough?"

"Well, that's all they are fitted for." [Quoted in *Bare Hands and Stone Walls*, p. 146]

When "the smoke of the battle finally cleared away," Russell reported, "Trinity had the usual vindication, the wickedness of the muckraker was satisfactorily demonstrated and all was once more peace." [*Bare Hands and Stone Walls*, p. 147] However, Trinity, having sustained damage during the previous three decades, and embarrassed by the charges, quietly began tearing down the tenement houses—while never acknowledging that it was the muckrakers who had forced the church into recognizing that it had not only a spiritual but moral and social obligation to the people.

Jack London (1876-1916) had seen what America was doing to itself, of the separation of classes that led to uncontrolled wealth and overwhelming poverty, and believed that only through a socialistic revolution could America awaken from its self-inflicted nightmare and restore its dreams of equality. He was not alone in his beliefs, as Charles Edward Russell among other muckrakers and reformers added their voices to the battle. However, it was London, the novelist, and Eugene V. Debs, the politician, whose voices gave the movement its strength.

London had already earned a reputation in his mid-twenties as one of the nation's better short story writers when he went to London to explore the class struggle, returning with the notes for *The People of the Abyss* (1903), a penetrating look at the problems of poverty. Two years later, after publication of four novels including *The Call of the Wild* (1903) and *The Sea-Wolf* (1904), two of the finest adventure stories published in the American experience, London wrote the socialistic treatise *The War of the Classes* (1905) and helped Upton Sinclair to secure publication of *The Jungle*. The year *The Jungle* was published was also the year that saw publication of London's *White Fang* (1906), the sequel to *The Call of the Wild*. Again turning to the socialist philosophy to show America what was happening to it, London wrote *The Iron Heel* (1907), a powerful novel that ripped into the widening chasm between the oppressed masses and the robber barons, prophecizing the unification of the great capitalistic monopolies into a fascist organization to control the nation's wealth; like all great novels, *The Iron Heel* was based upon fact. Among London's other muckraking novels were *The Strength of the Strong* (1911), *The Valley of the Moon* (1913), and *The Abysmal Brute* (1913).

Maximizing Profits on the Backs of Labor

On labor issues, the muckrakers continued hammering for reform, pointing to the continued exploitation of the worker, to the horrors of unsafe working conditions, and to the abuse of women and children in the labor force to arouse a nation into action.

In 1907, Benjamin Hampton (1875-1932) converted a mediocre 10,000-circulation *Broadway Magazine* into an editorially and economically strong half-million-circulation *Hampton's*, giving the public a mix of short stories, poetry, profiles and features—and a few powerful muckraking articles, the same formula *McClure's* found successful. In 1902, Marie and Bessie McGinney Van Vorst had written several articles for *Everybody's* about the exploitation of women in factory employment, just as Nellie Bly, Annie Laurie and other reporters for the *New York World, San Francisco Examiner,* and *New York Journal* had done in the 1880s and 1890s. The Van Vorsts had gone undercover as workers in a shoe factory, clothing mill, Southern cotton mill, and pickle factory to learn what Big Business was doing to the workers. The articles, collected into book form the following year as *The Woman Who Toils,* forced a naive America into recognition of the problems of the work force. However, the articles merely presented the facts of exploitation, not the causes or solutions, and didn't try to outline reasons why women were forced into factory work.

Now, in 1907, Rheta Childe Dorr (1866-1948) expanded the Van Vorst articles. Dorr was an excellent journalist who had spent four years on the *New York Evening Post,* and several years before that as one of New York City's better freelance newspaper reporters, having been unable to secure full-time employment because she was a woman. For more than a year, at $35 a week, a decent salary at the turn of the century, Dorr sent her notes to John O'Hara Cosgrave, editor of *Everybody's.*

Working in the sweatshops of the north, Dorr didn't merely tell about the working day of women, but looked to causes of the exploitation, to the conflict between what society had expected of a woman, and what some women wanted for themselves. She later recalled:

Although many women have since made personal investigations of the trades, I believe that I was the first woman to throw herself into the ranks of manual workers with a view of surveying their conditions in relation to the whole social fabric. . . . [I took up] one after another, the historic trades of women, cooking, sewing, washing and ironing, spinning and weaving, canning, preserving, and other household arts, following them from the home where they began to the factory which had absorbed them. My articles [described] the transformation of the trades themselves . . . and the effect of the change on the workers, their homes, and their point of view on life. My great object, of course, was to demonstrate that women were permanent factors in industry, permanent producers of the world's wealth, and that they must hereafter be considered as independent human beings and citizens, rather than adjuncts to men and to society. [Quoted by Susan G. Motes, "Rheta Childe Dorr," *American Newspaper Journalists, Vol. 25*, Gale Research, p. 81]

The series, co-authored by William Hard,[1] began in the October 1908 issue and continued for about a year.

Her first book, *What Eight Million Women Want* (1910), based upon a series of articles written for *Hampton's*, eventually sold almost a half-million copies, and established her as one of the nation's more respected journalists.

In one year, reported the American Institute of Social Service, more than 500,000 people were killed, maimed, or injured in the nation's work force. In "Making Steel and Killing Men," published in the November 1907 issue of *Everybody's*, William Hard described management indifference to the working conditions that had led to forty-six deaths, about four hundred permanent disabilities, and about two thousand injuries in one steel mill in one year in Chicago:

. . . The United States Steel Corporation, in the person of the Illinois Steel Company, was censured six times last year by coroner's juries. Here, at the time when ten men were injured in the pig-casting department, the Building Department of the City of Chicago was forced to intervene and to admonish the company that "a little diligent thought and precaution on your part would minimize the occurrence of such accidents." Here the number of the dead, who are reported to

---

[1]After a few months of investigation, Dorr was summarily dismissed—she was told she was merely a researcher, not a writer. Learning that her notes were to be compiled by Hard then published under his byline, Dorr sued and won the right of a co-byline. During that period of muckraking journalism, it was not unusual for one writer to compile notes from a researcher, then analyze and add to them, and write the articles under his own name; Gustavus Myers had been the unbylined researcher for David Graham Phillips' "Treason of the Senate." Hard later became an outstanding muckraker whose stories of labor were among the best of the period.

the coroner, furnishes the only clue to the number of the merely burned, crushed, maimed and disabled, who are reported to nobody. [p. 580]

No one knows just how many of those killed and maimed were children, but in a non-farm work force of 19.7 million, almost two million of whom were children, ten percent of the total, it would not be unreasonable to believe that about 50,000 of the 500,000 injuries and deaths a year were to children. Several newspaper reporters and editors in the nineteenth century, including Greeley, Hearst, and Scripps, had written against child labor and called for the enactment of state or federal legislation. But, their voices were silenced, often by families who needed the additional income just to survive.

In 1902, Ray Stannard Baker had described the "Children of the Coal Shadow," shocking a nation—but which did little to bring about reform. Now, four years later, poet-journalist Edwin Markham, assistant editor of *Cosmopolitan*, would add his voice to those calling for child labor legislation to prevent days as long as sixteen hours for children as young as five years old who worked for a fraction of what their sixteen-year-old brothers and sisters worked for. In "The Hoe-Man in the Making," an extended editorial published in the September 1906 *Cosmopolitan*, Markham strung his facts carefully, wringing tears from an audience of *Cosmopolitan's* one-half million subscribers. He focused upon the cotton mills, but his observations could be applied to any of the industries which employed, and exploited, the young:

Children rise at half-past four, commanded by the ogre scream of the factory whistle; they hurry, ill fed, unkempt, unwashed, half dressed, to the walls which shut out the day and which confine them amid the din and dust and merciless maze of the machines. Here, penned in little narrow lanes, they look and leap and reach and tie among acres and acres of looms. Always the snow of lint in their faces, always the thunder of the machines in their ears. A scant half hour at noon breaks the twelve-hour vigil, for it is nightfall when the long hours end and the children may return to the barracks they call "home," often too tired to wait for the cheerless meal which the mother, also working in the factory, must cook, after her factory-day is over. Frequently at noon and at night they fall asleep with the food unswallowed in the mouth. Frequently they snatch only a bite and curl up undressed on the bed, to gather strength for the same dull round to-morrow and to-morrow, and to-morrow.

When I was in the South, I was everywhere charmed by the bright courtesy of the cultured classes, but I was everywhere depressed by the stark penury of the working people. This penury stands grimly out in the graft monotonous shells that they call "homes"—dingy shacks, or bleak, barnlike structures. And for these dirty, desolate homes the workers must pay rent to the mill owner. But the rent is graded according to the number of children sent to work in the mill. The more the children, the less the rent. . . . [pp. 482-483]

The average child lives only four years after it enters the [cotton] mills. Pneumonia stalks in the damp, lint-filled room. . . . Hundreds more are maimed by the machinery. . . . One doctor said he had amputated the fingers of more than one hundred children, mangled in the mill machinery, and that a horrible form of dropsy occurs frequently among the overworked children. . . . [p. 483]

It was the New England shipper, greedy for gold at any cost, who carried the blacks to the South, planting the tree of slavery in our soil. And now it is the northern money-grubber who is grafting upon our civilization this new and more terrible white slavery . . . [p. 484]

By 1915, about two-thirds of the states had enacted child labor laws, and in 1916 Congress enacted legislation to prevent interstate commerce of products produced in factories and mills in which there were children employed who were under the age of fourteen; the following year, the Supreme Court ruled such legislation unconstitutional. There were several other legislative attempts to restrict child labor, including a Constitutional amendment approved by the Congress but which was defeated when it wasn't ratified. It wasn't until the Fair Labor Standards Act of 1938 that child labor was finally regulated.

Unable to Legislate Attitudes

Although Blacks had been legally emancipated for more than four decades, they still were subject to widespread abuse and denied even the most basic of rights. The nation had its Bill of Rights, and subsequent post-Civil War human rights amendments, the cities and states had their laws, but no legislation can modify human attitudes. And so it was that the majority continued to try to erase the nation's minorities, whether they were Blacks, Jews, or immigrants, women, the handicapped, or just anyone who didn't think—or look—or act—like the majority thought they should think, or look, or act. It was no different before the Revolution, it was no different after it.

While Lincoln Steffens, Ida Tarbell, and Ray Stannard Baker were digging into corporate excesses, S. S. McClure had assigned Carl Schurz (1829-1906) to look into the "Negro problem" in the South. Schurz, who had investigated the problems in the South for President Andrew Johnson in 1865, had been one of the nation's most influential newspaper editors and politicians, one of the founders of the Republican party, a former U.S. senator and leader of numerous reform movements. His books, *The New South* (1885) and *Life of Henry Clay* (1887), had been highly successful; his articles in major magazines were carefully read by politicians and the public. For the November 1903 *McClure's*, Schurz traced a history of post-Civil War oppression against Blacks, and took a harsh look at what the South was doing to try to restore the "old order" by denying voting and educational rights:

The only plausible reason given for that curtailment of their rights is that it is not in the interest of the Southern whites to permit the blacks to vote. . . . [p. 268]

Negro suffrage is plausibly objected to on the ground that the great bulk of the colored population of the South are very ignorant. That is true. But the same is true of a large portion of the white population. If the suffrage is dangerous in the hands of certain voters on account of their ignorance, it is as dangerous in the hands of ignorant whites as in the hands of ignorant blacks. . . .

[However,] with many of the Southern whites a well-educated colored voter is as objectionable as an ignorant one, or even more objectionable, simply on account of his color. It is therefore not mere ignorance in the voting body that arouses the Southern whites against the colored voters. It is race-antagonism, and that race-antagonism presents a problem more complicated and perplexing than most others, because it is apt to be unreasoning. It creates violent impulses which refuse to be argued with. . . . [p. 269]

We constantly read speeches in Southern newspapers and reports of public speeches made by Southern men which bear a striking resemblance to the pro-slavery arguments I remember to have heard before the Civil War, and they are brought forth with the same passionate heat and dogmatic assurance to which we were then accustomed—the same assertion of the negro's predestination for serfdom; the same certainty that he will not work without "physical compulsion"; the same contemptuous rejection of negro education as a thing that will only unfit him for work; the same prediction that the elevation of the negro will be the degradation of the whites; the same angry demand that any advocacy of the negro's rights should be put down in the South as an attack upon the safety of Southern society, and as treason to the Southern cause. . . . [p. 271]

What the reactionist really wants is a negro just fit for the task of plantation hand and for little, if anything, more, and with no ambition for anything beyond. Therefore, quite logically, the reactionist abhors the educated negro. In fact the political and social recognition of the educated negro is especially objectionable to him for the simple reason that it would be an encouragement of higher aspirations among the colored people generally. The reactionist wishes to keep the colored people, that is, the great mass of the laboring force in the South, as ignorant as possible to the end of keeping it as submissive and obedient as possible. As formerly the people of the South were the slaves of society, so they are now to be made the victims of their failure to abolish slavery altogether. . . . [p. 272]

To the lofty people who, for fear of compromising their own dignity, scorn to address a colored man as Mr. or a colored woman as Mrs. or Miss, they would give something to think by reminding them of the stateliest gentleman ever produced by America, a man universally reverenced, a Virginian, who, when a [Black woman], and a slave, too, had dedicated to him some complimentary verses, wrote her an elaborate and gravely polite letter of thanks, addressing her as "Miss Phyllis," and subscribing himself "with great respect, your obedient humble servant, George Washington." [p. 275]

"Can the South Solve the Negro Problem?" shocked *McClure's* readers, most of whom just assumed that there was no problem since no one ever denied *them* their rights. Unfortunately, instead of attacking themselves for allowing oppression to continue, they merely attacked "others" and conveniently blamed the problem upon the South.[2] The complacent North assumed the problems were all in the South, that the problems were the problems of the Confederacy, now more than four decades after the end of the Civil War. They were wrong.

Cosmopolitan's last significant series in its three years of muckraking was Ray Stannard Baker's "Following the Color Line," a two-part study

___

[2]McClure, although a reformer and catalyst for reform, was also was a fair and objective journalist, and later assigned novelist-journalist Thomas Nelson Page (1853-1922) to present other evidence, focusing upon the Southern perspective; his three-part series began in the March 1904 issue, and was eventually published as *The Negro, The Southerner's Problem.*

of racism in America, published in 1908, two years after the Atlanta riots, that told in solid factual terms the horror that one people were inflicting upon another. Baker went into the police stations to report about the methods of arresting Blacks; he went into the courts to report about discriminatory punishment.

The September 3, 1908 issue of *The Independent* published "The Race War in the North," William Walling's brutal look at lynchings and violence throughout the country, but which focused upon a race riot in Springfield, Illinois, that had led to several thousand Whites lynching two Blacks and driving others from the city. After several days of interviews, Walling was able to conclude:

"Why, the niggers came to think they were as good as we are!" was the final justification offered, not once but a dozen times. . . . [p. 530]

We at once discovered, to our amazement, that Springfield had no shame. She stood for the action of the mob. She hoped the rest of the negroes might flee. She threatened that the movement to drive them out would continue. I do not speak of leading citizens, but of the masses of people, of workingmen in the shops, the storekeepers in the stores, the drivers, the men on the street, the wounded in the hospitals . . . [p. 531].

In January 1909, Walling; Dr. Henry Moskowitz; and Mary White Ovington, a social worker living in a New York tenement, formed the National Association for the Advancement of Colored People. The petition to create the NAACP was signed by social workers Jane Addams and Ovington; educator John Dewey; government official Moskowitz; journalists William Lloyd Garrison, Charles Edward Russell, Lincoln Steffens, Oswald Garrison Villard, and Walling; Rabbis Emil G. Hirsch and Stephen Wise; and the Rev. John Haynes Holmes, the only Black in the group.

The violation of civil rights continued into the jails and prison systems throughout the country, their inhumane conditions described by innumerable newspaper journalists and reformers. In 1908, Fred R. Bechdolt and James Hopper probed the California prison system, fictionalized it, and wrote *9009*, a muckraking novel that helped Californians push for prison reform. However, it was in Georgia where the greatest muckraking occurred, where convicts with sentences of five years or more were "leased" to private contractors who subjected them to torture and forced working conditions as devastating as slavery in its worst moments. In "Following the Color Line," Ray Stannard Baker had pointed out reasons why Blacks were often convicted:

> One reason . . . lies in the fact that the state and the counties make a profit out of their prison system. No attempt is ever made to reform a criminal, either white or colored. . . . Last year [1907], the net profit to Georgia from its chain-gangs, to which the prison commission refers with pride, reached the great sum of $354,853.55.
>
> Of course a very large proportion of the prisoners are Negroes. Some of the large fortunes in Atlanta have come chiefly from the labor of chain-gangs of convicts leased from the state. The demand for convicts by rich sawmill operators, owners of brick-yards, large farmers, and others is far in advance of the supply. The natural tendency is to convict as many men as possible—it furnishes steady, cheap labor to the contractors and a profit to the state. Undoubtedly, this explains in some degree the very large number of criminals, especially Negroes, in Georgia. One of the leading political forces in Atlanta is a very prominent banker who is a dominant member of the city police board, where many convicts are employed.

In "A Burglar in the Making," published in the June 1908 issue of *Everybody's*, Charles Edward Russell described what life was like in a chain-gang camp:

> There is a commotion in the yard, and two of the guards appear, leading forward a convict to a place where a great barrel lies on its side. A big, authoritative man comes forward and gives orders. the convict is stripped. Then he is bent over the barrel. Two [men] hold his arms and his head. Two others hold his legs. He begs and pleads and struggles. The [men] hold him fast. Another man stands by with an instrument. It is made of sole leather, about three inches wide, three feet long, and three-eighths of an inch thick. It has a stout wooden handle. The man lifts the instrument high in the air. He brings it down, *swish*! upon the naked man on the barrel, the man on the barrel screams aloud with sudden agony. He does not shout or exclaim, he screams a horrible shrill scream of unutterable pain.
>
> The other man raises the instrument and brings it down, *swish*! again. Again the man on the barrel screams. A blow and a scream: a blow and a scream. Presently it is a blow and a sob: the man on the barrel is crying. Again a moment, and his blood trickles down his side; he is screaming, sobbing, crying now—and bleeding. The blows fall

upon his bruised and bloody back; he wriggles and twists about; the [men] can hardly hold down his head and his legs; the other men stand and gaze; the guards hold their rifles; and from the bluest of skies the soft sun of Georgia looks upon the frightful scene, and the sweet spring air from the southern woods blows over it.

But the man has done wrong: he has committed a fault.

Yes: from sunrise to noon he has wheeled fifty-seven loads of fresh brick [five to six pounds a brick, fifty to seventy bricks a load, 250-300 pounds a load, which he must wheel about four hundred feet]; the regulations of this hell on earth require that in such a time he shall wheel sixty loads. So, having thus transgressed, power and law and justice as administered in the State of

Charles Edward Russell

Georgia exact from him this penalty until he screams and cries and sobs—and bleeds.

He walks with difficulty, this offender against the majesty of the State of Georgia and its slave contracts. [He] is a cripple; he has chronic rheumatism in his back. [That] is why [there are] three missing loads from his tally between sunrise and noon. He is lame, he is no longer young, about fifty-five . . . He can not with ease wheel three-hundred pound loads. . . .

With the power of exposition, Russell described the meals:

George [a new prisoner who had been sentenced for having stolen $300] was led to one of the filthy sheds, where [he] received a breakfast of one slice of boiled salt pork and one piece of greasy corn bread. There were no knives nor forks, and George took the pork into his fingers. he felt something move under his fingers. He looked sharply at the pork. He saw what it was that had moved. It was worms. . . . For dinner [the prisoners] have each a piece of boiled salt pork, a piece of greasy corn bread. . . . For dinner, [the prisoners] have boiled salt pork and a piece of corn bread.

Tearing apart the inhumanity of man, Russell described what happened when one prisoner, undernourished and exhausted, dropped:

[His] companions in misery carry him to his filthy bunk . . . And so he lies there, and a million insects that inhabit his bed crawl over him and feed upon him, and for weakness he can hardly lift his hand to brush them from his face. So he lies there two days, three days, four days, five days, delirious part of the time, happily unconscious part of the time. The doctor comes and glances at him and goes his way; the slave contractor's agent look in the door and curses him.

With the publication of Russell's article, Georgia's newspapers began beating incessantly at the inhumanity of the work camps, calling for reform and the elimination of the hired contractor. The state—which had originally claimed no responsibility since it had "leased" the convicts to the highest bidders for specified periods of time—blamed the media for making trouble. But by the end of the year, the legislature did bring reform, eventually terminating the selling of convicts to private contractors.

The muckrakers during the first decade of the nineteenth century had exposed vice, graft, and corruption at all levels of society; exploitation of labor and of the poor; terroristic attacks upon minorities and apathy by the majority. Their efforts had led to widespread reform, but their moments on stage would soon be over as a nation beaten senseless by only a few dozen muckrakers out of thousands of journalists had grown tired of their performance. There was a new era coming, one less concerned with the ills of society and more concerned with getting on with its own lives.

CHAPTER 8

The Final Assault

The Roosevelt Progressive era had given freedom to the muckrakers; it had encouraged them, and it had taken the results of their investigations to try to improve America. Theodore Roosevelt—although having vented his rage at the reporters who had attacked the U.S. Senate, preferring to "rake the muck" while rejecting a celestial crown—nevertheless understood and respected the nation's press; he liked the reporters, confided in them, and encouraged their investigations. However, even Roosevelt had his limits, especially when he was the one being attacked.

In 1908, the *New York World,* which had never been a strong supporter of the nation's square deal rough rider, charged that the federal government had paid about $40 million for land in Panama when it was available for about one-tenth that; since Roosevelt was the president pushing the creation of the Panama Canal, the *World* essentially implicated the President for policies that may have led to graft in the construction of the canal. Furious, Roosevelt ordered his attorney general to file charges of criminal libel against the *World* and an Indianapolis newspaper which had reprinted the *World's* expose. On the sidelines, many anti-Pulitzer newspapers were cheering for the government to silence one of Roosevelt's harshest critics; few, newspapers or magazines even investigated the *World's* charges. Although the government's claims were later dismissed in federal court, Roosevelt emerged relatively unscathed by the *World's* charges. William Howard Taft wasn't as fortunate.

Before the era ended, the muckrakers who attacked senators and the wealthy, and looked into corruption, poverty, racism, and the exploitation of the workers, among many of America's other social problems, would finally attack the president of the United States. *Collier's*, under the direction of Norman Hapgood (1868-1937), showed the American public that not only had the Taft administration planned to sell—almost give away—about 100,000 acres of land in Alaska to monopolistic companies, but that both the secretary of the interior and President Taft had lied, and tried to cover-up evidence. *Collier's*, at great expense, and under extreme opposition, had tenaciously also proven that the Taft administration not only fired a federal official who tried to prevent the scheme, but established a commission that would "whitewash" the problem; the secretary of interior, "vindicated" by a high-level federation commission, would then file a multi-million dollar libel suit against *Collier's*, hoping to crush it.

The land-grab—it would eventually become a major case in the philosophical battle between the rights of private enterprise and the necessity for public conservation—had been brought to the attention of Washington by Louis R. Glavis, a field investigator for the U.S. General Land Office. A year later, after determining that there was probable fraud in the application and awarding of land grants, Glavis brought his investigation to President Taft—who ordered Richard A. Ballinger, secretary of the interior, to fire Glavis "for filing a disingenuous statement, unjustly impeaching the official integrity of his superior officers." [letter from President Taft to Ballinger, September 13, 1909, released to the press two days later.] In its November 13, 1909, issue, *Collier's* published Glavis' meticulously-researched article, "The Whitewashing of Ballinger," in which he reiterated the charges, what he believed was a subsequent cover-up, and events leading to his own firing. A month later, Christopher P. Connolly, who three years earlier for *McClure's* had exposed corruption in Montana, now nailed the case against the federal government. Defending Glavis while attacking Ballinger and Taft, Connolly stated a simple truth: "The Alaska Gold Mining Company, organized by Washington politicians, exploited Alaska with so high a hand that even Washington gasped at the brazenness. Then the spoil was gold—now it is copper and coal." ["Can This be Whitewashed Also?" *Collier's*, December 18, 1909.] Quickly, other muckraking journals, including *Hampton's* and the national urban newspapers, jumped on the story. E. W. Scripps himself told his newspapers to pursue the story, having become convinced that there had, indeed, been fraud and deceit.

Before the muckrakers finished with their investigations of the exploitation of land and the awarding of title to political cronies, Ballinger was under investigation by a joint House-Senate committee. After a four-month investigation, the Republican majority, by a 7-5 vote on May 20, 1910, held Ballinger blameless. Nevertheless, under fire by the public, Ballinger resigned about a year later, resolutely maintaining that he personally had nothing to do with the fraud. Nevertheless, President Taft would continue his four-year term under a mist of suspicion.

In 1909, the Taft administration passed a postal rate increase that quadrupled the rate for periodicals. Taft's supporters claimed that the increase was necessary to keep the Post office from serious deficit. Taft's opponents, however, rightfully claimed that since lower postage rates were built into the Constitution in order to encourage freedom of the press, the government's decision for a massive rate increase was done solely to silence the voices of protest. Nevertheless, the increase went into effect, forcing publishers to raise circulation rates by as much as fifty percent, thus losing subscribers and being forced either to raise advertising rates, thus losing some advertisers, or to lower the advertising rate to match the circulation base, thus lowering revenue. The administration's actions were just another shot of a volley that would kill the muckrakers.

Attacking Not Ideas But Life Blood

Benjamin O. Flower, in the July 1904 issue of *The Arena*, had written:
    No democracy can be maintained where the people or the public servants are subservient to any class or interest other than that of the whole nation or when the administration of government is placed in the hands of individuals, *not directly accountable to the people*. When there is class rulership, the people will always be oppressed or exploited in the interest of the dominating class, while the latter will steadily acquire wealth which others have earned and power that is destructive to free institutions. ["Twenty-Five Years of Bribery and Corrupt Practises . . ." p. 49]
But now, in a different time, the indignation that Flower and the other muckrakers felt was being lost upon a nation rushing into a new hedonism, a world war, and oblivious to the nation's social ills, willing to listen to the voices of capitalism that claimed the muckrakers had abused their right of criticism. For a couple of decades, it was *right* for there to be social criticism; but now it was a different time, and Big Business was able to mount its greatest campaigns for preservation. The first warning shots were fired shortly after Roosevelt's muckraker speech in early 1906 when several of the nation's magazines almost immediately abandoned investigative journalism in deference not only to what they thought were the President's wishes, but what they knew to be advertisers' wishes. And Charles Edward Russell, pointing to only one of thousands of events that

would portend the end of the era, recalled one speech by one businessman:

Speaking at a chamber of commerce banquet in a Western town, the president of a New York City bank made the emphatic declaration that there would be no more muck-raking in this country. In plain terms he declared that business had suffered all the attacks it intended to endure and that the slanderers of the leaders of the nation's commerce would be silenced. [*Bare Hands and Stone Walls*, p. 145]

According to Louis Filler:

The strength of popular demand, as well as the disunity between advertisers, more than counterbalanced the efforts of reaction to check the muckrakers. But the urge to combat exposure could hardly be expected to wane, despite the optimistic predictions of some muckrakers that a good time was coming when business would be perfectly free, competitive, and honest. The cheerful avowals of less realistic muckrakers simply proved that they did not understand their own success. Men who believed that "honesty is catching" were not likely to survive the shock of disillusion. For reform could not proceed on its own momentum. Big Business was not to be argued into social consciousness. . . .

What [the muckrakers] failed to understand and record was that the trusts could not be reformed by exposure. The bureaus were intended for permanence, which meant that either they or muckraking would have to go. Both could not exist side by side. [*Crusaders for American Liberalism*, p. 360]

And so it was that it was the muckrakers who went, after two glorious decades of shaking the American social order and forcing reform down the public's throats. Populism and agrarian reform were now a part of history. Even the public, which had created the climate that had led to the muckraking movement, now found they were no longer "excited" by the exposes, and had begun accusing the media of being part of an anti-capitalist plot to destroy the country.

The newspapers and magazines soon found that Big Business developed newer and better ways to threaten the magazines. To attack the facts would be futile—to attack their lifeblood would not. The newspapers and magazines also found that banks—most controlled by interlocking directories—were unwilling to extend credit, no matter how financially solvent the magazine was, blackmailing them into either stopping their muckraking or face financial ruin. Such was the case at *Collier's*, where Norman Hapgood finally admitted defeat and resigned; at *Success*, which was forced into bankruptcy, extinguished in 1911, resurrected under a different format and finally died in 1928; and at *Hampton's*.

Benjamin Hampton had been one of the first to realize the vengeance of the trusts after he assigned Charles Edward Russell to write a series of powerful articles about America's railroads and their grab for power. From the New York, New Haven, and Hartford Railroad of Charles Mellon came a visitor one day who charged that the yet-unpublished article—which a spy had gotten to the railroad—was a pack of lies:

"Well," said Mr. Hampton, "we will not print in this magazine anything we know to be untrue. Here are the proofs of the article. Suppose we go over it and you point out the things that are untrue and if you can show that they are so we will omit them."

It's all untrue," said the young man. "It's just one string of lies from beginning to end."

Hampton picked up the proofs and read the first sentence.

"Is that true or untrue?" says he.

"Oh, well, of course, I don't mean that," said the visitor. "I mean when you get down into the heart of the thing."

"You said it was all untrue," said Hampton. "We must read it all and see if you are right." He read the next sentence.

"Is that true or untrue?"

"Wait till you get past the introduction."

They went on, Hampton pausing at the end of every sentence and the young man impatiently waving him to proceed until they came to a sentence that declared that in ten years the capital stock of the railroad had been increased 1501 percent.

"There," shouted the young man, "that statement is a damn lie."

"Is it?" said Hampton, and he reached into a drawer in his desk from which he fished a copy of *The Congressional Record* containing explicit testimony to the assertion the article made.

So they proceeded to the end, Hampton referring to *The Record* or an investigating committee's report whenever a statement was challenged.

"Where's the lie?" said Hampton.

"Well, you may have documents and things enough to make out a case, but the article is injurious to the railroad and we demand that it be suppressed."

"It will be printed," said Hampton.

"Then I must tell you that if you print that article your magazine will be put out of business. That's all." And he went out. [*Bare Hands and Stone Walls*, by Charles Edward Russell, pp. 188-189]

Probably in collusion with the J. P. Morgan banking interests, the railroads forced creditors to stop credit, bankers to cancel loans, and finally Hampton to sell his interest in the 480,000 circulation magazine to avoid bankruptcy. In the August 1911 issue, Hampton had said that the banks refused his loans because of the magazine's "fearless, aggressive editorial policy [which] had offended the powers of Wall Street." [p. 258] In *The Profits of Religion* (1918), Upton Sinclair claimed that " . . . the story of [*Hampton's*] wrecking by the New Haven criminals will some day serve in school text-books as the classic illustration of that financial piracy which brought on the American social revolution." [p. 181] Within a year, the new owners skimmed almost $200,000 from the magazine, effectively killing it by 1911. although it struggled as *Hampton-Colombian Magazine* then *The Hampton Magazine* for another year.

Unable to sustain losses from lack of circulation, Benjamin Flower's *The Arena*—which had been at the front of the movement for social change and in denunciation of racism—in 1909 was merged into the decidedly not muckraking *Christian Work*. Flower himself moved to the *Twentieth Century* where he improved both editorial and circulation, but never saw the magazine achieve the reputation of *The Arena*; eventually, he lost control when the banks refused to extend credit.

The *American Magazine*, which was infused by the blood of the era's greatest muckrakers, soon turned away from muckraking, and was eventually sold in 1911 to a corporation backed by J. P. Morgan, target of many of the muckrakers during the previous two decades. By 1915, most of the staff, after innumerable arguments with management, had resigned, and *American Magazine*, with a circulation approaching two million subscribers in the early 1920s, was now clearly a "family magazine," with virtually no investigative spirit.

Everybody's, which had seceded from the tyranny of the American News Co. in 1906 to form its own distribution network, and wasn't as harmed as some of the other muckraking magazines, continued muckraking until about 1913, but had become more of a general interest magazine, then after World War I became an all-fiction magazine; with a circulation of only 50,000, it was combined with *Romance Magazine* in 1929.

Pearson's, billing itself as "the magazine which prints the facts that others dare not print" now entered the world of muckraking, becoming, as Charles Edward Russell stated, "the last vehicle in which Big Business could be exposed." In *Bare Hands and Stone Walls*, Russell recalled:

Colonel Arthur Little [*Pearson's* owner] kindly took us in from the doorstep on which we [muckrakers] were shivering . . . By dint of Colonel Little's indomitable will it lasted three years. Then exactly the same tactics that had been applied to *Success* and to *Hampton's* were turned upon him and he too went down, though with flags flying. [p. 190]

As for *McClure's*, the magazine that became identified as one of the nation's best-edited magazines? It soon fell away from muckraking about 1911-1912, when S. S. McClure sold the magazine. Although McClure returned to the magazine in 1924, it was a different product than he had left it; two years later, McClure again sold, this time to the Hearst empire which changed its focus to "The Magazine of Romance," as its new subtitle proclaimed. In March 1929, it was dead.

Gustavus Myers, known as the "Historian of the Muckrakers" for his carefully-documented research and history of the movement, had quickly learned that although some of the newspapers and magazines were publishing his investigations, the book publishers were resolutely silent, afraid of controversy, concerned with profits. After numerous rejections, Myers had personally financed *The History of Tammany Hall* (1901), the definitive study of machine corruption, then sold the book through mail order ads. Then in 1910, Myers' *History of the Great American Fortunes*, which had been rejected by almost every American publisher for more than a decade, was finally published by the socialist Kerr Co. The book became a best-seller, and was widely accepted as the definitive study of the rise and power of the wealthy. But, many distributors, in collusion with, or fearful of, the political and business interests, wouldn't touch.

Eventually, the American News Co., the nation's largest distributor of magazines, refused to carry the muckraking journals, or pressured its news stands, by not accepting returns of unsold copies, into not ordering certain magazines. Without the monopolistic distributor, muckraking fell apart.

Advertisers and Big Business couldn't shake the power of the Hearst empire, but the *New York American* and *Journal* just didn't publish as many anti-trust articles as before, and their stories supporting the rights of the working class and the impoverished just diminished; even *Cosmopolitan* just stopped publishing muckraking stories about four years after it had begun. It is highly possible that Hearst's defeat for the governorship and presidency had soured him on the American people, for in his heart he truly believed he was campaigning not to promote himself but to help the people—and the people turned on him. By World War I, Hearst had begun turning away from some of the principles that had made him a champion of the people, and soon opposed the labor movement. After the war, Hearst—once denounced in the press as a socialist—attacked anyone he believed were socialists or communists, including Charles Edward Russell who had been one of His closest supporters, and who probably had learned the principles of socialism from him. Although Hearst was instrumental in securing necessary convention votes for Franklin D. Roosevelt, campaigned for his election in 1932, and supported proposed New Deal legislation, within two years he declared it to be a "Raw Deal," and viciously attacked anti-monopoly and pro-labor legislation, as well as the Works Progress Administration programs for the poor. By the mid-1930s, Hearst was one of the most powerful people in the United States, directing an empire that included more than 40,000 employees, twenty-six newspapers, thirteen magazines, eight radio stations, two major motion picture companies, and three international news syndicates; the newspapers accounted for about one-fourth of all circulation of Sunday newspapers. By World War II, the Hearst crusading spirit was long dead.

Joseph Pulitzer died in 1911, but Frank I. Cobb, whom Pulitzer had trained as his replacement, continued the tradition of excellence. In 1923, Cobb died. During the next half-century, the great New York newspapers died or were merged into a loss of identity. In 1924, The *Herald* and *Tribune* merged into the *Herald Tribune*, and became even greater than its parents; but, it too died. In 1931, Pulitzer's *World* was merged into Roy Howard's *Telegram*; later, the *World-Telegram* and *Sun* merged, to become part of the Scripps empire, without the spirit of E. W. Scripps. In 1960, Hearst closed the morning *American* and merged it into the *Evening Journal* to become the *Journal-American*. In 1966, the merged newspapers—the *Herald Tribune*, *World-Telegram and Sun*, and the *Journal-American*—merged into some monolithic monstrosity known as the *World Journal Tribune*, the newspaper formed from the ashes of Pulitzer, Hearst, Greeley, Bennett, Scripps, Wisner, Day, and Charles A. Dana, but without the soul of their founders. By mid-1967, the *WJT* too was dead.

A Scattering of Muckrakers

The muckrakers themselves scattered politically and geographically after World War I. Socialists Charles Edward Russell, Lincoln Steffens,

Upton Sinclair, and William Walling turned more militant, becoming involved in many social causes. Russell, while attacking the pro-establishment bias of the American media, worked to help the Irish republic, the labor movement, and the American urban Jews; Steffens reported the Mexican and Russian revolutions, and became active in providing food and clothing for the Russians trapped by famine after their Revolution; and Walling helped to establish the NAACP, while continuing his campaign to fight for the rights of all minorities. Each wrote books which became popular, with Steffens' autobiography becoming required reading in several hundred high schools and colleges during the 1940s and 1950s.

Sinclair himself wrote more than eighty books, with *Dragon's Teeth* (1942) winning the Pulitzer prize in fiction. Sinclair's other novels include *The Metropolis* (1908), a study of decadence resulting from wealth; *King Coal* (1917), based upon the conditions in the Colorado mines leading to a strike and the company-led Ludlow Massacre; *The Profits of Religion* (1918); *The Goose-Step* (1923) and *The Goslings* (1924), studies of the American education system; *Oil!* (1927), a plea for the establishment of socialism following the scandals of Harding administration; and *Boston* (1928), a fictionalized version of the trial and execution of Sacco and Vanzetti, whose primary crime appeared that they were anarchists.

Three of the four became involved in their own political campaigns to further the cause of social justice. Russell was the socialist candidate for U.S. senator from New York in 1914; Walling was the progressive Democratic candidate for Congress from New York City in 1924; Sinclair, after a brilliant campaign in the primaries, became the Democratic candidate for governor of California in 1934, only to lose when machine Democrats teamed with Republicans to vote a Republican into office. Josephus Daniels eventually became Secretary of the Navy under Woodrow Wilson, but continued his ownership of the *Raleigh News & Observer*, retiring in the early 1940s.

Some muckrakers became more conservative after World War I. Ida Tarbell, continuing her first pursuit of being a biographer, wrote relatively affable features about corporation presidents. Mark Sullivan became a columnist, first for the *Evening Post* then the *Herald Tribune*. The six-volume *Our Times* was one of the best literary histories of the first three decades of the twentieth century.

Ray Stannard Baker's eight-volume biography of Woodrow Wilson became the definitive work, the last two volumes earning him a Pulitzer Prize in 1940. Under the pseudonym David Grayson, he wrote several popular novels. George Kibbe Turner, like many of the outstanding journalists in the 1920s and 1930s, wrote screenplays. David Graham Phillips' powerful best-seller about poverty, *Susan Lenox*, was published in 1915, four years after he was murdered in New York City. Samuel Hopkins Adams, one of the nation's leading fighters for adequate health care, wrote biographies and novels, one of which was *The Clarion* (1914), a powerful indictment of the patent medicine industry; another of his novels was turned into the megabucks film, *It Happened One Night*. Will Irwin (1873-1948), who had spent a year as an editor at *McClure's*, and later wrote the definitive criticism of American journalism for *Collier's Weekly* in 1911, increased his reputation as one of the nation's greatest reporters; two of his plays became Broadway hits, most of his novels became best-sellers. William Hard became a Washington correspondent for *The Nation*, then an editor for *Reader's Digest*. Frank Norris died at thirty-two from a ruptured appendix. Thomas Lawson became a gardener. Edwin Markham, like other former muckrakers, worked to eliminate poverty, while also providing significant assistance to helping create a Jewish homeland. Rheta Childe Dorr became one of the nation's leading war correspondents; but much of her life as one of the nation's more militant feminists was filled with her campaigns to bring equality and better working conditions to women.

Because They Loved the World

Two of the most-respected muckrakers, defending the decades of investigative concern for what had happened to the American dream, tried to put their decade into perspective. Upton Sinclair, in *The Independent* of September 3, 1908, pointed out that the muckrakers wrote "not because they love corruption, but because they hate it with an intensity that forbids them to think about anything else while corruption sits enthroned." A socialist with a mission not only to reform but to improve upon the social conditions of the world, Sinclair clearly stated:

As a rule, the Muckrake Man began his career with no theories, as a simple observer of facts known to every person at all "on the inside" of business and politics. But he followed the facts, and the facts always led him to one conclusion; until finally he discovered to his consternation that he was enlisted in a revolt against capitalism.

He is the forerunner of a revolution; and, like every revolutionist, he takes his chances of victory and defeat. If it is defeat that comes;

if the iron heel wins out in the end—why, then, the Muckrake Man will remain for all time a scandal-monger and an assassin of character. If, on the other hand, he succeeds in his efforts to make the people believe what "everybody knows"—then he will be recognized in future as a benefactor of his race. ["The Muckrake Man," *The Independent*; September 3, 1908; p. 519]

And Ray Stannard Baker pointed out, "We really believed in human beings. We 'muckraked' not because we hated our world but because we loved it. We were not hopeless, we were not cynical, we were not bitter." [*American Chronicle*, p. 226]

In the December 1903 issue of *McClure's*, Baker had written:

One . . . man, no matter how obscure, quiet, simple, can get results amazing in their importance; one such man is worth about four thousand so-called resectable citizens who stay at home and talk about the shame of boss-rule . . . If this republic is to be saved it must be saved by *individual effort*. ["The Lone Fighter," p. 197]

Less than a decade later, not only were individuals not attacking the establishment, neither were the journalists. After 1912, there would be fewer journalists who would still be unafraid to challenge corruption and stupidity, to force America to look at, and try to solve its problems. There would still be some investigations; there would still occur some changes. But now, in a different age as people once again became restless, with an approaching war in Europe, the muckrakers were no longer relevant. They had done their job and had done it exceedingly well. But their time was up and no one could change that.

the Progressive

Founded in 1909
by Robert M. LaFollette Sr.
•
Morris H. Rubin
Editor, 1940-1973
•
EDITOR
Erwin Knoll
MANAGING EDITOR
Linda Rocawich
CONTRIBUTING EDITOR
John Buell
BOOK EDITOR
Mary Sheridan
CONTRIBUTING WRITERS
Nat Hentoff, Molly Ivins, June Jordan
ADMINISTRATIVE SECRETARY
Teri Terry
PROOFREADER
Diana Cook
EDITORIAL INTERN
April Rockstead
EDITORIAL ADVISORY BOARD
Ben H. Bagdikian, Kathryn F. Clarenbach,
Samuel H. Day Jr., Jean Bethke Elshtain,
Richard Falk, Francis J. Flaherty,
John Kenneth Galbraith, Herbert Hill,
John B. Judis, Barbara Koeppel,
Colman McCarthy, Betty Medsger,
Keenen Peck, Carol Polsgrove,
Daniel Schorr, Lawrence Walsh,
Roger Wilkins, Maurice Zeitlin
•
ART DIRECTOR
Patrick JB Flynn
ASSOCIATE ART DIRECTORS
Donna Magdalina
Lester Doré
•
PUBLISHER
Matthew Rothschild
CIRCULATION DIRECTOR
Joy E. Wallin
ASSISTANT CIRCULATION DIRECTOR
Scot Vee Gamble
ACCOUNTANT
Dale Munger
MEMBERSHIP COORDINATOR
Jeffrey B. Kosmacher
TELEMARKETING COORDINATOR
Cris Brennand
TELEMARKETER
Eileen Cyncor
BUSINESS SECRETARY
Maria Martinez
•
BOARD OF DIRECTORS
Erwin Knoll, Chairman
Mary Sheridan, Warren Randy,
Brady C. Williamson, Scot Vee Gamble,
Matthew Rothschild

THE PROGRESSIVE
is set in type at Impressions, Inc.,
Madison, Wisconsin.
The magazine is printed and bound
at Royle Publishing Co.,
Sun Prairie, Wisconsin.

MEMO *from the Editor*

On the Library Front

Michael Elmendorf, a sixteen-year-old sophomore at Shaker High School in Colonie, New York, knows what he likes and doesn't like. He likes Lieutenant Colonel Oliver North, and circulated a petition in his support last year among fellow students. He doesn't like *The Progressive*, and circulated a petition this spring to have it banned from his high school's library.

The Progressive is to be found in several hundred high-school libraries across the country. I wish it were in many more. I'm pleased to be able to tell you that after due consideration of young Elmendorf's petition (which was signed by 123 of his fellow students), it will continue to be found in the library at Shaker High.

Elmendorf's objection to *The Progressive* was related only in broad, ideological terms to his admiration for Colonel North. In fact, he was apparently more deeply offended by advertisements published in this magazine than by its editorial contents. According to news stories in *The Albany Times Union*, his complaints centered on classified ads headed PROOF JESUS FICTIONAL, WOMEN LOVING WOMEN, and "ANARCHIST COOKBOOK," as well as full-page ads placed by the Jewish Committee on the Middle East.

"If someone wants to read [*The Progressive*], fine," Elmendorf told a six-member committee appointed by school authorities to hear his formal complaint, "but don't spend my family's tax dollars on it." And he cited a peculiar statement he attributed to John Adams: "Our Constitution was made for moral people. It is wholly inadequate for any other."

Fortunately, *The Progressive* received a vigorous defense from Joyce Horsman, the school's director of library and audiovisual services, who presented a petition signed by 395 students committed to their own, and their fellow students', freedom to read. (Presumably, another 900 or so students at Shaker High didn't care much either way.)

"Libraries should provide information on all points of view," Horsman told the committee.

In its report to School Superintendent Charles Szuberla, the panel said *The Progressive* "would have to be of little value as a library source or be incendiary in nature to warrant a recommendation for its removal. There is no support for either conclusion." And it added: "Mr. Elmendorf's request for removal constitutes a call for unwarranted censorship of a rep-

utable publication that has been, with good reason, included in the media center's collection for more than ten years." The Superintendent agreed with the panel's recommendation.

We're not all that keen to be called "reputable"—"disreputable" would suit us just as well—but it's good to know that the right to read has friends in Colonie, New York.

Elsewhere on the library front, we've been presented with conclusive evidence that the Federal Government does, indeed, face a budget deficit of calamitous proportions. Alpha G. Rose, serials librarian at the U.S. Department of State, recently wrote to *The Progressive*'s Managing Editor, Linda Rocawich:

"We . . . would like to add your journal to the Department of State Library's collection. Due to budgetary constraints, however, we are unable to purchase new subscriptions at this time. Would you consider giving the Library a complimentary subscription?"

I had no idea things were *that* bad. I assume that before asking *The Progressive* for a free subscription, the officials in Foggy Bottom considered and, for their own good reasons, rejected such possibilities as trimming $50—the price of a library subscription—from the military-aid total for El Salvador, or from the entertainment budget of the Paris embassy, or from the funds allotted to harassing Cuba via TV Martí.

Unwilling to compound the budget deficit in any way, or to force President Bush and what is laughingly termed the Congressional leadership into a 10-a-year tax increase, we decided to take up Alpha Rose's offer of a State Department publication in exchange for a subscription to *The Progressive*. We'll be receiving *Background Notes on the Countries of the World*, and intend to read it regularly. Watch for appropriate excerpts on the No Comment page.

Obviously, there's no need for generous readers to endow the State Department with a gift subscription to *The Progressive*. But if you'd like to make provision for your favorite high-school (or college, or public) library, do let us hear from you.

CHAPTER 9

The Modern Muckrakers

The fire that burned within the nation's greatest muckrakers, that was re-ignited during the radical 1960s in a minority of journalists willing to probe America's social problems even when they had to live in poverty to dig out the truth, was all but extinguished during the "me first decade" of the 1980s. Nevertheless, although it breathes hard, muckraking still lives.

Just as it didn't begin with the muckraking magazines of the first decade of the twentieth century, neither did it end with their assassination. During the decades following World War I, a few newspapers, magazines, and journalists continued to investigate social problems that could have torn apart the American democratic structure—and were often vilified by the people and their colleagues that by writing the truth they themselves were tearing apart the structure that was the "American dream."

In a case of history repeating itself, the Warren G. Harding administration found itself on the verge of collapse after Paul Y. Anderson, working with the full assistance of O.K. Brovard, editor of the Pulitzer-owned *St. Louis Post-Dispatch*, survived numerous personal and professional attacks in order to report the Teapot Dome Scandal that resulted from a rape of American oil resources in order that a few persons, including the secretary of the interior, opponents of environmental issues, and senior White House officials, would benefit financially. Harding had apparently learned many of the details several months after oil leases were issued to private companies, but chose not to make an issue of it; his death in 1923, during the third year of his presidency, stopped any official inquiry into Harding's complicity. In 1929, Anderson won the Pulitzer Prize for reporting.

Among the more aggressive newspapers was the *Jewish Daily Forward*, edited by socialist Abraham Cahan from 1903 to 1951. The

133

newspaper dominated New York's Lower East Side, and became the voice for world Jewry during the Nazi era; Cahan—whose first thrust into journalism had been as a reporter for city editor Lincoln Steffens on the *New York Commercial*—became one of America's leading opponents of the exploitation of labor and immigrants. Emerging during the 1930s, as a part of America flirted with the concepts of socialism and Communism, were several left-of-center publications, including the *Daily Worker* and Dwight MacDonald's *Politics*; most of the publications fought for social justice, the rights of the worker, and a redistribution of wealth.

'To Help People Understand'

As has been the case for over two centuries, America's muckrakers are seldom praised, usually vilified, and are only a small part of journalism.

Drew Pearson (1897-1969) came to prominence at a time when press releases dominated the media's coverage of the federal agencies. *The Washington Merry-Go-Round* (1932), written by Pearson, a reporter for the *Baltimore Sun*, and Robert S. Allen (?-1981), of *The Christian Science Monitor*, but published anonymously, exploded onto the national scene with gossipy exposes of how the federal government conducted its business. With the success of the book, Pearson and Allen left their staff positions to write a daily syndicated column, eventually published by more than six hundred newspapers, with Pearson's commentary carried by more than two hundred radio stations. Pearson continued the column alone after 1942 when Allen resumed his military obligations, and became a highly-decorated officer in World War II. After the war, Allen began "Inside Washington," a syndicated column that continued until his death in 1981. Pearson, continuing "The Washington Merry-Go-Round," helped organize a massive food drive to help the people of Europe, while also fighting the resurgence of Ku Klux Klan activity throughout the United States.

Using a network of tipsters, while fiercely protecting their identities, Pearson was feared, hated—and respected—as he investigated scandals at all levels of government, digging out innumerable stories of influence peddling, bribery, and incompetence in the government. Chalmers Roberts, in the *Washington Post*, summarized Drew Pearson as . . .

. . . a muckraker with a Quaker conscience. In print, he sounded fierce; in life, he was gentle, even courtly. For thirty-eight years he did more than any man to keep the national capital honest. [September 1, 1969]

In 1947, Jack Anderson (1922-) became one of Pearson's top investigative researchers; in 1958, Pearson added Anderson to the column's byline; upon Pearson's death nine years later, Anderson continued the column's mandate to uncover governmental scandal at all levels, and is currently considered to be the nation's leading muckraking reporter, his column appearing in nine hundred newspapers with combined circulation of about forty million.

During the past three decades, Anderson was assisted by several top investigative reporters including Les Whitten, Brit Hume, and Dale Van Atta. The Anderson team has uncovered myriad instances of governmental deceit, corruption, cover-up, conflict of interest, and vendettas against those who try to expose bureaucratic waste and inefficiency. Anderson's Pulitzer Prize in 1972 was for uncovering evidence that proved the Nixon administration was providing secret assistance to Pakistan in its war against India. Other "scoops" included several Watergate revelations and proof that the U.S. Department of Justice ended its antitrust action against the International telephone and Telegraph Co. (ITT) not long after ITT had donated $400,000 to the national Republican party.

Like all muckrakers, the problems Anderson had were more than just with trying to uncover the truth. In *Inside Story* (1974), Brit Hume pointed out that Anderson, "an investigative reporter long before it was fashionable," like most muckrakers "had endured years of litigation, suppression, and, among many of his colleagues, scorn, to keep at it while others scurried to cover safe topics such as foreign affairs and election campaigns." [p. 283]. Among Anderson's books are *Washington Exposé* (1966), *Case Against Congress* (1968), and *Confessions of a Muckraker* (1979).

Unlike Pearson and Anderson, Isidore Feinstein (1907-1989) better known as I.F. Stone, a radical and cantankerous journalist, didn't have millions of readers for his reporting. In fact, the iconoclastic *I. F. Stone's Weekly*, even at its peak, had no more than 75,000 circulation. But by the end of the *Weekly's* life in 1971, almost all of the Senate and House, and their staffs, along with a sizable chunk of four Presidential administrations from Eisenhower to Nixon had read the newsletter which consistently attacked governmental excesses and corruption.

Like the muckrakers at the beginning of the century, Stone was vilified equally for his undeterred pursuit of truth and for his membership in radical left organizations. From the late 1920s to the early 1950s, he was a staff writer for the *Camden* (N. J.) *Courier, Philadelphia Inquirer, PM,* and the *New York Compass*, forming his weekly newsletter of social and political comment upon the death of the *Compass*.

His penetrating analysis of the Korean War policies, *The Hidden History of the Korean War*, made him even more unpopular with the establishment during the nation's swing to the extreme right during the period after World War II. In the introduction, Stone had sent a warning shot for what would become the way he dealt with American society, both during war and peace:

It is a case study in the cold war. It is also a study in war propaganda, in how to read newspapers and official documents in wartime. Emphasis, omissions, and distortions rather than straight lies are the tools of the war propagandist.

During the early and mid-1960s, he was virtually a social outcast for his fact-based articles that showed the nation why it had no business being involved with the Vietnam War. The federal government variously tried to ignore and destroy him; even the people he once thought as friends backed away. Eventually, the United States recognized that its "good intentions" in Vietnam were tearing apart the American people, just as Stone had said. By the end of the *Weekly's* life in 1971, the Left had returned to praise the gadfly journalist as one of their own, after deserting him when he wrote against human rights violations in the Soviet Union. Even the nation's "power brokers" had recognized that Stone, in his own muckraking way, once you stripped the polemic from his articles, was writing truth.

In an interview two years before his death, Stone had summarized his beliefs as a muckraker:

Larceny is inseparable from government, has to be kept under control, and ought to be exposed. But that's very unimportant. The main job of the press is to help people understand what is happening— the issues, the struggles of the time, how to deal with them, how to prevent human conflict, how to run a good society with peaceful change—so they can make wise choices among the different points of view. [Quoted by Larry Van Dyne, "The Adventures of I. F. Stone," *Chronicle of Higher Education*; February 5, 1979; p. 6]

Dubbed "Queen of the Muckrakers" by *Time*, Jessica Mitford (1917-1990) was a careful and meticulous journalist who, like the earlier muckrakers, looked at the American social structure and tried to improve it. Among her targets were prisons, television executives, a "fat farm" that preyed upon the wealthy, and a nationally-popular correspondence course for "aspiring writers" which did little more than take their money. However, her greatest fame had come early in her career when she wrote *The American Way of Death* (1963), a probing look at the crass commercialism, over-priced funerals, and high-pressure sales tactics of the funeral industry that might have shamed even the worst of the used car dealers.

The article which led to the book began in the late 1950s, from a suggestion of her activist-lawyer husband who, says Mitford "had been doing a good bit of legal work for unions . . . and he was just appalled at the way undertakers took nearly all the survivors' death benefits." That first article, "St. Peter Don't You Call Me," a seemingly innocuous overview of funeral costs, was turned down by several magazine publishers before it was finally published in the November 1958 issue of *Frontier*, a 2,000 circulation liberal monthly, published in Los Angeles. An interview in the *Saturday Evening Post* led to a national concern about the practices of the funeral industry, and that led to the book which led America to realize that it did have a right to determine what it wanted with its own funerals, and not be subjected to the tactics of the undertakers. Mitford was able to report in 1964:

> The mortuary press report a decrease of 30 percent in the average funeral sale. . . . Casket manufacturers in New York State say there has been a "run on cheaper boxes." In four American states, official investigations of the entire funeral industry have been launched by the legislatures. Clergymen tell me their congregations are beginning to insist on funerary moderation. [*Poison Penmanship*, p. 91]

However, as with other muckrakers, Mitford had to endure vilification of her personal life by shotgun charges thrown out by her subjects. For an interview with Pat Jensen in the *Writer's Digest*, Mitford had said, "I report things as I see them, and the people I'm reporting about usually scream, 'It's not objective!'" In an article in *Nova*, published a year after the book shook apart the nation, Mitford noted:

> Of course [the funeral industry attacked] me in absolute fury. . . In [their] journals I read month after month about the "Mitford Bomb," "the Mitford war dance," "the Mitford missile," "Mitford blast," and "Mitford fury." They have condemned the movement for cheaper funerals as a Red Plot, and have found an ally in Congress: Congressman James B. Utt of California who read a two-page statement about my subversive background into the *Congressional Record*. Of undertakers he said, "I would rather be buried by one of our fine, upstanding American morticians than to set foot on the soil

of a Communist country," and of my book he added cryptically, "Better dead than read." [*Poison Penmanship*, p. 91]

The year *The American Way of Death* appeared, CBS-TV aired a documentary about the funeral industry, and several magazines published articles that elaborated upon Mitford's charges. In 1965, Hollywood produced *The Loved One*, an outrageous farce billed as "something to offend everyone," adapted by Terry Southern and Christopher Isherwood from the writings of Mitford and Evelyn Waugh.

Mitford was born into British nobility; as journalist Lena Jager noted in the June 13, 1964, issue of the *Manchester Guardian*, "Her life has been a protest—a protest against her own privileged, arid, aristocratic background; against snobbery and political selfishness and reactionary regimes wherever they existed." A market researcher, bartender, sales person, and typist, Mitford didn't begin writing until she was about thirty-eight. By then, her political enemies were able to dredge up her past as a Communist sympathizer during the Spanish Civil War, and her membership in the American Communist party—she didn't resign from the Party until 1958—as reasons why she was blatantly not only unAmerican, but unChristian as well. Nevertheless, the truth of her investigations dissolved much of the opposition, and by the 1980s, she was respected as a crusading journalist who, with wit and a scalpel not meat cleaver approach to muckraking, was able to help America understand its problems.

It began simply enough:

There was once a town in the heart of America where all life seemed to live in harmony with its surroundings. The town lay in the midst of a checkerboard of prosperous farms, with fields of grain and hillsides of orchards where, in spring, white clouds of bloom drifted above the green fields. In autumn, oak and maple and birch set up a blaze of color that flamed and flickered across a backdrop of pines. The foxes barked in the hills and deer silently crossed the fields, half hidden in the mists of the fall morning.

By the time it ended, Rachel Carson (1907-1964) had scared America into rethinking its belief that pesticides were universally good, and *Silent Spring* became one of the most powerful books ever written in defense of the environment. With the knowledge of a biologist and the skill of a literary journalist, Carson carefully wove her story of how DDT and other pesticides not only killed off insects from leaves and crops, but was being absorbed into the nation's food chain, polluting its drinking supply, its air, and its food, causing disease and death.

Carson had planned to be a writer, but a course in biology at the Pennsylvania College for Women (now known as Chatham College) had led her to a zoology degree, graduate work at Johns Hopkins, and a two-decade career as a journalist-scientist, much of it as a staff writer and biologist, then as editor-in-chief of publications for the Fish and Wildlife Service. Several articles about the environment preceded "Undersea," published in 1937 in the *Atlantic Monthly*. That article led to *Under the Sea-Wind* (1941), a critically praised non-seller, published the month of the Pearl Harbor attack. One decade later, *The Sea Around Us* (1951) established Carson as one of the nation's finest writers, as Carson make oceanographic geology a dinner-table topic; for eighty-six weeks, thirty-nine of them in the top position, the book dominated the *New York Times* best-sellers list. *The Edge of the Sea* (1956) was the last of the her major writing about the oceans. It would be her attack upon the poisoning of America that would now give America a chance to save the planet she so lovingly had written about.

During the previous decade, several scientists had questioned the use of DDT as a pesticide. According to journalist Frank Graham Jr.:

During the war, when [Carson] was still working for the Fish and Wildlife Service, she had been aware of the early studies made on DDT to determine its ultimate effects on the environment. Though some biologists had expressed their apprehensions, there was nothing definite to sustain them. What were thought to be DDT's special assets effectively served to mask its defects. Because it does not break down in the environment, but persists in its toxic state or years, and perhaps decades, it seemed marvelously convenient for the farmer or forester who could get by with only an occasional application of it to his crops. At the same time, it is not acutely toxic to animals as many other pesticides are, and therefore seemed to be relatively harmless in every way to "non-pest" species.

Since DDT is cheap and easy to make, it became the most widely used of the new chemical insecticides. Thus it also became the most intensively studied of them all. DDT was hailed, on the basis of this short-term test, as a "savior of mankind," and the rest of the new chemicals [of the chlorinated hydrocarbon group] rode on its coattails with clean bills of health. [*Since Silent Spring*, pp. 14-15]

In 1957, biologists detected that certain birds which fed on the fish in Clear Lake, California, were dying; their investigation showed that a pesticide in the water was being absorbed by microscopic plants and animals which were part of the grebes' food chain. In 1958, Dr. Roy

Barker, scientist in the Illinois Natural History Survey, pointed out that residue DDT originally sprayed onto leaves to kill insects was being digested by earthworms which were eaten by birds. However, his findings, like others who had raised cautions against the pesticides, were largely ignored or dismissed as "incomplete."

After several years research, thousands of hours of interviews with scientists throughout the world, and with the seemingly unlimited and unselfish assistance of Clarence Cottam, her former boss at the Fish and Wildlife Service, Carson was ready to show America what it had done to itself. She cared about the destruction of the environment, but she knew that only if she showed what pesticides were doing to mankind's health could she evoke the greatest concern.

Silent Spring, abridged and serialized in the *New Yorker* prior to book-length publication, was immediately controversial. As expected, the chemical industries viciously attacked her, launching a seemingly unlimited barrage of news releases, public statements, and ads to convince the public that pesticides were safe; even the American Medical Association was led into the trap, and suggested that its members check not with the environmentalists but with the chemical industry to learn the truth about the pesticides and possible medical effects. However, the greatest attacks came, surprisingly, from agencies of the federal government and the American scientific community which had arrogantly claimed not only were pesticides safe—Carson had called them "biocides"—but that she was not a "true" scientist and didn't understand the "whole picture." The U.S. Department of Agriculture, which had done an extraordinary job of fact manipulation, and which had a history of trying to force its employees into accepting widespread pesticide programs, condemned her and her book. (A "fact-finding" report two years earlier had "whitewashed" the problem.) In "Silence, Miss Carson," published in *Chemical and Engineering News*, Dr. William J. Darby, a nutritionist at the Vanderbilt University School of Medicine, fired the most potent shot:

> Her ignorance or bias on some of the considerations throws doubt on her competence to judge policy.... [Her] book adds no new factual information not already known to such serious scientists as those concerned with their developments nor does it include information essential for the reader to interpret the knowledge. It does confuse the information and so mix it with her opinions that the uninitiated reader is unable to sort fact from fancy . . . In view of her scientific qualifications in contrast to those of our distinguished scientific leaders and statesmen, this book should be ignored . . . [Nevertheless,

scientists] should read this book to understand the ignorance of those writing on the subject and the educational task which lies ahead.

In *Conservation News*, the New Jersey director of the Department of Agriculture, claimed: "In any large scale pest control program we are immediately confronted with the objection of a vociferous, misinformed group of nature-balancing, organic-gardening, bird-loving, unreasonable citizenry that has not been convinced of the important place of agricultural chemicals in our economy." Others attacked her, without having read the book, claiming she was for banning *all* insecticides, although she had made no such statement in print or to the press. Her concern was that what insecticides were used must not pollute the environment or enter the food chain and harm other life.

In the U. S. Senate, Abraham Ribicoff spoke out against pesticide usage; at the Department of Interior, secretary Stewart Udall expressed his strong concerns about the problems associated with DDT and forbid its use in Department of Interior programs if there was any doubt about its safety; Udall's actions opened a public fight that put Interior in direct opposition to Agriculture. In 1963, after intensive investiogation, enderin, a chlorinated hydrocarbon, was found by the U.S. Public Health Service, to have been the cause of the death of five million fish in the Mississippi River; although the fish had died in Louisiana, the poison had originally been used in Tennessee and spread south with the current.

Eventually, it would be a federal report, ordered by President Kennedy, that would lead to the banning of DDT and similar pesticides. Against significant opposition from the Department of Agriculture and several other governmental agencies, the President's Science Advisory Committee not only condemned the chemical companies and governmental complicity, but concluded that Carson had been accurate in her statements that the pesticides were not only destroying the ecological balance of the nation but as it entered the food chain were probably causes of death. The President's report led to further public outrage over what the government and chemical industries were doing. Even the President's report, even public outrage, even Carson's death in 1964 from cancer, could do nothing to stop the controversy and the attacks against her and her research. In *Silent Spring*, Carson had argued:

We have subjected enormous numbers of people to contact with these poisons, without their consent and without their knowledge. If the Bill of Rights contains no guarantees that a citizen shall be secure against lethal poisons distributed either by private individuals or public officials, it is surely only because our forefathers, despite their considerable wisdom and foresight, could conceive of no such problem.

In 1964, Dr. Robert I. Rudd, professor of biology at the University of California, finally saw his book, *Pesticides and the Living Landscape*, published. The manuscript, completed shortly before Carson finished *Silent Spring*, was turned down by commercial publishers as too controversial; at the University of Wisconsin Press, which eventually published it two years after Houghton Mifflin published *Silent Spring*, it underwent internal attack while it languished in the academic publishing world as more than a dozen reviewers, many of them pro-pesticide, ruled on its "acceptability." Nevertheless, Rudd's book, along with Carson's, became the two weapons that would bring change in America's almost unquestioned acceptance of pesticides, and would force America to take a more intelligent stand regarding its own environment. By massive protests, the people would make sure their own rights would no longer be violated. Individually, in small circles, in large public interest groups, the people would force their state and federal governments to see massive fish kills, to realize that they would no longer tolerate being poisoned. In 1969, the federal government announced DDT and similar pesticides would be phased out during the next two years.

On the Princeton University campus in the early 1950s, almost a decade before *Silent Spring* would change America's attitudes about their environment, a young government and economics student tried to stop that Ivy League university from spraying DDT on campus trees. He failed. At the Harvard Law School, he tried to turn the *Harvard Law Review* into a magazine of social reform. He failed to do that, too, and most of his classmates entered the worlds of corporate law or privileged private-interest law. "The most important thing a lawyer can do," Ralph Nader (1934-) later said, "is become an advocate of powerless citizens. I am in favor of lawyers without clients. Lawyers should represent systems of justice." During the next three decades, Nader would lead a national campaign that would not only investigate corporations and government, but lead to sweeping reforms in consumer protection.

However, had it not been for the arrogant stupidity of the nation's largest corporation, Nader's campaigns might have been little more than bubbles in the air. Just as many of the muckrakers' greatest fame had come from one investigation, so had Nader's—at the same time he was investigating automobile safety, General Motors was investigating him. By the time the investigations had ended, Ralph Nader had made *Unsafe at Any*

Speed (1965) an indictment of the automobile industry and a call for action that led the U. S. Senate to speed up passage of what became the Traffic and Motor Safety Act of 1966—and the president of General Motors to publically apologize on national television for having hired private detectives not only to follow Nader and dig up derogatory references to the young muckraker, but of having orchestrated a campaign of harassment. *Unsafe at Any Speed*, an outgrowth of "American Cars: Designed for Death," published in the *Harvard Law Record*, was an insightful probe that claimed that America's automobile corporations were responsible for the death of thousands of people not because of driver error or road conditions, but because of defects in the design and manufacturing process. Charging that the corporations were more concerned with style over safety, with profits over people, Nader attacked GM's Chevrolet Corvair, calling it "one of the nastiest-handling cars ever built."

Like Mitford's *American Way of Death* and Carson's *Silent Spring*, Nader's *Unsafe at Any Speed* attacked corporate America by concentrating upon an issue that directly affected each American. Nader later said, "People might not be concerned about the structure of the modern corporation, but they are concerned about local artifacts—consumer products." [Quoted in "Stages of Nader," by David Ignatius, *New York Times*, January 18, 1976].

A muckraking folk-hero of the '60s, Nader used his newly-acquired fame and grass-roots support to push the federal government into passing legislation that established revised safety standards in underground coal mining and in inspection standards for meat slaughterhouses—problems which muckrakers had written about at the turn of the century, and which the people had been led to believe were no longer problems after the passage of federal laws almost a half-century earlier.

In 1969, Nader founded the Center for Study of Responsive Law. With a staff largely composed of college students and recent graduates, and funded by grass-roots support and their willingness to work long and hard for little financial benefits, "Nader's Raiders," as they became known to the media, dug into the political and social fabric of America to expose greed and a blatant disregard of the people. The guiding principle for the Raiders was one of the knight in shining armor (his Raiders) out to rescue the fair maiden (the people) from the abuses of the evil witch (the corporate and governmental powers). "What we now have is a democracy without citizens," said Nader. No one is on the public's side. And the bureaucrats in the administration don't think the government belongs to the people."

In 1970, GM agreed to pay Nader $425,000 for its campaign of harassment. Nader promptly put most of the $284,000 he had after paying his attorneys into creating the Corporate Accountability Research Group and the Public Interest Research Group; a year later, he created Public Citizen, Inc., a Washington-based lobbyist group for the people.

Frustrated when Congress deleted key clauses and weakened others in his proposal for a Consumer Protection Agency, Nader created Congress Watch, and threw a large organization of volunteer and low-paid staff into a massive two-year project to investigate the Congress and regulatory agencies. The result was publication of six books and forty "Nader Reports," most of them charging that the government was more a tool of special interests than of the people—charges not any different from what the earlier muckrakers had stated. However, unlike many of the earlier muckrakers who illuminated the problems and hoped that the nation would rise up in indignation, Nader and his Raiders—including Ted Jacobs who directed day-to-day operations of the Raiders, and Joan Claybrook who headed up his lobbying group—forcefully became a part of the legislative process. Using their knowledge of public relations and the law, they forced the federal government into recognizing a greater social responsibility to the people as it established, after extensive Nader lobbying, the Environmental Protection Agency in 1970, the Freedom of Information Act of 1974, and the Occupational Safety and Health Administration of 1976.

However, by the mid-1970s, as America successfully shook off its activism of the 1960s, Nader had begun to lose much of the glamor the media had accorded him a decade earlier. The attacks, by corporate and political America, as well as the establishment press, became more direct, more vicious. In 1971, Lewis Powell, soon to become a Justice of the Supreme Court, attacked Nader as "the single most effective antagonist of American business," and urged "no hesitation" to attack those who attack the American business community. Others began to pick on his hard-headed unwillingness to compromise, his "Lone Ranger" mentality, and even his self-imposed relatively impoverished lifestyle. During the 1980s, Nader's organizations investigated the insurance and nuclear power industries, and continued their mission in consumer interest, working with utilities to help the poor afford heat and water.

In a *New York Times* profile of January 18, 1976, David Ignatius tried to sum up Nader's life, contributions to the people, and where he fit into American social history:

With his constant stream of exposes, Nader helped to revive the muckraking tradition . . . that if you can bring nasty facts to the attention of the public, reform will follow automatically. This belief in the efficacy of The Facts became a watchword for Naderism. The ideology of the movement could best be summed up in Justice Louis Brandeis's famous dictum, "Sunlight is the best disinfectant."

However, like the muckrakers almost a century earlier, Nader has been frustrated by public apathy to reform, citing low voter turnouts and the public's acceptance of pollution, safety hazards, and governmental inefficiency. "How much effort [are] citizens [willing to spend to exercise] their civic responsibility," Nader has asked, concluding, "We can't possibly have a democracy with 200 million Americans and only a handful of citizens."

Drew Pearson, Jack Anderson, I. F. Stone, Jessica Mitford, Rachel Carson, and Ralph Nader are only some of the people who are the "modern muckrakers." Among the current establishment newspaper journalists who have developed solid reputations for investigative reporting are Dean Baquet, formerly of the *Chicago Tribune*, now with the *New York Times*; Donald Bartlett and James Steele, *Philadelphia Inquirer*; Carl Bernstein, freelance writer; Gilbert Gaul, *Philadelphia Inquirer*; Bob Greene, *Newsday*; Mary Hargrove, *Tulsa Tribune*; Rich Maurer, *Anchorage Daily News;* David Morrissey, *Arizona Republic*; Eric Nalder, *Seattle Times*; Jim Savage, *Miami Herald*; Charlie Shepard, *Charlotte Observer*; Olive Talley, *Dallas Morning News*; John Ullman, formerly of the *Minneapolis Star and Tribune*, now a freelance consultant; and Bob Woodward, the *Washington Post*. Recognized for excellence in investigative journalism are *Newsday*, the *Philadelphia Inquirer,* and the *Boston Globe*.

However, investigative journalism and muckraking journalism often have different purposes. The investigative journalist wants to bring out abuses of the public trust, to write of conflict of interest, of closed meetings, of nefarious schemes to bilk the people of their riches. The muckraker wants to expose not the superficialities of corruption, but the social fabric of society. Like Samuel Adams and Thomas Paine, Charles Edward Russell and Upton Sinclair, I. F. Stone, Jessica Mitford, and Ralph Nader, they want to change society, believing that exposing certain problems is useful but that until society itself is improved the problems will always exist. A nation may reluctantly tolerate an investigative reporter; it has little tolerance for a muckraker.

Just as the radical press of the 1760s helped prepare the Colonies for the war of liberation, the alternative and radical press of the 1960s had prepared America for a war against the indifference to social problems that seemed to have been a mist over the country during the Eisenhower era. Among the better alternative newspaper-magazines which called for civil rights enforcement, civic reform, improvement of living conditions in the inner cities, protection of the environment, and the end of America's presence in Vietnam were the *Berkeley Barb, San Francisco Bay Guardian, Kaleidoscope* (Madison, Wisc.), *Kudzu* (Jackson, Miss.), *Los Angeles Free Press, The Realist, San Diego Free Press and Street Journal, Village Voice*, and the radical feminist publication, *Off Our Backs*. Providing news and features to many of the alternative press were the Liberation News Service and the Underground Press Syndicate. At various times during the 1960s and 1970s, almost all the alternative publications were targets of harassment by governmental authorities, including the FBI, and of private groups determined that there should only be one "correct" voice allowed in a society that claims to support the Constitution. Among the current leaders of the alternative press are *In These Times, The Progressive, Mother Jones, Ramparts, Rolling Stone, Texas Observer*, and the *San Francisco Bay Guardian*, all of which have strong muckraking emphases, and usually win their share of awards in national contests.

The *Progressive*, founded in 1909 by Robert La Follette, has been a consistent voice of reform, publishing articles about health, environment, the nuclear industry, and world politics. However, it was an article that almost wasn't published that brought the *Progressive* to world attention—and a spot in American legal history.

The *Progressive* had planned to publish Howard Moreland's article, "The H-Bomb Secret" in the April 1979 issue. The purpose was not to give away military secrets, but to expose America's vulnerability—all the facts in the article on how to make a hydrogen bomb were in public documents. Upon arguments of the Departments of Defense, Justice, and State, the federal district court ruled that in this case prior restraint was justified, that the security of the State was far greater than the protection of First Amendment rights.

While the nation's establishment media claimed that the *Progressive* had chosen the wrong issue and the wrong time to test the First Amendment, and had refused to assist in a classic First Amendment fight, the *Progressive* incurred financial loss in order to carry forth the principles of a free press. When first the *Penninsula Times-Tribune* of Palo Alto, California, published Charles Hansen's similar artticle about how to make an H-Bomb, then the *Milwaukee Sentinnel* published Jerry Fass's article along the same lines, the Department of Justice chose to drop the case. The article, with editor commentary, finally appeared in the November issue.

Going Beyond Anti-Littering Campaigns

The nature of both radio and television is such that they are entertainment not news media. Former CBS-TV anchor Walter Cronkite noted that TV news, for the most part, is a "headline service," and that the entire thirty-minute evening newscast of any network would not even fill the front page of a daily newspaper. The average story is measured not in column inches but in seconds. Because of what television and radio are, muckraking is largely ignored in all but the largest markets, and even then, may only be fresh updates to what metropolitan newspapers have been reporting. In the face of possible revenue loss, a few radio and television stations have gone beyond editorializing about why cancer should be wiped out, and why it's un-American to litter.

During the "Golden Age" of radio, during the 1930s, radio news became an important commodity, and the names—and voices—of H. V. Kaltenborn, Floyd Gibbons, Lowell Thomas, Boake Carter, and Edwin C. Hill became as well known as the most popular movie stars. However, the 1930s and 1940s were not times for major investigative reporting.

In 1951, when CBS converted Edward R. Murrow's radio show, "Hear it Now" into television's "See it Now," investigative reporting received a new emphasis. Murrow and Fred Friendly, Murrow's producer, believed in solid factual reporting, and were among the few who were unafraid to clearly state their position. For several years, Murrow had spoken out against Sen. Joseph McCarthy's unsubstantiated attacks upon Americans whom he and others accused of being Communists or Communist sympathizers. Once again, America had been gripped by the fear of "Commies" and "Pinkos," the result being the establishment of extensive blacklists in the entertainment industry, the establishment of loyalty oaths and the firing of teachers, government workers, journalists, actors, and innumerable others in the creative arts, and wholesale volumes of arrests and indictments. Many journalists had been speaking out against McCarthy for years, although most avoided the issue and accepted a self-imposed censorship on issues contrary to the Senator's wishes, which they had believed reflected the mood of the country. But now the mood of the country, after a half-decade of accusations, was changing, if ever so slightly. For several months, Murrow and Friendly, using film clips of Sen. McCarthy, had been working on an investigative documentary that would show McCarthy's errors, letting the Senator's words be his own noose. The Aluminum Company of America (Alcoa), sponsor of "See It Now" had been threatened with an economic boycott if the show aired; CBS, Friendly, and Murrow each were threatened with a wide range of reprisals, including federal subpoenas. But, on March 9, 1954, with Alcoa's sponsorship, CBS aired the special documentary; for at least a small piece of time, television showed it had guts.

Television had followed newspapers and magazines in attacking the evils of McCarthyism; however, general circulation newspapers and magazines followed specialized publications and fiction. The outstanding muckraking attack upon the climate of fear came from playwright Arthur Miller, author of *All My Sons* (1947) and *Death of a Salesman* (1949, Pulitzer Prize in Drama), who now risked his career to write *The Crucible* (1953), set in Salem during the witch trials of the seventeenth century, but in reality a loosely-disguised allegory detailing fear and self-interest in the McCarthy era. Miller was attacked by reporters and editorial writers, by politicians, teachers, and businessmen, but the play became a classic in American theatre, although it never received the Pulitzer Prize.

In 1960, the CBS team of Edward R. Murrow and David Lowe produced "The Harvest of Shame," a powerful one-hour documentary detailing the exploitation of migrant workers by corporate growers. However, when NBC aired Martin Carr's "Migrant," in 1970, it ran into a corporate buzz saw. Citing the Coca Cola Co. as a primary exploiter of labor in the Florida citrus fields, the documentary showed that nothing had changed to better the working conditions since the CBS report a decade earlier. Coca Cola and the Florida Fruit and Vegetable Association unleashed a brutal campaign of harassment about a month before the documentary aired on July 16, writing letters not only to the network and its affiliates, but also to key political leaders, the media, and even the Federal Communications Commission. In a letter to the FCC, made available to network affiliates, the Association blatantly threatened their license:

[A biased presentation] could result in grave injustice to the people and the state of Florida, particularly the workers and their employers. . . .

If the film is shown by a licensee [NBC affiliate] of the [FCC] and is in fact a slanted news presentation, the Florida Fruit and Vegetable Association will request the Commission to specify and issue as to whether such licensee is adequately discharging its responsibility as to warrant its continuing to be a licensee.

Without advertising, NBC did air the documentary. One week later, a Senate subcommittee opened hearings on the problems in the migrant labor force. The president of Coca Cola acknowledged that NBC was accurate in its presentation, condemned the treatment of migrant workers, and began a seven-year plan of action that gave the workers full company benefits, better pay and housing. However, in January 1971, the Coca Cola Corp. moved a $2 million ad budget from NBC to the other two networks.

Also during 1970, during the Vietnam War, the CBS investigative documentary, "The Selling of the Pentagon," detailed the megabucks public relations program of the Department of Defense. The Pentagon, in characteristically non-PR fashion, labelled the documentary a "pack of lies," demanded equal time—which it got, only to watch CBS counter the Department's rebuttal. A Congressional committee ordered CBS to surrender all film it did not use, hoping to prove that CBS, by selective reporting and editing, as charged by the Department of Defense, was not only unfair but biased in its presentations. CBS was cited for contempt, but the full House chose not to pursue the matter. The FCC eventually determined that although there was some distortion and selective editing, CBS essentially met all criteria for truthfulness in broadcasting.

Other major network documentaries include "Biography of a Bookie Joint," 1961, CBS; "Hunger in America," 1967, CBS; "Whose Right to Bear Arms?", 1967, NBC; and "Who Killed Lake Erie?" 1969, NBC; "Health in America," 1970, CBS; and "Mission Possible," a three-part series on the environment, broadcast in 1970 by ABC.

In Fall 1968, CBS-TV premiered "60 Minutes," a news magazine program, produced by veteran journalist Don Hewitt, and featuring journalists Mike Wallace and Harry Reasoner. When Reasoner moved to ABC-TV, Morley Safer, in 1970, and Dan Rather in 1976 were added to the team; Reasoner returned in 1979; when Rather became CBS Evening News anchor in 1981, Ed Bradley became the fourth reporter. In 1984, Diane Sawyer became the fifth reporter, replaced in 1989 by Steve Kroft and Meredith Vieria.

In an era during which form almost drowned content, and "TV News" came to mean the "Ken and Barbie look," with an abundance of toothy smiles and frosted or blow-dried hair rather than journalistic competence, "60 Minutes" started off poorly in the ratings. In its first three seasons, "60 Minutes" dropped in ratings (from 13.0 to 9.7), in share of the market (from 25 percent to 17 percent), and in comparison to other prime-time shows (from 83rd to 101st of 103). However, CBS News president Bill Leonard fought to keep "60 Minutes" on the air. With a tradition of journalistic respectability forged by Douglas Edwards, Edward R. Murrow, and Walter Cronkite, CBS shuffled the program, hoping to find a place for it. Slowly, as Americans began to appreciate the formate of three major features and a "blister"—a short human interest feature or commentary at the end of the show—the ratings rose. When CBS shuffled "60 Minutes" into a 7 p.m., Sunday, time slot in 1975, following professional football, the public began to realize that there truly could be substance as well as entertainment in TV news.

On November 26, 1978, "60 Minutes" became the first news documentary to take over first place in the ratings. The following year, with an average rating of 28.4, "60 Minutes" topped the year-end final ratings, and was either first or second in year-end ratings from the 1979-1980 season through the 1984-1985 season, and has never been out of the "Top 10" since. With the public accepting the "60 Minutes" format, the advertisers began lining up to get time; a 30-second spot in 1990 sold for $125,000-$200,000, the rate per advertiser depending upon a number of factors. CBS was able not only to pay its correspondents, writers, and producers star salaries, but also have the financial security that allows the development of major stories of importance. Because of an audience estimated as many as fifty million viewers, the "60 Minutes" impact is such that even when a local newspaper does much of the investigative work, "60 Minutes" follow-ups are influential enough to bring about action.

Among the many investigations that "60 Minutes" undertook were investigations into mail-order diploma mills, medical "cures," problems in mental health units, and the Gulf of Tonkin incident that had led to America's increased involvement in the Vietnam War. In 1979, it tuned to nuclear power, reporting numerous safety problems in the Illinois Power Plant; in 1981, it did an expose of gun-smuggling to the Irish Republican Army (IRA) by some Americans and Libyans; in 1983, after several Texas newspapers raised pointed questions following their own probes, the "60 Minutes" investigation by Morley Safer, watched by several million Americans, finally led to the release of a young Black engineer who was sentenced to life imprisonment for armed robbery after police and the prosecuting attorney suppressed evidence that could have established the defendant's innocence.

The year that "60 Minutes" premiered, NBC placed "First Tuesday" into prime time, then tried shuffling it, renaming it, re-reshuffling it, then eventually dropped it. Other successful TV news magazines have been "20/20," with anchors Hugh Downs and Barbara Walters, and Lynn Scherr on consumer issues; and "Nightline," hosted by Ted Koppel on ABC. Among the nation's better network journalists are Sam Donaldson, for White House coverage, ABC-TV; Fred Francis, covering the Department of Defense, NBC-TV; Jeff Greenfield, politics, ABC-TV; Cokie Roberts, Congress, NPR; reporter Brian Ross and producer Ira Silverman, general assignment investigative, NBC-TV; and Garrick Utley, foreign affairs, NBC-TV.

Several local TV stations now have consumer affairs specialists; many are little more than advice columnists who do minimal research. However, several have taken on national corporations by investigating the validity of advertising claims and other business practices. Among the best of the consumer investigative reporters are Dr. Herb Dennenberg (WCAU-TV, Philadelphia), former controversial Pennsylvania insurance commissioner and state consumer advocate; and David Horowitz, whose "Fight Back" themes were first seen by viewers of KNBC, Los Angeles, then by the National Broadcast Company.

Local television stations WBRZ (Baton Rouge), WCCO (Minneapolis), and the Oregon Public Broadcasting Network all devote considerable airtime to reporting significant social issues.

A Common Bond of Assistance

Two major organizations have helped give an identity and unification to the modern muckrakers. Investigative Reporters and Editors (IRE), with headquarters at the School of Journalism of the University of Missouri, is an association for those who are active in public affairs/ investigative journalism or who teach the subject. Among the many activities of the IRE are national and regional conferences and workshops, publications to assist reporters, and a large file of current investigative articles from all media. IRE was also responsible for creating the framework and carrying through the Arizona Project in 1977 following the murder of reporter Don Bolles. The six-month investigation by fifty journalists uncovered massive statewide corruption.[1]

The Center for Investigative Reporting (CIR), founded in 1977 by David Weir and Dan Noyes, is headquartered in San Francisco. With a staff of twelve, nine of whom are journalists, the CIR provides well-

---

[1]See "Overview: The Arizona Project," by Tom Collins.

researched stories to the regional and national media; like the IRE, it will assist other reporters in pursuing their own stories. The CIR specializes in stories focusing upon the environment and violation of the public trust; it is also active in freedom of information issues. Its stories have appeared on ABC, CBS, and NBC television networks, including "60 Minutes" and "20/20."; in major national magazines, including *Mother Jones, Esquire, The New Republic, U.S. News and World Report*, and *Ramparts*; and major newspapers, including the *Boston Globe, Chicago Sun-Times, Los Angeles Times*, the *Times of London, USA Today*, and the *Washington Post*. Among major articles, CIR journalists have uncovered evidence of spying by the FBI upon Americans critical of the Reagan administration, innumerable accidents on board American and Soviet nuclear ships, and the exporting of toxic wastes to Third World countries. Among the book-length investigations from CIR have been *Circle of Poison* (1981), by David Weir and Mark Schapiro, a study of pesticides and agriculture; *Troubled Water* (1985), by Jonathan King, a penetrating study of America's water supply; *Yakuza* (1986), by David E. Kaplan and Alec Dubro, an investigation of the Japanese Mafia; *The Bhopal Syndrome* (1987), by David Weir, a study of the world's worst industrial disaster; and *The Electronic Sweatshop* (1987), edited by Diana Hembree, several studies of the effects of VDT technology upon the workplace. CIR has also established a comprehensive internship program for students.

Still Only a Particle

However, even with the work of IRE and CIR, even with special investigative teams in some of the nation's media, muckraking today, as it has always been, is still only a particle of journalism. Although there are still muckrakers who have the intelligence and fire to investigate America's social infrastructure, who will go beyond trying to invoke flea bites, who are unafraid of controversy or consequences of investigative reporting, the media are, now as in the past, products of a society, neither at the cutting edge nor trailing the pack. Only a few of the hundreds of thousands of journalists will feel the fire of reform, rather than solely the lure of a Pulitzer Prize. It is was no different during the Revolution or during the "era of the muckraker." It is no different today; it won't be any different tomorrow.

Epilogue

The era of the muckrakers didn't flourish just because a few journalists were indignant about corruption and social injustice, but because an oppressed and exploited urban America and a few courageous owners of newspapers and magazines, often lured by possible circulation gains, allowed it to flourish. Muckraking, whether during the Revolution or in the present, is an exception to the patterns that have created and reinforce American society, for the nature of the American press is such that it is not radical nor can it be any more socially aware than the society in which it exists. Why there is little muckraking is a reality shared by society, which can't tolerate change and, thus, seemingly moves not at all, allowing certain elements the opportunity for exploitation; by the owners of the media who, whether they own a small weekly or a television network, are an economic muscle that dictates certain of society's rules; and by the journalists themselves, who, contrary to their beliefs, are molded into the image of what the society and its owners expect.

Reporters may honestly believe they are socially and politically aware, while trying to foster the image of independence, but they are no different from the image that the owners of the media want, which roughly translates into a down-the-middle, not too much left or right consciousness of middle-class society itself. They believe that journalists have to be impartial, independent, but don't understand that they have already been modified and codified by pre-existing standards and values assigned to the social class known as "reporter." They don't wear headbands or oversized jewelry; they do wear suits or sports jackets if men, hose if women; they cut their hair fashionably long or modishly short, depending upon the current standards of "acceptability"; they drive the cars they believe are assigned to their social class; they buy the perquisites of social life within the parameters of their paychecks. They may grumble at business methods, mutter obscenities at governmental incompetence, or complain about how PR has made image more important than substance, but they wouldn't think of massive social reform, of going forth in battle to change the philosophical nature of the State.

Further, the nature of reporting hasn't changed much in two centuries. With only a few refinements since the "Penny Press Era," the average news staff has settled into a routine of chasing ambulances and fires, news releases and social news, city council meetings, Lions Club lunches, and visits to the local Chamber, School Board, or Legislature for their stories, making believe that they are really hard-hitting "investigative" journalists just because on occasion they may stumble onto a story that others have known for years. For the media, it is far easier to chase superficial public document stories (the kind where there are easy-to-get public records, such as at a police station or in the courthouse), to spend equal time interviewing all the sides—making sure, of course, to transcribe their words exactly—than to dig even further into the records, to spend days poring through seemingly unrelated pieces of paper, to talk to innumerable sources, then to piece together a series about discrimination, slum housing, the rape of natural resources, the exploitation of the worker, or governmental and business corruption and greed, all of them obscured by packs of the Big Lie from corporate America and the government. Far too frequently, the press believes that it is "muckraking" when it complains about odors from the local sewer treatment plant or when it attacks what it believes to be high teacher salaries (which are usually higher than those of non-unionized reporters.) The reality is that a gung-ho "I'm-gonna-win-a-Pulitzer" reporter, often encouraged by desk-bound editors, will clumsily dig into a story that is little more than a flea bite upon society's ass, and overlook the story that can tear at its heart.

Thus, it was not unusual for the masses of White, male, middle-class, college-educated, white shirt/brown suit reporter of the 1950s and early 1960s to miss the story of the urban civil rights struggle; it was not peculiar that reporters through most of the 1960s almost unquestioningly accepted military statements and body count numbers while a nation was rising up in protest to the war in Vietnam; it was not strange that the mass of journalists arrived late—or not at all—on stories of the environment, the homeless, safety at nuclear power plants; and the savings and loan scandals. When governmental investigative bodies or non-profit agencies for social change or even the few existing muckraking journalists, such as I. F. Stone, Jack Anderson, and Jessica Mitford, noted the problems, then and only after a sufficient time for the public to decide whether it was going to buy into the revelations, did the media jump onto the story and ride forth in righteous indignation, waving banners of an independent and courageous press, unafraid of anyone or anything.

However, the failure to dig into the nation's social fabric, to expose waste and greed and social injustice doesn't lie entirely with the reporters of the American scene, for in order for journalism to become more than a superficial recording of current events, it's necessary that publishers go beyond the superficial. Although some publishers may argue they owe nothing to a community other than providing a forum for news and advertising, most do agree that there is a necessity for a newspaper, especially in a one-newspaper town—all but about thirty American cities are "one-newspaper towns"—to acknowledge a social responsibility to the community which has given it its profit. However, publishers become torn between the necessity of appearing to have a social conscience and their need to "maximize profits," a battle cry of American business (combined with the necessity of paying repair bills for their BMW and gardening bills for their summer cottage.) Indeed, in the media as in corporate America there is an extremely high correlation between "maximizing profits" and "minimizing social responsibility," for as one rises, the other must decline; the function of a publisher should be, although it is often not the case, of tempering one with the other to benefit all segments of society.

On the larger dailies and many of the national magazines, even those under collective bargaining agreements, the salaries, working environment, and fringe benefits are far from what good journalists can earn working in public relations, a field which about half of all journalism majors enter upon graduation, or in non-media employment, which about one-fourth enter. Ideally, publishers should determine the number of reporters and expenses necessary to give a newspaper community respectability, pay premium wages to attract the best journalists, then add at least one or two more reporters to the staff to give the newspaper a cushion so the managing editor can separate a reporter from daily routine reporting in order to concentrate upon a critical social issue. Such, of course, is not the case, as publishers have long ago learned that they can pay low wages and still attract freshly-minted journalists, willing to work for $5,000-$10,000 a year less than entry-level employees in other occupations. It was not uncommon for non-unionized daily newspapers to start reporters at $11,000-$14,000 a year, with radio and television stations often paying less than that for entry-level professional positions, although the median top minimum on unionized Guild newspapers was about $33,000 in 1990. Further, the expenses necessary to support an investigation can easily exceed the total editorial expense budget.

Although publishers and editors claim they wish to attract the best—and can show mounds of employment applications to back up their belief that there's no shortage of qualified applicants—the reality is that some of the best aren't submitting applications and planning on careers in newspaper journalism; and those who are the better reporters stay just long enough to fatten their resumés but not long enough to understand the community they live in, as they move from one newspaper to another, one station to another, in order to improve their own working conditions, wages, and opportunities for advancement. The result, of course, is that since few reporters will stay long enough to get to know the community and its players, there is even less a chance that a newspaper will cover the issues critical to the community—as well as uncover corruption in all its forms.

Further, profit is not made in investigative reporting. The "output" in column inches of any investigation, even one researched and written in less that a week, is significantly less than the output of routine assignment. On a small or mid-size editorial staff, each reporter producing as many as a dozen stories a day—from rewrites of routine news releases to cursory overviews of city council meetings—it's difficult to separate out even one reporter to write absolutely nothing for a week, a month, maybe several months, then produce "only" a series of a half-dozen solid articles at the end of the investigation. Even on editorial staffs of forty or fifty, the average size of a mid-size daily, giving one or two of the two dozen or more field reporters long-term special assignments severely cuts into the total output of column inches, significantly reducing the amount of routine news each newspaper must publish to satisfy its audience.

Both the print and electronic media are dependent upon advertising revenue for operating expenses; on newspapers, it is usually more than two-thirds of their revenue; on radio and television stations, it is virtually all their revenue. Advertisers who become unhappy with a newspaper, can reduce or eliminate advertising. However, since almost all of America has no competing local newspaper, then the possibility of an advertiser deliberately reducing advertising to "hurt" a newspaper is usually not economically feasible, even with strong radio or television stations in the immediate area. Indeed, most publishers, while conscious of advertiser influence, will keep the editorial and advertising staffs separate. Even magazines, which have significantly more circulation overlap, can count on a higher percentage of circulation revenue to total income than newspapers, and are in a continual fight to hold the advertisers they do have, aren't as vulnerable. But, virtually the entire country is blanketed by competing radio and television stations. No matter where you stand in the country, there is almost a one hundred percent chance that you can hear at least two or three radio stations or view at least two television stations; fifty-five million American homes with television have cable—a dozen or more VHF and UHF stations and one or two dozen cable-only stations can be received; for about $1,000, front lawn satellites can pull in more than one hundred competing stations. Thus, newspapers in their monopoly can afford to antagonize, radio and television with their dependence upon the ratings, usually don't.

In *Television: The Business Behind the Box*, Les Brown, television editor of *Variety*, explained the reality of television:

> Good documentaries were bad business for broadcast companies that had allowed themselves to become extensions of the advertising industry and had no insulation from the petty political purposes of legislators and governors, who could retaliate in a number of different ways. Not only was there the expense of producing and presenting the programs, but also the added costs of legal defense, flights to Washington for testimony, and occasional losses of business from advertisers. And added to the burden of paperwork and correspondence were the man-hours, particularly the absorption of top management officials diverted from gainful business activities.
>
> Courage is a requisite for good journalism, and courage is not easy to ask from companies that must answer to stockholders, advertisers, affiliated stations, and the source of their own valuable licenses—the government—before they answer to the public. [p. 197]

The result, of course, is that television often sensationalizes rather than reports the news, knowing that large audiences lured to the "happy news" format of the Ken-and-Barbie doll anchors will lead to increased advertising revenue.

Finally, and perhaps most importantly, the public has some responsibility for the lack of social justice reporting. If the public prefers tabloid entertainment and horoscopes to social issues journalism, refuses to fight for its own rights, refuses to raise its voice to support the owners of the media and the journalists who want to expose corruption, incompetence, and social injustice, then why would the media lords and their reporting staffs wish to risk financial stability?

Even if the media lords sacrificed more of their profit, even if journalists by some Divine intervention became truly independent, even if the public rose up in mass protest to their own ignorance, muckraking would still be a very small part of the media, an even smaller particle of the nation itself. Yet, even in its smallness, even when the forces of government, business, and the public arose to muzzle it, the voice of the muckraker has been heard as it sounded the call of a social revolution.

Case Overviews

CASE OVERVIEW:
The Civil Rights Era

Most investigative journalism centers around corruption and the violation of the public trust; some of it focuses upon social issues. Horace Greeley, William Lloyd Garrison, Jacob Riis, Carl Schurz, and Ray Stannard Baker among other journalists, the *New York Tribune, New York World*, and many of the muckraking magazines had led the rest of the American media to recognize and then report upon discrimination and the effects of racism in America.

However, since the media are a part of the society, if the society chooses to be racist, then the media itself must also be racist, non-judgmental, or face ostracism, physical threats, and severe economic crises (represented by significant losses in advertising, circulation, and job-shop income). When the newspaper tries to rise beyond the racism within its environment, then by its courage shows the potential that all media have.

Shortly after it was created in 1916, the Pulitzer Prize board at Columbia University, sensitive to the values Joseph Pulitzer tried to instill in American journalism, recognized the difficulty the media had in several attempts to speak out against the rising violence of the Ku Klux Klan, the "invisible empire" of pointed-sheeted families dedicated to the elimination of minorities and views which it didn't like. After World War I, the *New York World*, long identified as a champion of the immigrant and exploited worker, and of American minorities, launched one of its greatest editorial crusades. With Frank I. Cobb, one of the nation's best editors and writers leading the fight, the *World* attacked the resurgence of the Klan, pointing to innumerable cases of secret meetings and attacks upon Blacks.

In 1922, the Pulitzer Prize for Meritorious Public Service was awarded to the *Memphis Commercial Appeal* for "its courageous attitude in the

161

publication of cartoons and the handling of news" regarding the Klan. By issuing the nation's most prestigious award in journalism first to a newspaper that published an investigation of the Klan, then the following year to a Southern newspaper that tried to keep the light on Klan activities, the Pulitzer Prize board was formally telling the nation's media that not only would it recognize similar efforts, but that there was no place in the media, and in society, for racism.

Although most the media didn't get the message, some found themselves "socialized" into action. In 1926, The Pulitzer board awarded the Pulitzer Prize in Meritorious Public Services to the *Columbus* (Ga.) *Enquirer-Sun* for "the service which it rendered in its brave and energetic fight against the Ku Klux Klan; against dishonest and incompetent public officials and for justice to the Negro and against lynching." Two years later, the *Indianapolis News* won the award for a series of articles detailing the influence of the Klan in Indiana politics. For editorials against lynching and for the rights of Blacks, Grover Cleveland Hall, editor of the *Montgomery* (Ala.) *Advertiser*, in 1928; and Louis Issac Jaffe, editor of the *Norfolk Virginian- Pilot*, in 1929, won the Pulitzer Prize for editorial writing. The Pulitzer Prize for Reporting for 1938 was awarded to Raymond Sprigle, of the *Pittsburgh Post-Gazette* for a series of articles, based upon stolen documents, which proved that U. S. Supreme Court Justice Hugo Black had been a member of the Klan in Alabama. In 1953, the *Whiteville News Reporter* and the *Tabor City Tribune*, two North Carolina weeklies, were awarded the Pulitzer Prize for Meritorious Public Service for their campaigns, at great economic and personal risk, that resulted in the conviction of more than one hundred Klansmen.

The Civil Rights era, beginning shortly after World War II ended, but which became a major social force in America for a two decade period beginning in the mid-1950s, produced an awareness of the rights of all minorities. The media were not expected to lead the campaign to eliminate segregation and racial and religious intolerance. But, the editors and reporters who did use their newspaper as vehicles to try to get their communities to accept all people as equals, found support in the Pulitzer Prize Board when it again made its position known by awarding the Pulitzer Prize for editorial writing to several editors for their opposition, often at economic or personal risk, to racial intolerance. Those who received the Pulitzers were Hodding Carter, editor of the *Delta Times-Democrat* (Greenville, Miss.) (1946); Buford Boone, *Tuscaloosa* (Ala.) *News* (1957); Harry S. Ashmore, executive editor, *Arkansas Gazette* (1958); Ralph McGill, editor, *Atlanta Constitution* (1959); Lenoir Chambers, editor, *Norfolk Virginian-Pilot* (1960); Ira B. Harkey, Jr., editor, *Pascaqoula* (Miss.) *Advertiser* (1963); Hazel Brannon Smith, editor-publisher, *Lexington* (Miss.) *Advertiser* (1963); Horace G. Davis, Jr., *Gainsville* (Fla.) *Sun* (1971); and John Strohmeyer, editor, *Bethlehem* (Pa.) *Globe-Times* (1972).

While spouting phrases that journalism was a profession that accepted all kinds of people and all kinds of opinions, editors and publishers during much of the nation's media history, especially during the mid-twentieth century, excluded minorities and non-conformists from newsroom staffs. By the 1960s, the prevailing attitude was that journalists must have degrees, wear suits and ties if men, dresses and hose if women, write *and speak* Standard English, and have conventional opinions. Long hair, love beads, the music of the Grateful Dead—and left-of-center, especially socialist, views weren't tolerated. It was be this adherence to conformity that led the media to miss much of the drama that was unfolding in the 1960s.

In 1965, the *Los Angeles Times,* which had more than earned a reputation as a lethargic, often reactionary, giant, suddenly came alive during the Watts racial riots which had left thirty-four dead, more than one thousand wounded. For its coverage of the riot, the *Times* earned the 1966 Pulitzer Prize for local spot news reporting. However, there were no awards for the *Los Angeles Free Press*, an alternative weekly, or for other social issues publications which had previously published stories about the racial problems prior to the Watts riot, and which would continue to look into the social problems of America's slums—stories which the establishment press often avoided as either "too messy to deal with" or "not the kind of story our [college-educated] reporters of [white] readers would care about."

Seldom in American history has there been accurate reporting about the American Indian, and especially the continual conflict between American Indians and the Bureau of Indian Affairs. If the media are to be believed, Indians either don't exist—there's so little reporting about their lives and problems—or, if they do exist, they killed settlers, fought the cavalry, and are now drunks living on reservations. Certainly, the way most media portrayed American Indians during the first two centuries after the Declaration of Independence led most Americans to believe the horror stories of uneducated savages. Even worse than horror stories was neglect.

For years, the Palm Springs, Calif. *Desert Sun* had known that the Aqua Caliente Indians, who once owned most of the desert that became an oasis for the visibly affluent, had been cheated by business people in the court system of their rightful claims for the land. However, the news that had often dominated the newspaper centered around who was in town and what parties they were attending. A large segment of migrant laborers and nearly-impoverished Indians were overlooked since Palm Springs was a "glamor" capital, and the newspapers, firmly entrenched into the society of glamor that had been created around it, was not able to perceive any problems worth the editorial space. Some in Palm Springs even feared that should there ever be scandal—other than that surrounding the basic marital difficulties of the wealthy—that people would no longer be interested in Palm Springs; to "protect" the society—and, thus, the people— scandal was only whispered, never shouted, certainly never printed. Thus, it was left to the *Riverside Press- Enterprise*, sixty miles away to investigate corruption in the court system that denied the Agua Caliente Indians their property and estates. The series of articles earned the newspaper the 1968 Pulitzer Prize for Meritorious Public Service, and a clear, though unsaid, statement that local newspapers have a responsibility not only to courageously face possible economic sanction, but to become more interested in all parts of their community, not just that of the power-brokers. During the two decades following the Agua Caliente story, the *Desert Sun* published numerous articles about the Indians, and of government problems, establishing itself as a responsible local newspaper.

CASE OVERVIEW:

Reporting a Massacre

Between 8 and 11 a.m., March 16, 1968, the 1st Platoon, Charlie Company, 1st Battalion, 20th Infantry, 11th Brigade, U. S. Army, entered the Vietnamese village of My Lai 4, about 340 miles north of Saigon, expecting to find a large Viet Cong force. The Viet Cong, however, had left the area, leaving only civilians.

Psyched up to kill, aware of the Army's policy to produce "body counts," the 1st Platoon then massacred the civilian population, randomly killing old men, women, children, babies. By the time the massacre had ended, 347 civilians had been killed at MyLai 4, and the village torched. Random acts of murder and rape occurred throughout that day and the following day in other villages near My Lai 4, with 155 murdered at nearby Mykhe 4. During the massacre, several Charlie Company soldiers had tried to stop the killing; an enlisted man in the 1st platoon had directly refused orders to set up a machine gun and kill a trench-full of civilians; a helicopter pilot had ordered his gunner to kill American troops if they proceeded to advance upon a trench of civilians.

Nevertheless, to most soldiers in the company, the "victory" over My Lai 4 was not too unlike a football victory; they laughed, retold the events, and cheered once again. Photographs of the carnage, taken by an Army photographer, were never released to the media.

The "cover-up" began when the Army decided not only to modify casualty counts, but to claim the dead as Viet Cong, and to report that the operation was successful. The story, largely as presented by the Army, was picked up by the wire services; *The New York Times* played the Army's story on its front page.

South Vietnamese officers and village chiefs, after long deliberations whether they wished to antagonize the Americans further, sent reports to American commanding officers about a "possible" killing of civilians. Nevertheless, most officials—American and South Vietnamese—wanted to "cover up" the incident, believing that the murder of the civilians would further antagonize the South Vietnamese, and could lead not only to increased anti-American feeling within South Vietnam, but increased anti-war sentiment within the United States. The news media continued to accept the Army's reports.

As word of the massacre spread—after all, soldiers are expected to brag about their day's work—thousands of soldiers cheered an American victory, even though they knew civilians were killed. However, many also felt revulsion at both the massacre itself and the deliberate cover-up.

Shortly after the massacre, Ronald L. Ridenhouer, a helicopter gunner, flew over My Lai 4, saw the devastation, and vowed to find out what had happened. Upon his discharge at the end of 1968, against the advice of many of his friends who urged him to "forget it, it'll only hurt the country," Ridenhouer began writing letters to members of Congress, the Army, and the Department of State. Most offices threw the letters away or referred them to the Army. Rep. Morris Udall, however, followed through. At first it appeared that the Army would again bury the investigation. After some reluctance, the Army began another investigation, this one conducted by the Inspector General's office, which should have conducted the original investigation. And still there was no media coverage.

On Sept. 6, 1968, the Associated Press transmitted a 190-word "filler," based upon information from the Army, indicating that the Army planned to court martial Lt. William Calley, platoon leader. Most member newspapers didn't even publish the article, and there was no follow-up.

A few weeks later, a friend tipped reporter Seymour Hersh that there was likely to be much more to that story. As he began investigating, with the Army maintaining that the problem was just that of a mediocre officer who had gone berserk, Hersh began to unravel not only the massacre but also the cover-up. With financial assistance from the Fund for Investigative Journalism, Hersh travelled throughout the United States to dig out the story, eventually finding and interviewing Ridenhouer, members of the platoon, and Calley. Nevertheless, although Hersh had strong journalistic credentials, the media were reluctant to publish his stories; editors gave innumerable reasons, including the fear of libel, but the "gut" feeling of many was that Americans don't massacre civilians. None of the media would accept his investigation—except for Dispatch News Service, a small syndicate incorporated by journalist Michael Morrow the year before to market stories from freelance writers in Vietnam. David Obst, a young marketing specialist who managed DNS, literally begged newspapers to take Hersh's story, after having assured them that it had been reviewed by an attorney. Almost forty newspapers finally ran the first story in mid-November. *The New York Times* didn't run the DNS story, going with its own reporter who hadn't interviewed Calley or any of the First Platoon soldiers.

Still, American media and the public had doubts. Then, at the end of November, Hersh found a 22-year-old My Lai veteran, tormented by murders, who volunteered not only to talk about what had happened, but to tell a national television audience. With Walter Cronkite of CBS-TV asking questions, the soldier confirmed Hersh's reporting, confessing that under orders he killed civilians. Hersh's detailed second story finally was bought by newspapers throughout the world.

Hersh wrote several more stories about the massacre, and eventually a book which was published in Spring 1970, about the time he had won the Pulitzer Prize for international reporting—without having once gone to Vietnam. Two more books followed, detailing the massacre and cover-up, including the alteration or destruction of official records, and the failure of the Army to convict anyone other than Calley.

Calley was eventually sentenced to life imprisonment, spent three days in a stockade then ordered to spend the remainder of his term in house arrest. Three years later, he was paroled by the secretary of the army, and is currently a well-respected jeweler living in Columbus, Georgia.

Hersh continued writing stories about the Vietnam war, spending several days in Hanoi, became a nationally-known antiwar speaker, and was eventually hired as an investigative reporter for the Washington bureau of *The New York Times* where he became involved with several Watergate "scoops." During his career, although praised by the public, Hersh was, nevertheless, condemned by some of the media for some of the tactics he used to dig out his investigations, and was widely condemned for an "overriding ego," charges not unlike those hurled at many of the muckrakers more than a half-century earlier.

Three years after the massacre at My Lai 4, a year after Calley was convicted, Americans soldiers, in direct violation of Army policy regarding engagement of the enemy, strafed a Vietnamese village, killing ten civilians. Their punishment? All were issued reprimands by a two-star general; none were court martialed.

CASE OVERVIEW:

The Resignation
of a President

On August 9, 1974, almost two years after being reelected to the presidency in a landslide vote, and now facing possible impeachment proceedings, Richard M. Nixon resigned in disgrace. Nixon had been accused of several offenses, including obstruction of justice following the break-in on June 17, 1972, of the office of the Democratic National Committee in Washington, D.C.'s Watergate Building. Soon, the name "Watergate" would come to mean everything that was wrong with the President's administration—and with politics in general.

At first, it seemed to be, as presidential press secretary Ron Ziegler called it, "a third-rate burglary." But as *Washington Post* reporters Carl Bernstein and Bob Woodward saw it, there was far more to the story. Shortly after the break-in, they had preliminary evidence that the trail led to the White House, possibly even to the President himself.

The *Post*—which had been scooped on the Pentagon Papers case[1] late in its denunciation of the Vietnam War, and generally raised little opposition to whomever was president—however, now found itself almost alone in its stories about the burglary. Most of the capital's press corps were busy with the political campaign, writing reactive news—most stories were essentially reports of what someone in the campaign, whether that of Nixon or of Sen. George McGovern his Democratic opponent, said or did. It is always much easier—and more accepted—to write reactive news; besides, almost no one could believe that White House officials would be so stupid as to authorize a burglary, especially since the polls indicated that the president was an overwhelming favorite to be reelected. Most of the nation's news media remained almost silent on what became the Watergate Conspiracy, spiking most of the AP or UPI reports of what was being reported in the *Post*. The *Post* had risked its integrity that its evidence indicated a conspiracy within the White House to obstruct the investigation of the burglary.

The first few months were difficult for the *Post*, especially since it received almost no support from the other media. Further, it now faced a secret but elaborate scheme by the Nixon administration to discredit *Post* stock, and to challenge the licenses of TV stations owned by the *Post's* owners. Spending hundreds of hours poring over documents and interviewing federal employees, Bernstein and Woodward learned that the president himself had either initiated or approved an elaborate, and unconstitutional, series of actions to attempt to "cover-up" the trail that led to the White House. It was this "cover-up"—in all probability, the president did not authorize or condone the break-in—that brought about his resignation.

As the cover-up became apparent, the nation's media began increasing their Watergate coverage, now with a self-imposed guilt of having run insipid stories for too long, and with the vengeance of one betrayed and now trying to prove that it is able to keep up with the pack. But, the media were usually a few steps behind the *Post*, and *The Los Angeles Times,*

---

[1]The Pentagon Papers were hundreds of secret government documents tracing the history of the Vietnam War. After *The New York Times* secured possession of these documents, the Supreme Court was forced to rule on the federal government's pleas for prior restraint to publication, citing national security as its reason for requesting the exception to First Amendment law. The Court, by a 6-3 vote, declared that national security would not be violated if the media published the documents.

which had made several major discoveries in the case. However, both newspapers were at least one step behind the federal committees established to investigate the Nixon administration.

As important as the work of the *Post* was in bringing the situation to the American people, Bernstein and Woodward were forced to rely upon official testimony for the core of their stories. The *Post* had shown that there could be a trail; the Office of the Special Prosecutor, as well as House and Senate committees, had to blaze that trail. By the time the Office of the Special Prosecutor completed its investigations into the activities of the Committee to Reelect the President, and the President's subsequent actions to the burglary, federal grand juries issued indictments against almost fifty individuals, including two U.S. attorneys general, the secretary of the treasury, senior White House aides, and either the chairmen of the boards or senior executives of sixteen major American corporations; the president became an unindicted co-conspirator. Twenty-five persons would eventually be imprisoned for their part in the Watergate Conspiracy. The *Post* and other media, by their reporting, had kept the story "alive" by making the public aware of the official investigations and by giving the investigators a sense that the American people were supporting them in their actions.

However, the *Post* reporting also left a number of veiled news sources. Did these unnamed people, such as Deep Throat who had provided significant information to the *Post*, really exist, or were they composites or even figments of the reporters' imaginations? And, if they did exist, why weren't they willing to let their names be known—were they truly afraid or were they just trying to "get" the President while hiding behind the veil of anonymity? Even the *Post* reporting techniques of verification from a second independent source was not enough evidence for many readers and journalists to believe that the *Post* wasn't out to "get Nixon." Further, Bernstein and Woodward were reprimanded by Federal District Court Judge John Sirica for deliberately violating federal law by talking to one of the persons on the Grand Jury. Equally as important, of thousands of facts, there were hundreds of factual errors, some minor, a few major, probably none intentional. It would be these inconsistencies that would allow the Nixon administration to try to scuttle the *Post* investigation by reinforcing the belief of an "Eastern liberal-bias media" out to "get" the President. And then there was the question of the tapes, a story that provided thousands of inches of news. After castigating Richard Nixon for having secret tapes made of his conversations in the White House, reporters found themselves, reluctantly at first, admitting that not only did they themselves secretly tape conversations but that other presidents, including John F. Kennedy, had also maintained secret recordings.

Nevertheless, the nation had a new president; the *Post* was awarded the Pulitzer Prize for Meritorious Public Service; thousands of students decided that they'd like to become journalists so they, too, could become investigative reporters and "get" people—between 1974 and 1983, enrollments in journalism doubled—and Richard Nixon was now in a quasi-exile in San Clemente, Calif., tormented by both a society that would not forgive and by the knowledge that what he had done, and was now mercilessly being attacked for, had been done many times before by many different federal officials and many presidents, with almost no repercussions. And, he knew, there were other presidents who committed greater offenses against the American people, whose administrations were shaken, but who retained the office and survived the accusations.

CASE OVERVIEW:

Uniting Journalists for a Common Cause
by Tom Collins

One of the most exhaustive investigations ever undertaken into corruption in a state has been conducted [in Arizona] for the last six months by a team of reporters and editors from newspapers all over the country.

The unusual experiment in collective journalism is the result of the murder last summer [1976] of Don Bolles, an investigative reporter for the Arizona Republic. Bolles had written a number of stories about corruption in Arizona and was pursuing what he believed was an important lead when he was lured to a meeting and blown up in his car.

He died eleven days later. Aside from the information that the team of journalists has unearthed, the point it wants to make is that if one reporter

---

This article previewed a series of twenty-three articles that were nationally distributed, beginning Sunday, March 13, 1977. ©1977, Investigative Reporters and Editors, Inc. Reprinted with permission of IRE.

is killed, others will show up to carry on his work.

"This is not an act of vengeance," said Robert Greene, the Suffolk editor of Newsday, who directed the project for Investigative reporters and Editors (IRE), a national organization. "We did not come to find the killer of Bolles and we expressly did not work on the Bolles murder. It was a reasoned response to the killing of a reporter by continuing his work."

Despite the almost theatrical overtones inherent in the situation—a dead reporter, a group of journalists, many of whom never knew him, collaborating in his memory—the investigation was conducted in a calm, professional manner.

The team established its headquarters on the top floor of the Adams Hotel and converted it into a combination city room and dormitory in which the journalists worked and lived. A detailed, comprehensive filing system containing information on more than 40,000 individuals, organizations and businesses in Arizona was set up; areas of investigation were defined, reporters assigned to help put the material together in story form.

Some members of the team were able to work on the project for months at a time, while others could stay only a few weeks; most had been given paid leaves by their newspapers to participate. One reporter, Ross Becker, quit his job and sold his car to finance his participation in the project, and a few others donated their vacation time and paid their own expenses.

They arrived in this desert city from newspapers large and small and as far apart as Chicago; Eugene, Oregon; and Washington, D. C. They worked 12- and 14-hour days, interviewed hundreds of people, filed memos and returned to their own news organizations.

They talked at length to politicians, Mafia hoodlums, pimps, prostitutes, bankers and businessmen, sifted through countless public documents, combed through the garbage of individuals who were the targets of the investigation in a search for leads; checked drug-smuggling operations on the Mexican border; and dodged an armed guard on a ranch which employed illegal aliens.

Their reports, focusing on the penetration of organized crime into Arizona life, have been written, rewritten, edited and re-edited and will culminate in a series of stories totaling 100,000 words that will begin in participating newspapers . . . on Sunday, March 13, 1977.

According to Harley Bierce, executive secretary of Investigative Reporters and Editors, which is sponsoring the investigation, about fifty reporters have been in and out of the project and an equal number of newspapers have contributed direct support in either money or manpower.

Numerous press, organizations and individuals also have helped out in cash donations, services and moral support. IRE's contribution to the costs of the investigation may run as high as $80,000, Bierce said, and the total cost, including the salaries and expenses of the reporters which have been paid by their organizations, probably will exceed $250,000.

With the exception of one reporter who left the team, the group has been exceptionally close-knit, possibly due to the circumstances of working on behalf of Bolles. "I haven't seen one scrap of jealousy," said Mike Satchell of the *Washington Star*. As an experiment, said Alex Drehsler of the *Arizona Daily Star*, "it has definitely worked." Despite the fact that they "were all reporting for a filing cabinet, with no individual names on a story," said Greene, "there were no ego clashes."

Jack Driscoll, assistant executive editor of the *Boston Globe*, noted that he as well as almost everyone else on the team went through the process of having a story bounced back for additional information and rewritten for style as well as content. "Each story is edited three or four times," he said, "but there's no ego thing involved. Cooperation has been tremendous."

Newsday's involvement in the project began last summer when an IRE convention, held coincidentally a few days after Bolles' car was blown up, asked Green to go to Phoenix and explore the possibilities of a team effort there. Greene, who is a member of the IRE board and whose investigative talents had helped win two Pulitzer Prizes for *Newsday*, made the trip, decided that the project was worthwhile, and was asked to head the team by the IRE board. With the approval of *Newsday* publisher William Attwood and Executive Editor David Laventhol, he began assembling files last summer. Both he and IRE began lining up participating newspapers. *Newsday's* Tom Renner, who is also an expert on organized crime, made several trips through the West and Southwest to gather preliminary information from police intelligence officials that would be used in the investigation. Anthony Insolia, a *Newsday* managing editor, joined the team in the later stage of the investigation to assist in outlining and editing the series.

The project, however, is not without its detractors and skeptics, and has already generated some controversy in journalistic circles, mainly on the complaint that it is an exercise in "pack journalism," a phrase that journalists abhor. The team has also been characterized as a group of outsiders riding herd over a situation that might have better been left to the locals.

Two of the country's most influential newspapers, for example, the *New York Times* and the *Washington Post*, declined to join the group, and the *Post* in particular has been critical of it. *Post* media critic Charles Seib characterized it as "elitist" and said that the project "seems to be saying that the murder of a reporter is a super-murder, triggering a super response," which "smacks of vigilantism."

The Seib article, and the *Post's* attitude in general, rankled the team. "We expected reasonable and reasoned criticism, but it would probably be wise to wait until it's over," said Dick Cady, an investigative reporter from the *Indianapolis Star* who joined the project in December. "How can you start taking shots at it until the book is closed?"

Greene also notes that the state's largest newspapers, the *Arizona Daily Star* and the *Arizona Republic*, have been cooperating with the project and have not evidenced any discomfort over the presence of outsiders. The *Star*, whose editor, William Woestendiek, was an early supporter of the project, has contributed the services of two reporters; the *Republic* and its sister newspaper, the *Phoenix Gazette*, while not actually a part of the group, have provided assistance and assigned reporters to act as liaisons to the team.

Among those who have raised questions about the project have been the *Post's* Benjamin Bradlee; Otis Chandler, vice chairman of the Times-Mirror Co., which owns the *Los Angeles Times* and *Newsday*; and A. M. Rosenthal, executive editor of the *New York Times*. Bradlee has referred to the investigation as "gimmicky" and both he and Chandler have questioned whether outside newspapers should cross into someone else's turf. "I don't know how I'd feel if outsiders came into California," Chandler remarked to an Arizona newspaper group earlier this year, "but I don't think I'd be too pleased about it."

Rosenthal, in a recent telephone interview, said he had nothing against the project, but he "did not want to participate in pool journalism." Such an enterprise, he said, could lead to future projects and result in the press being perceived as "a single weapon, a juggernaut," when its great strength has always been its competitiveness and independence. "There has never been any doubt in my mind that these are good people and will do a good job, but my question is whether it is good for journalists," he said.

However, those editors and reporters who have joined or supported the investigation—and which constitute an overwhelming majority—disagree. They contend that newspapers are already engaged in various forms of collective journalism through the news services they operate and subscribe to. The *Times* and *Post*, for example, operate their own news services and subscribe, like most newspapers, to AP and UPI, among other news wires. Also, they argue, the Arizona project is an example of how newspapers can combine their resources for the public good in an investigation that they could not individually afford and which otherwise would not take place. Maxwell McCrohon, managing editor of the *Chicago Tribune*, which contributed the services of reporter Ron Koziol, said he had "no misgivings at all" about the project and James Bellows, editor of the *Washington Star*, suggested that it could be expanded in the future into other areas besides crime. Joseph Shoquist, managing editor of the *Milwaukee Journal*, which also sent a reporter, saw the investigation as "answering—in a way that newspapers could—the elements that killed Don Bolles. I don't see how that undermines our independence or conflicts with our principles."

Adding to the controversy is some dissension within IRE itself about certain aspects of the project. Some board members, concerned that it might appear that IRE was capitalizing on Bolles' death, have objected to the hiring of a literary agent and a proposal for a book and television documentary to be done on the project. Media critic Ben Bagdikian is to do the book and [producer] David Susskind may do the documentary, with some part of the proceeds to be donated to IRE for a resource center. There also have been questions about the organization's fund-raising policies and whether law enforcement agencies should have access to some of the information the team has compiled.

On that point, Greene said, several agencies had been extremely helpful to the project and in return some files have been opened to them, including the FBI, where it was believed the information might lead to an indictment and where the team was convinced the agency was doing an honest job. However, no sources of information have been revealed, he said.

The question of cooperation with police agencies is an important one and raises the issue of whether the press should ever give the appearance of being an investigative arm of the law. Reporters have gone to jail in a number of instances rather than turn over their notes, tape recordings and TV outtakes to law enforcement officials seeking them. One IRE board member, Jack White, who heads an investigative team at the *Providence Journal*, said he had serious reservations about the practice, but that Greene's explanation at a board meeting in January had satisfied him and others who were present. Bierce, the IRE executive secretary, said the practice was acceptable on a limited basis but that it should not become automatic.

Even some of those on the team had doubts about the project before they joined it—and wondered whether a group of investigative journalists of no small egos could work harmoniously together. Bill Montalbano, a foreign corespondent for the Miami Herald, said his editor told him before he came out, "'We don't know which way this is going to go but we want access to the copy. Take a look. If you don't like it, come home.' I'm still here," he added.

Cooperation from the community has generally been good, although Arizona business people have been apprehensive about the series' effect on the state's image.

"We don't like it. But as long as we have problems, we might as well get them out in the open and get it over with. If it is done responsibly, we may all learn something." This attitude, expressed by Phoenix attorney and civic leader Richard Mallery, summed up the typical reaction in Arizona to the IRE team project in that state. Many Arizonans, because of deep pride in the Grand Canyon State and concern for the economy, were worried about the effects of more bad publicity. But they saw the value of having some of Arizona's problems defined.

There was also a vocal minority against, as articulated by Sen. Barry Goldwater (R-Ariz.), who dodged our repeated requests for an interview. Opponents of our investigation gave these grounds: 1) team members should stay home and clean up their own cities; 2) it is impossible for outsiders to understand Arizona; 3) the team is an expression of eastern establishment panic over Arizona's success at attracting industry; 4) the publicity will destroy tourism and further business growth.

Among the leading proponents is Mallery, a spark-plug of the reform-minded Phoenix Forty, which despite its roots in old vested interests, has shown both clout and imagination recently in pushing for broad changes. He is a rising member of the law firm of Snell and Wilmer, which so personified the old order of doing things that it became the cornerstone of the state business power structure.

From midpoint in our project, Mallery established liaison with the team for reform-minded elements of the Phoenix business community. A series of meetings with business leaders ensued during which the purpose and essential findings—without specifics—of the IRE project were discussed. The same was done with key legislative leaders who had sought out IRE even before the current legislative session began. Arizona business support for the project was underlined even before the investigation began last September, when the Arizona Association of Industries led by Motorola, AiResearch and Standard Oil agreed to raise money to support the project on a no-strings attached basis. AAI raised more than $24,000.

Some results are already evident: Business, prodded by Mallery and others, has raised $150,000 to fund a study of Arizona's governmental structure and desired state goals by the prestigious Hudson Institute of New York.

A Phoenix Forty task force is presently analyzing the structure and effectiveness of state regulatory agencies such as the liquor commission and the real estate department with an eye toward tougher laws, modernization and better staffing. There are, for example, no spot checks for watered liquor or switched brands. The task force is also researching much-needed additions to the state penal law.

The state House of Representatives, in addition to introducing a number of tough new laws, is appropriating more money to beef up narcotics enforcement and, as a direct result of meetings with IRE staffers, has proposed a professionally staffed permanent committee on organized crime with subpoena power and the right to hold public hearings.

IRE has had other vocal supporters. Attorney General Bruce Babbitt said: "I wish they could send 100 more reporters." Phoenix Police Chief Larry Wetzel said that since IRE came to Phoenix "it has brought about an awareness that will help law enforcement [through an expanded justice system]." In the long run, predicted Wetzel, "it's going to be a good thing for Phoenix and Arizona."

Phoenix Mayor Margaret T. Hance said: "Sure, it [the IRE project] will have some effect on our image as a tourist and convention city ... but whatever the [impact] is, I say we should take our lumps and get it over with." And state Senate Majority leader Alfredo Gutierrez feels the probe "is one of the healthiest things that could have happened to the state."

Goldwater and others disagree. In a recent Phoenix TV interview, Goldwater said: "I'm not the least bit pleased by these . . . visiting newsmen who have difficulty understanding what Arizona is all about attempting to write stories about which they know nothing. . . . I'm afraid the good name of Arizona is going to get damaged and a lot of people in it, and I just don't like that kind of football. . . . I think the whole approach is wrong. I think there's too many Pulitzer-minded people in the country. Maybe they ought to eliminate the prize."

The senator is not alone. Former Maricopa County Attorney Don

Harris, who lost the Bolles case investigation to Babbitt, has ben quoted as saying that he felt the objective of the IRE team reporters was to come to Arizona and then go back East and "make a million dollars writing books."

Some Arizonans are also naturally fearful about the possibility of their names appearing in print—"and some have legitimate reason to be concerned," said the *Star's* Woestendiek. One Phoenix resident sent the team a postcard, thanking it for coming to the state. "There have been more indictments and more sentences for fraud . . . since you have been here than in the last 10 years. You should have come to Arizona sooner."

Surprisingly, says Greene, the Mafia itself seems resigned to the public attention that will result from the investigation. He said the Mob's attitude was, "A reporter was killed, right? It was stupid, right? You gotta expect this." Mobsters interviewed by IRE were fatalistic. "We expected it," said Bonanno associate Eddie Duci of Phoenix.

Bolles' murder is still a very real factor in the minds of the journalists and a reminder of why they participated in the project. "This man was killed while he was doing his job and because he was doing it," said the *Chicago Daily News'* Phil O'Connor, who with his fellow reporter, Ed Rooney, donated some of his vacation time to the project. "I have five children and Ed has six, and so we could identify with him." Said the *Globe's* Driscoll, "He started a story and we'll finish it."

Greene said that the series will reveal the extent of organized crime's information about political corruption, land fraud operations, and the increased use of Arizona as a corridor for drugs moving out of Mexico. He expects it to be a "blockbuster."

Beyond that, he said, it will demonstrate that Arizona society on all levels was indirectly responsible for Bolles' death because it "helped perpetuate an incredible arrogance and an attitude in which all things seemed buyable and in which you could get away with anything—to the point where one guy would finally say, 'Okay, let's kill Bolles.'"

The bottom line, in journalistic terms, is how much national impact the material will have. When it is weighed by the team's peers, will the immense undertaking, with its high costs, long hours, risks, and separations from families, seem worthwhile? The team is aware that the rest of the journalistic world will be watching and judging its performance. As the project drew to a close a few weeks ago, *Newsday's* Insolia summed up the feeling among the group: "It's getting close to opening night and we're all getting a little nervous." . . .

CASE OVERVIEW:
A Question of Ethics

There was corruption in Chicago—actually, there is almost always corruption in Chicago—and the *Chicago Sun- Times* was going to ferret it out. The Better Government Association, a reform group that worked with Chicago's investigative reporters, claimed that almost no bar or tavern could operate in Chicago without becoming involved in bribery and kickbacks. So, the *Sun-Times* bought a bar, renamed it the Mirage, and assigned two reporters and a photography team to go "undercover," with the assistance of the Association.

A four-month investigation revealed extensive graft, with state and local health, safety, and liquor inspectors, as well as Chicago Police agreeing to "look the other way" upon payment of "fees." Some taverns that did meet the laws, however, found that inspectors could "find" violations if payments were not made.

The twenty-five article series, published January 8- February 5, 1978, eventually resulted in twelve inspectors being fired, several more suspended, and the establishment by Chicago of stricter enforcement controls. The series earned reporters Zay N. Smith and Pamela Zeckman, working with William Recktenwald of the Association, the public service award of the Society of Professional Journalists—and a rebuke from the Pulitzer Prize board which overturned the recommendation of one of its juries, and refused to award Smith and Zuckman the Pulitzer Prize for investigative reporting, claiming that the story was obtained by fraud and deception.

The decision further opened the division between the public and the nation's media. Opponents of investigative undercover journalism believe that journalists must always identify themselves, and that "undercover" investigative work is the responsibility not of the media, but of law enforcement agencies. By doing the work that society has reserved for law enforcement agencies, journalists, who are forever trying to assert their independence from governmental and economic restriction, overstep their boundaries, thus violating the public trust that establishes clear distinction between "reporter" and "cop." Further, the possibility of entrapment is significant as the journalists, some with a "hired gunslinger" mentality, sniff out a "good" story. Reporting the news, not making it is the function of the media, they claim.

However, those who believe in undercover journalism argue that reporters who merely report the news are "clerical transcribers," taking notes on what they are told, asking others to confirm or deny statements, then translating information for the public. The media responsibility, they argue, involves not only the reception of information, but also extensive data collection, synthesis, and analysis of that data to help society not only see itself but understand its own problems. Because corruption, whether in government or private industry, violates a public trust, it is the responsibility of the media, as a part of society, to make society aware of the problem. It is the responsibility of the law enforcement agencies to decide if there is sufficient cause for prosecution. The greater good of society, they claim, is served by conducting the investigation, making people aware of the problem, then letting society correct the problem.

The use of deception to get a story has always been a part of the journalistic tradition. Nellie Bly, for Joseph Pulitzer's *New York World* posed as a patient at a mental hospital to get a story about inhumane conditions in the treating of the institutionalized mentally ill; the Van Vorsts and Rheta Chile Dorr posed as factory workers. Upton Sinclair, in 1905, posed as a worker in a meat packing plant to learn more about worker exploitation and the unsanitary health standards in the industry; the result was *The Jungle*, one of the most powerful books in American literature. During the 1920s, in an era known as "jazz journalism," reporters perfected the art of "getting the story at any price," deliberately lying to news sources, claiming to be whomever it was beneficial to be in order to get the information, often violating the law or court orders in the belief that the story was the most important thing, and that the greater good was in getting the information to the public than in following confining rules and regulations. Among current undercover reporters, Hal Bernstein worked in a migrant labor camp and on the Alaska pipeline to uncover worker exploitation and corruption.

During the Civil Rights era, several newspapers published articles about racism in the housing and real estate industry detailing the experiences of the difficulty Blacks had in finding housing. In most cases, a Black couple would check out possible housing, followed by a White couple. For variation, there might be a "mixed" couple in addition to the White and Black couples. In almost all cases, none of the prospective "tenants" or "homeowners" identified themselves as reporters.

It is no longer unusual for reporters to pose as potential welfare recipients to investigate what the bureaucracy does to the poor, as drunks to investigate jail conditions, as frustrated care owners to check the honesty and competency of service stations owners, as migrant laborers to check exploitation, or as patients suffering from cancer or backaches to investigate all kinds of phenomenal cures. Should anyone challenge their stories, the reporters answer their critics by pointing out that the reporters were only "eavesdropping" on what was occurring, that they did not require anyone to do anything that person would not already have been doing.

Almost from the time that tape recorders were invented, reporters have taped conversations with news sources. Most recordings were made with the knowledge of the sources—the recording serving to aid the reporter in note taking, and in the accurate writing of the sources's statements. However, reporters have also used micro recorders, hidden in their inside coat or purse pockets, and have also taped telephone conversations without the knowledge of the other party. The FCC requires that a "beep" be sounded whenever a telephone conversation is being recorded; many reporters have "overlooked" that requirement. In addition, thirteen states require that both parties to a telephone conversation agree if there is to be any recording made. Further, the use of the "hidden cameras"—at first the still photograph, later film and videotape—has raised questions of the conflict between the public's right to know and the right of personal privacy.

In *Detman v. Time* (1971), the U. S. Court of Appeals for the 9th Circuit, abruptly stopped any lingering beliefs that the commission of a crime by journalists, even if "for greater public good," would not be tolerated. In issuing her opinion, Judge Shirley Hufstedler ruled that the "First Amendment has never been construed to accord newsmen immunity from torts or crimes committed during the course of news gathering."

Although several journalistic codes of ethics forbid lying to get information, acceptable reporting techniques allow journalists to lead a source to believe that the reporter knows more than is actually known. Often, journalistic interrogation can make the source believe that police questioning can't be all that bad. Both reporter and source also know that no one tells all the truth; the source knows that lying is wrong, but that not telling all the facts is acceptable—after all, it's the journalist's job to find those facts; the journalists know that there will always be more facts to the story than the source is telling.

In a sense, it's a game that each plays with the other. It's when the informal rules are broken, when there is a deliberate "cover-up" of an entire story that will lead journalists to become zealous in their pursuit of what they believe is truth; it is deliberate lying by the journalist, no matter what the reasons, that causes significant credibility problems to the journalism profession. Nevertheless, journalistic codes of ethics in order to be accepted as guides of conduct must be enforced; as yet, there is minimal enforcement, and the only penalties, and these are extremely rare, is to suspend the journalists from membership in whatever professional organizations they belong to, and which has the one clause or statement that was violated.

Bibliography

Baker, Ray Stannard, *An American Chronicle*, Charles Scribner's Sons (New York), 1945.

Bannister, Robert C., *Ray Stannard Baker*, Yale University Press (New Haven, Conn.), 1966.

Barry, Peter N., *"The Decline of Muckraking: A View from the Magazines,"* unpublished doctoral dissertation, Wayne State University, 1973.

Beard, Charles A. and Mary R., *The Rise of American Civilization*, Macmillan (New York), 3 vols., 1927-1939.

Bleyer, Willard G., *Main Currents in the History of American Journalism*, Houghton Mifflin (Boston), 1927.

Bloomfield, Maxwell, "Muckraking and the American Stage: The Emergence of Realism, 1905-1917," *The South Atlantic Quarterly*, Spring 1967.

Bleum, William, *Documentary in American Television*, Hastings House (New York), 1964.

Bok, Edward W., *The Americanization of Edward Bok*, Scribner's (New York), 1920.

Bowers, Claude G., *Beveridge and the Progressive Era*, Houghton Mifflin (Boston), 1932.

Boyer, Richard O. and Herbert M. Morais, *Labor's Untold Story,* Marzani & Munsell (New York), 1955.

Bragaw, Donald H., *Soldier for the Common Good; The Life and Career of Charles Edward Russell*, doctoral dissertation, Syracuse University, 1970.

Brandes, Werner, *Lincoln Steffens—Publicist, Patriot, 'Plutogoge*, doctoral dissertation, University of Munich, 1967.

Brasch, Walter M. and Dana R. Ulloth, *The Press and the State*, University Press of America (Lanham, Md.), 1987.

Brown, Dorothy M., "The Quality Magazines in the Progressive Era," *Mid-America,* July 1971.

Brown, Les, *Television: The Business Behind the Box,* Harcourt Brace Jovanovich (New York), 1971.

Cassedy, James H., "Muckraking and Medicine: Samuel Hopkins Adams,"*American Quarterly,* Spring 1964.

Chalmers, David, *The Muckrake Years,* Van Nostrand-Reinhold (New York), 1974.

_____, *The Social and Political Ideas of the Muckrakers,* Citadel Press (New York), 1964.

Chamberlain, John, *Farewell to Reform,* John Day (New York), 1932.

Channing, Edward, *History of the United States,* Macmillan (New York), 1927.

Chelslaw, Irving G., *An Intellectual Biography of Lincoln Steffens,* doctoral dissertation, Columbia University, 1952.

Clark, C. Walter, Jr., *The Political Thought of Lincoln Steffens,* doctoral dissertation, Indiana University, 1970.

Commager, Henry Steele, *The American Mind,* Yale University Press (New Haven, Conn.), 1950.

Cross, Whitney R., "The Muckrakers Revisited: Purposeful Objectivity in Progressive Journalism," *Neiman Reports,* July 1952.

Dudden, Arthur P., "Lincoln Steffens' Philadelphia," *Pennsylvania History,* October 1964.

Eastman, Joel W., "Claude L'Engle, Florida Muckraker," *Florida Historical Quarterly,* January 1967.

Ellis, Elmer, *Mr. Dooley's America,* Alfred A. Knopf (New York), 1941.

Emery, Edwin and Michael Emery, *The Press and America,* Prentice-Hall (Engelwood Cliffs, N.J.), 6th ed., 1987.

Fairchild, Roy P., "Benjamin O. Flower: Father of the Muckrakers," *American Literature,* May 1942 and November 1950.

Faulkner, Harold U., *The Quest for Social Justice, 1898-1914,* Macmillan (New York), 1931.

Felt, Jeremy P., "The Progressive Era in America, 1900-1917," *Societas,* Spring 1973.

Feurberg, Gary H. *Principles of Muckraking,* doctoral dissertation, University of Oregon, 1970.

Filler, John, "The Muckrakers in Flower and in Failure," *Essays in American Historiography,* edited by Donald Sheehan and Harold C. Syrett, Columbia University Press (New York), 1960.

Filler, Louis, *Crusaders for American Liberalism*, Harcourt, Brace (New York), 1939.

_____, *The Age of the Muckrakers*, Pennsylvania State University (University Park), 1976.

Francke, Warren T., *Investigative Exposure in the Nineteenth Century: The Journalistic Heritage of the Muckrakers*, doctoral dissertation, University of Minnesota, 1974.

Fretz, Lewis A., *"Upton Sinclair: The Don Quixote of American Reform,"* doctoral dissertation, Stanford University, 1970.

Grenier, Judson Jr., *The Origins and Nature of Progressive Muckraking*, doctoral dissertation, UCLA, 1965.

Grenier, Judson, "Muckraking and Muckrakers: An Historical Definition," Journalism Quarterly, Autumn 1960.

Glantz, Rudolph, "Jewish Social Conditions as Seen by the Muckrakers," *Yivo Annual of Jewish Social Science*, 1954.

Hapgood, Norman, *The Changing Years*, Holt, Rinehart & Winston (New York), 1930.

Johnson, Warren B., "Muckraking in the Northwest: Joe Smith and Seattle Reform," *Pacific Historical Review*, November 1971.

Harris, Leon, *Upton Sinclair*, Thomas Y. Crowell (New York), 1975.

Harrison, John M. and Harry H. Stein, *Muckraking: Past, Present and Future*, Pennsylvania State University Press (University Park, Pa.), 1973.

Harrison, John M., "Finley Peter Dunne and the Progressive Movement," *Journalism Quarterly*, Autumn 1967.

Harvey, Robert D., *The Rhetoric of the Muckrakers: A Contribution to the History and Theory of Social Realism in the American Novel, 1900-1920*, doctoral dissertation, University of Chicago, 1965.

Hicks, Granville, "Lincoln Steffens: He Covered the Future," *Commentary Magazine*, February 1952.

Hinds, George L., *The Speeches and Speaking of Joseph Lincoln Steffens*, doctoral dissertation, Northwestern University, 1952.

Hofstadter, Richard, *The Age of Reform*, Alfred A. Knopf (New York), 1955.

Horton, Russell M., *Lincoln Steffens*, Twayne (Boston), 1974.

Huddleston, Kathryn D., *The Literary and Social Significance of Everybody's Magazine from 1903 to 1913*, doctoral dissertation, Peabody Institute, 1975.

Josephson, Matthew, *The Robber Barons*, Harcourt, Brace & Jovanovich (New York), 1934.

Kaplan, Justin, *Lincoln Steffens: A Biography*, Simon and Schuster (New York), 1974.

Kendrick, Alexander, *Prime Time: The Life of Edward R. Murrow*, Little, Brown (Boston), 1959.

Kobre, Sidney, *Development of American Journalism*, William C. Brown (Dubuque, Iowa), 1969.

Lasch, Christopher, *The New Radicalism in America*, Alfred A. Knopf (New York), 1965.

Leonard, Lianne J., *Lincoln Steffens and the Search for Progressive Political Philosophy*, master's thesis, Stanford University, 1959.

Lloyd, Henry Demarest, *Wealth Against the Commonwealth*, Harper & Bros. (New York), 1894.

Lyon, Peter, *Success Story: The Life and Times of S. S. McClure*, Scribner's (New York), 1963.

Mann, Arthur, *The Progressive Era: Liberal Renaissance or Liberal Failure?*, Holt, Rinehart, and Winston (New York), 1963.

____, *Yankee Reformers in the Urban Age*, Harper and Row (New York), 1966.

Marcosson, Isaac F., *David Graham Phillips and His Times*, Dodd, Mead (New York), 1932.

Maxwell, Robert S., "A Note on the Muckrakers," *Mid-America* January 1961.

May, Henry F., *The End of American Innocence*, Quadrangle Books (Chicago), 1964.

McClure, S. S., *My Autobiography*, Frederick A. Stokes (New York), 1914.

Moody, John, *The Truth About Trusts*, Moody Publishing (New York), 1904.

Mott, Frank Luther, *A History of American Magazines*, Belknap Press of Harvard University Press (Cambridge, Mass.), 5 vols., 1938-1964.

____, *American Journalism*, Macmillan (New York), 1962, 3rd edition.

Mowry, George E., *Theodore Roosevelt and the Progressive Movement*, University of Wisconsin Press (Madison), 1946.

Nevins, Allan, *American Press Opinion, Washington to Coolidge*, Heath (Boston), 1928.

Older, Fremont, *My Own Story*, Macmillan (New York), 1926.

Parrington, Vernon, *Main Currents in American Thought*, Harcourt, Brace Jovanovich (New York), 1927.

Phillips, David Graham, *The Treason of the Senate*, edited by George E. Mowry and Judson A. Grenier, Quadrangle (Chicago), 1964.

Pringle, Henry F., *Theodore Roosevelt*, Harcourt, Brace & Jovanovich (New York), 1931.

Reiger, Cornelius C., *The Era of the Muckrakers*, University of North Carolina Press (Chapel Hill), 1932.

Reynolds, Robert, "The 1906 Campaign to Sway Muckraking Magazines," *Journalism Quarterly*, Spring 1963.

Russell, Charles Edward, *Bare Hands and Stone Walls*, Charles Scribner's Sons (New York), 1933.

Schlesinger, Arthur M., *The Rise of the City, 1878-1898*, Macmillan (New York), 1932.

Schramm, LeRoy H., *Organized Labor and the Muckrakers, 1900-1912*, doctoral dissertation, Cornell University, 1972.

Schultz, Stanley, "The Morality of Politics: The Muckrakers' Vision of Democracy," *Journal of American History;* December 1965.

Sedgwick, Ellery, *The Happy Profession*, Little, Brown (Boston), 1946.

Semoche, John, "Theodore Roosevelt's Muck-Rake Speech: A Reassessment," *Mid-America*, April 1964.

_____, *Ray Stannard Baker: A Quest for Democracy in Modern America*, University of North Carolina Press (Chapel Hill, N.C.), 1969.

Shapiro, Herbert, *Lincoln Steffens: The Evolution of an American Radical*, doctoral dissertation, University of Rochester.

Shapiro, Herbert, ed. *The Muckrakers and American Society*, D.C. Heath (Boston), 1968.

Smith, Mickey C., "The Medical Muckrakers," *Pharmaceutical Marketing and Media*, December 1966.

Stein, Harry, "American Muckrakers," *Journalism Quarterly;* Spring 1979.

_____, "Lincoln Steffens: Interviewer," *Journalism Quarterly*, Winter 1969.

_____, "American Muckrakers," *Journalism Quarterly;* Spring 1979.

_____, "Theodore Roosevelt and the Press: Lincoln Steffens," *Mid-America* 54:94-107 (April 1972).

_____, *Lincoln Steffens: An Intellectual Portrait*, doctoral dissertation, University of Minnesota, 1965.

_____, "The Muckraking Book in America, 1946-1973," *Journalism Quarterly*, Summer 1975.

Stinson, Robert, "McClure's Road to *McClure's*: How Revolutionary Were 1890s Magazines?" *Journalism Quarterly*, Summer 1970.

Sullivan, Mark, *Our Times*, Scribner's (New York), 1926.

Swados, Harvey, *Years of Conscience*, World (Cleveland), 1962.

Tarbell, Ida M., *All in the Day's Work*, Macmillan (New York), 1939.

Thompson, John H., "American Muckrakers and Western Canadian Reform," *Journal of Popular Culture*, Spring 1971.

Titus, Warren I., "The Progressivism of the Muckrakers: A Myth Reexamined through Fiction," *Journal of the Central Mississippi Valley American Studies Association*, Spring 1969.

Weinberg, Alvin M., "Scientific Choice and the Scientific Muckrakers," *Minerva*, Autumn-Winter, 1968.

Weinberg, Arthur and Lila Weinberg, *The Muckrakers*, Simon & Schuster (New York), 1961.

West, Katherine S., *"The Influence of Newspapers on the Magazine Muckraking Movement,"* master's thesis, University of Wisconsin, 1943.

Wilson, Harold S., *McClure's Magazine and the Muckrakers*, Princeton University Press (Princeton, N.J.), 1970.

Index

NBC-TV 146ff
Nelson, William Rockhill 19-20
New York American 127
New York Central Railroad 69, 96
New York Evening Post 6, 23, 111
New York Herald 7, 90, 128
New York Herald Tribune 128
New York Journal 31ff, 111, 127, 128
New York Journal-American 128
New York, New Haven & Hartford
   Railroad 70
New York Sun 7, 12, 23-24, 94
New York Telegram 128
New York Times 23, 95, 165, 167,
   173, 174
New York Tribune 8, 12, 26, 128
New York World 31, 33, 77, 94, 111,
   121, 128, 161
New York World-Telegram 128
New York World Journal Telegram 128
Newsday 145, 172ff
Nichols, Francis H. 43-44
9009 (Bechdolt and Hopper) 117
Nixon, Richard M. 167-170
Norfolk Virginian-Pilot 162
Norris, Frank 70, 130

O'Connor, Phil 177
Oil! (Sinclair) 129
Older, Fremont 21-22, 92
Orchard, Harry 65
Oregon Public Broadcasting 150
Our Times (Sullivan) 129
Ovington, Mary White 117

Page, Walter H. 87
Page, Thomas Nelson 116n
Paine, Thomas 4, 145
Patent Medicines 78-83
Pearson, Drew 134
Pearson's 126-127
Peltret, Frank 30
Penninsula Times-Tribune 146
Pennsylvania Railroad 68
Penny Press 6-8, 27
Penrose, Boise 46
Pentagon Papers 168n
Peruna 80
Philadelphia General Advertiser 4
Philadelphia Inquirer 145

Phillips, John S. 37ff, 40-41, 63-64
Phillips, David Graham 69, 94ff,
   103, 112n, 130
Phillips, David Graham 112n
Pilgrim's Progress (Bunyan) 3
Pinkerton Agency 69-70
Pinkham, Lydia 81
Pittsburgh Post-Gazette 162
Platt, Thomas C. 95-96, 97
Police Gazette 78
Popular Science Monthly 107
Populism 19-21, 124
Powderly, Terence 17
Progressivism 20, 26-29, 121, 128, 161
Pullman Co. 68-69
Pure Food and Drug Act 86, 87, 88

Quay, Matthew 68

Railroads 16, 22, 30, 67-75, 96
Railroads 16, 22, 30, 67-75, 96
Raleigh, Henry 101
Raleigh State Chronicle 22
Ramparts 145
Rather, Dan 149ff
Reasoner, Harry 149ff
Recktenwald, William 178ff
Reconstruction Era 10-17
Renner, Tom 172
Review of Reviews 45
Rhodes, Harrison 107
Ribicoff, Abraham 140-141
Ridenhouer, Ronald L. 165-166
Ridgway, Erman J. 77, 84-85, 87
Riis, Jacob 12-13
Riverside Press-Enterprise 164
Roberts, Cokie 150
Roberts, Chalmers 134
Rockefeller, John D. 15-16, 54ff, 93,
   96, 107
Rolling Stone 145
Romance Magazine 127
Rooney, Ed 177
Roosevelt, Franklin D. 20
Roosevelt, Theodore 3-4, 13, 20, 23, 28,
   33, 34, 45, 74-75, 83, 87-88, 97, 101-
   102, 105, 121, 128; Muckrake speeech
   3-4, 97-98, 105, 123
Rosenthal, A. M. 173
Ross, Brian 150

The Hon. John Grigsby (Klein) 107
The Independent 117, 130
The Iron Heel (London) 110
The Jungle (Sinclair) 86, 88-92, 110, 118
The Lion and the Mouse (Klein) 107
The Making of an American (Riis) 12
The Metropolis (Sinclair) 129
The Nation 57
The Octopus (Norris) 70
"The Owners of America" 107
The People of the Abyss (London) 110
The Pit (Norris) 70
The Profits of Religion (Sinclair) 129
The Progressive 145-146
The Realist 145
"The Selling of the Pentagon" 148
The Shame of the Cities (Steffens) 51
The State 22-23
The Strength of the Strong (London) 110
The Valley of the Moon (London) 110
The War of the Classes (London) 110
The Washington Merry-Go-Round
    (Pearson and Allen) 134
The Woman Who Toils (Van Vorst) 111
Thomas, Isaah 4
Thomas, Lowell 146
Thurston, John M. 33
Tolstoy, Leo 14
Tramping With Tramps (Willard) 42
"Treason in the Senate" 94-99, 106
Trinity Episcopal Church 108-110
Turner, George Kibbe 38, 52, 65, 130
Twain, Mark 30, 34
Tweed, William "Boss" 23

U. S. Steel 59, 112-113
U. S. v. The Progressive 146
U. S. S. Maine 33
Udall, Morris 165
Udall, Stewart 141
Ullman, John 145
Underground Press *Syndicate* 145
Union Pacific Railroad 69
Unsafe at Any Speed (Nader) 142-143
Utley, Garrick 150

Van Vorst, Marie 111
Van Atta, Dale 134
Van Vorst, Bessie McGinley 111
Vanderbilt, Cornelius 16, 70

Vanderbilt, William Henry 16, 27, 69, 96
Veiler, Bayard 107
Vieria, Meredith 149
Villard, Oswald Garrison 117

Walker, David 5
Wallace, Mike 149ff
Walling, William 117, 129
Walters, Barbara 150
Wanamaker, John 46
Washington, George 4, 116
Washington Post 168-170, 173, 174
Washington Exposé (Anderson) 134
Watergate 167-170
WBRZ-TV 150
WCCO-TV 150
Weir, David 151
Western Union 69
Westliche Post 26
Wetmore, Claude 47
Wetzel, Larry 176
What Eight Million Women Want
    (Dorr) 112
White, William Allen 19-20, 64
White, William Allen 52
White, Jack 174
Whiteville News 162
Whitten, Les 135
"Who Killed Lake Erie?" 148
Wiley, Harvey Washington 78-79, 88
Willard, Josiah Flynt 41-42
Williams, Jesse Lynch 107
Wise, Stephen 117
Wise, Thomas 107
Wisner, George 7, 128
Wister, Owen 53-54
Woestendiek, William 173
Woodward, Bob 145, 167ff
World's Work 77, 88
World's Week 107

Yakuza (Kaplan and Dubro) 151
Yellow Journalism 31-34, 93

Zeckman, Pamela 178ff
Ziegler, Ron 167

About the Author

Dr. Walter M. Brasch is an award-winning writer-journalist and university professor of journalism. Among his nine books are *Black English and the Mass Media, Cartoon Monickers,* and *The Press and the State* (with Dana R. Ulloth)

In a two-decade career in journalism, he was a newspaper reporter and city editor, specializing in public affairs reporting; editor-in-chief of two magazines and a book publishing company; writer/producer of multi-screen multimedia productions; television writer/associate producer; and a public relations/media consultant for political campaigns and the entertainment industry.

Dr. Brasch is a specialist in media history and social issues, and the interelationships between the media and government. He earned an A.B. in sociology from San Diego State College, an M.A. in journalism from Ball State University, and a Ph.D. in mass communication/journalism from The Ohio University.